AF837745

Practices of Care in an Italian Eating Disorder Clinic

WYSE Series in Social Anthropology

Editors:
James Laidlaw, William Wyse Professor of Social Anthropology, University of Cambridge, and Fellow of King's College, Cambridge
Joel Robbins, Sigrid Rausing Professor of Social Anthropology, University of Cambridge, and Fellow of Trinity College, Cambridge

Social Anthropology is a vibrant discipline of relevance to many areas – economics, politics, business, humanities, health and public policy. This series, published in association with the Cambridge William Wyse Chair in Social Anthropology, focuses on key interventions in Social Anthropology, and is based on innovative theory and research of relevance to contemporary social issues and debates. Former holders of the William Wyse Chair have included Meyer Fortes, Jack Goody, Ernest Gellner and Marilyn Strathern, all of whom have advanced the frontiers of the discipline. This series intends to develop and foster that tradition.

Recent titles:

Volume 19
Practices of Care in an Italian Eating Disorder Clinic: Rethinking Food, Family and Ethics
Giulia Sciolli

Volume 18
Critiquing Neoliberalism: Art and Activism in Post-Recession Dublin
Natalie Morningstar

Volume 17
Building Social Worlds: Thinking Forwards with Esther Newcomb Goody
Edited by Barbara Bodenhorn, Alicia Fentiman and Mary Goody

Volume 16
Asian Lives in Anthropological Perspective: Essays on Morality, Achievement and Modernity
Susan Bayly

Volume 15
An Anthropology of Intellectual Exchange: Interactions, Transactions and Ethics in Asia and Beyond
Edited by Jacob Copeman, Nicholas J. Long, Lam Minh Chau, Joanna Cook and Magnus Marsden

Volume 14
Against Better Judgment: Akrasia in Anthropological Perspectives
Edited by Patrick McKearney and Nicholas H.A. Evans

Volume 13
New Perspectives on Moral Change: Anthropologists and Philosophers Engage with Transformations of Life Worlds
Edited by Cecilie Eriksen and Nora Hämäläinen

Volume 12
Where Is the Good in the World?: Ethical Life between Social Theory and Philosophy
Edited by David Henig, Anna Strhan and Joel Robbins

Volume 11
Making Better Lives: Hope, Freedom and Home-Making among People Sleeping Rough in Paris
Johannes Lenhard

Volume 10
Selfishness and Selflessness: New Approaches to Understanding Morality
Edited by Linda L. Layne

Volume 9
Becoming Vaishnava in an Ideal Vedic City
John Fahy

For a full volume listing, please see the series page on our website: https://www.berghahnbooks.com/series/wyse

Practices of Care in an Italian Eating Disorder Clinic

Rethinking Food, Family and Ethics

Giulia Sciolli

berghahn
NEW YORK • OXFORD
www.berghahnbooks.com

First published in 2026 by
Berghahn Books
www.berghahnbooks.com

© 2026 Giulia Sciolli

All rights reserved. Except for the quotation of short passages for the purposes of criticism and review, no part of this book may be reproduced in any form or by any means, electronic or mechanical, including photocopying, recording, or any information storage and retrieval system now known or to be invented, without written permission of the publisher.

Library of Congress Cataloging-in-Publication Data
A C.I.P. cataloging record is available from the Library of Congress
Library of Congress Cataloging in Publication Control Number: 2026001413

British Library Cataloguing in Publication Data
A catalogue record for this book is available from the British Library

EU GPSR Authorized Representative
LOGOS EUROPE, 9 rue Nicolas Poussin, 17000, LA ROCHELLE, France
Email: Contact@logoseurope.eu

ISBN 978-1-83695-524-5 hardback
ISBN 978-1-83695-525-2 epub
ISBN 978-1-83695-526-9 web pdf

https://doi.org/10.3167/9781836955245

A Michela, sole di tutti i girasoli

Contents

Illustrations

Acknowledgements

This book would not have been possible without all the people who inhabit, each in their own way, the residential and semi-residential facility of the eating disorder treatment centre that I call Il Giardino. The extent to which they let me be part of their lives is something I would have never expected. To guarantee their anonymity I cannot name them here, but I hope that what I have written will, in small part, reciprocate the enormous gift they gave me.

I would like to start by thanking the clinical director for answering so enthusiastically when I first contacted her, for trusting me to access the delicate space of the treatment centre, and for the illuminating conversations we had on eating disorders.

My most heartfelt gratitude goes to the patients I met, for their interest in my research at a time when many might just want to be left alone; for letting me be part of their treatment path – including the moments when they were most vulnerable – and for sharing with me their life stories and struggles. I cannot thank them enough. Wholehearted thanks also go to their families and especially their parents, for letting me participate in their weekly support meetings and for dedicating time to discuss painful parts of their lives with me, often at moments when they already felt everything around them was falling apart. I am immensely grateful to the members of the treatment team, including the interns, volunteers and the president of the association for patients' families. I thank them all for welcoming me so warmly from the very beginning, for being so curious about my work, for finding time to talk to me despite being overwhelmed with their job, and for sharing with me the many challenges of their difficult work. By tempering the often-intense atmosphere of the centre with heartwarming laughter, they made my fieldwork not only a fascinating journey but also something that I looked forward to every morning. A special thanks goes to those I call Mauro and Serena, for being the most nurturing temporary 'second family' that one could wish for, and for their enduring friendship. I thank them all – patients, family carers and healthcare professionals – also for the precious feedback they gave me when I presented the 'results' of my research and when I sent them parts of what later became this book. In addition to the many helpful comments and questions that I received, knowing that what I was writing resonated with their experiences and with what they think is important was the strongest motivation to keep working on it and publish it. This book, with much love, is to all of you.

In Cambridge, my first thanks go to my Ph.D. supervisor Maryon McDonald, for giving a chance to my research project, for the countless hours of dedicated feedback and for always pushing me to sharpen my ethnographic lens. The Ph.D. colleagues who attended the writing-up seminar have offered stimulating feedback on some of the chapters – thank you all for always doing that with kindness and generosity. Among them, special thanks go to my friends Danny Cardoza, Claire Moll, Angel Naydenov, Laura Tradii, Liangliang Zhang and Ruiyi Zhu, for the many in-person and online conversations we had and, most of all, for providing me with a vital support network during what have been challenging and isolating years. Many thanks also go to my academic advisor James Laidlaw, for his thought-provoking questions and comments. I am deeply grateful to my postdoctoral mentor Perveez Mody, for always being so enthusiastic and supportive about my work and plans for the future. The small but persistent reading group on 'care' at the University of Cambridge has been a formidable safe space in which to experiment with ideas. Many, many thanks go to Patrick McKearney for putting the reading group together and for giving precious and insightful feedback on my work. Similarly, I warmly thank Ignacia Arteaga for being an inspiring anthropologist and a rock of support – she gave helpful comments on earlier drafts, talked through ideas with me and always encouraged me. Mikkel Kenni Bruun and Rebecca Hutten also provided generous feedback on part of what is now Chapter 5, as editors of a recent collection on the anthropology of psychology. Finally, in Cambridge I want to thank all the undergraduate and M.Phil. students I have supervised between 2021 and 2026: by teaching and discussing about food, kinship and care with them during seminars and supervisions, I often came to see things more clearly than when they were just in my head.

Beyond the borders of little Cambridge, I am grateful to Janet Carsten, whose work on food and kinship has been the very first thing that made me fall for anthropology, and whose encouraging feedback as my external Ph.D. examiner filled me with the tenacity which is always necessary to publish one's work and to keep doing what brings one joy. Joanna Cook has also been a source of inspiration since my days as a Medical Anthropology student at UCL, and of encouragement and enthusiasm for seeing this work published. Emilija Zabiliute and Hannah McNeilly gave careful feedback on the draft of what later became part of Chapter 6, as editors of a special issue which was born from a workshop on care, kinship and chronic conditions held at the University of Edinburgh. Many thanks also go to Aruna Dahal for sharing with me the exciting beginning of my journey as an anthropologist and for providing, since then, constant boosts of confidence; and to Letizia Bonanno for invigorating conversations about care and mental health and for periodically reminding me, with her ethnographic drawings, of the magic that anthropologists can do with their work.

The Cambridge college Clare Hall, the Social Anthropology Department, the Cambridge Trust, the University of Cambridge, and the Economic and Social Research Council of the UK (Grant Ref ES/X00743X/1) have provided funding and support for the research project and for some of the writing work that turned into this book.

I am also grateful to James Laidlaw and Joel Robbins, editors of the Wyse Series in Social Anthropology at Berghahn, for considering and supporting my book proposal; to the four anonymous peer reviewers for their careful and constructive feedback on the proposal and full manuscript; to the editorial team at Berghahn Books for their enthusiasm and assistance, especially Tom Bonnington and Divjot Kaur; and to the production team for the meticulous copy-editing and proofreading, especially Annie Rose and Rowena Ockenden.

In Italy, my first thanks go to Cinzia Caporale and to all my colleagues at the Interdepartmental Center for Research Ethics and Integrity of the National Research Council (CID Ethics-CNR), for supporting the final drafting of this book and for nurturing my research interests. Among them, special thanks go to Giorgia Adamo, Marco Annoni, Marco Arizza, Ludovica Marinucci and Roberta Martina Zagarella for the stimulating discussions on some of the book content and for their consistently warm and cheering attitude.

In the world of Italian anthropology, I thank Angela Molinari and Manuela Tassan for the feedback they provided on a paper that is now part of Chapters 3 and 4, as convenors of a panel entitled *Alimentare il Sociale* (Feeding the Social) at the third National Conference of the Italian Society of Cultural Anthropology (SIAC), held in Rome in September 2023. In the world of Italian psychiatry, I deeply thank Ignazio Ardizzone, Massimo Cuzzolaro, Laura Dalla Ragione, Riccardo Dalle Grave and Leonardo Mendolicchio for welcoming a social anthropologist into spaces and conversations from which anthropologists are often still excluded, for showing me the good that psychiatry can do and most of all for fighting for a world in which there is more care for eating disorders and mental health.

From my personal world in Italy – now partly scattered across Europe – I thank Beatrice, Fanny, Marco, Melody, Roberta and Serena for being those precious people you always feel 'there' even if they are far away. And my parents and grandparents for being there when I needed them.

Finally, I thank Giulio, for that spark that one only feels in conversations that challenge you lovingly, for being the greatest supporter in my best, average and worst days, and for being the home I want to explore the world with and return to every day.

Introduction

Thinking about Eating Disorders through Anthropology, and the Other Way Around

It is an unexpectedly chilly morning in early June 2019. I am walking to the residential facility for eating disorders called Il Giardino[1] (literally The Garden) as I have been doing almost every day for nearly a year now. One can glimpse the distinctively orange walls of the sixteenth-century villa hosting the facility from above and below, whether one is ascending or descending from the small grey-coloured town in central Italy where it is located. The five-minute walk from my flat is usually very quiet, but today I find cars stuck in line one after the other. As soon as I turn the last corner, I see a red car blocking the way in front of the entrance to the building, with two people standing just outside, talking to someone in the car. While getting close to the red car I bump into the nutritionist Irma, who greets me with 'Oh thank God you are here Giulietta, today we really need help. It's one of those days that you want to forget. Look at what I have to do'. Irma then moves closer to the car and starts talking to someone inside. I can see now that it is a young girl, eleven or maybe ten years old. She is holding tight to the car seat. I infer that the two adults standing near Irma are the girl's parents. 'Come on Carlotta, let's go up. The drawing group is starting in a bit, it will be fun!', Irma tries to convince her. But Carlotta keeps shaking her head. At that point, the girl's father enters the car to pull his daughter out. Carlotta starts screaming that she does not want to go, while her father releases her from the rope attached to her seatbelt, which had reportedly been necessary to prevent her from trying to jump out of the car during the trip. Carlotta's father pulls her out by force and then drags her into the building with Irma's help. Carlotta's mother follows them tearfully, and keeps repeating: 'If mummy and daddy leave you here, it's only to help you; we can't help you at home'. They all disappear behind the orange walls, as I step up across the street to follow them inside, briefly encountering the startled look of a passer-by.

Just what goes on inside this building is, in fact, not obvious. Observing it while descending from the town centre, which is perched on a hill, one might guess that there is a large garden within its walls, as centuries-old trees reach over the top. Sometimes, especially in spring and summer, one can hear distant voices of girls coming from within. At times they are chatting, at times crying, at times laughing, and at times – it seems – acting. What happens here is closely connected to a much more recognisable and prosaic space, just a ten-minute walk from the orange villa as you continue to descend towards the ancient city walls: the local health centre (*centro salute*). Only by reading the small plaque placed on the front door of the villa can one make the connection: 'Residential Facility for Eating Disorders Il Giardino' is written under the name of the respective local health unit[2] and the name of a local charity fund. Similarly, if one goes to the health centre further down the road, one can read that the third floor hosts the 'Eating Disorder Day Service Il Giardino', provided by the same local health unit. Seemingly different spaces are thus brought together for apparently the same 'thing' – that is, 'eating disorders'.

Classified as 'mental illnesses' in the *Diagnostic and Statistical Manual of Mental Disorders*[3] (*DSM-5*) of the American Psychiatric Association (2013), what are now known as 'eating disorders' are a growing concern globally. First appeared in the clinical literature as 'eating disorders' in 1981 with the creation of the *International Journal of Eating Disorders* (Yates 1989: 814), eating disorders have been defined as 'a social epidemic' linked to 'Westernisation' (Gordon 2000): every year in the world millions of people are reported to fall ill, and international research suggests that the numbers keep growing (Miskovic-Wheatley et al. 2023; Schmidt et al. 2016; The Lancet Diabetes and Endocrinology 2023). Among eating disorders, 'anorexia nervosa' and 'bulimia nervosa' are defined in the *DSM-5* as 'a persistent disturbance of eating-related behaviour' due to body weight and shape becoming an 'obsessive preoccupation'. They are described as being characterised by 'insufficient or excessive food intake', often accompanied by 'self-induced vomiting, purging and compulsive exercise' (American Psychiatric Association 2013). With a mortality rate between 4% and 5%, anorexia nervosa, together with bulimia nervosa and substance use disorders (in particular opioid use), is reported to have the highest mortality rate of all mental health conditions, figuring among the most common causes of death for young Europeans and North Americans after road accidents (Arcelus et al. 2011; Auger et al. 2021; Chesney, Goodwin and Fazel 2014; Smink, van Hoeken and Hoek 2012). This is linked, the scientific literature reports, to the high rates of relapse after treatment (Khalsa et al. 2017). Although a fixed definition of 'recovery' is problematised both by those living with eating disorders and by scholars (Eli 2016; LaMarre and Rice 2021), according to clinical definitions fewer than half of patients with anorexia or bulimia nervosa fully recover in the long term

(Miskovic-Wheatley et al. 2023; Schmidt et al. 2016) and between 10% and 23% of cases develop into 'chronic conditions' (Berkman, Lohr and Bulik 2007; Fichter et al. 2017; Quadflieg and Fichter 2019).

Most people in Europe, North America and Australia today are familiar, even if to different extents, with eating disorders. This is likely the result of, on the one hand, the efforts of healthcare professionals, associations of parents and sufferers themselves to bring more attention to the issue, and, on the other, of an increased media attention due to the apparently 'exploding' numbers of new cases in recent years, especially since the beginning of the Covid-19 pandemic and the impact of lockdowns and social distancing measures on mental health (see Devoe et al. 2023; Linardon et al. 2022; Schneider et al. 2023). We now find eating disorders featuring not only in memoirs, novels and graphic novels,[4] but also in recurrent articles on national newspapers,[5] and in movies,[6] TV series[7] and documentaries[8] on popular TV channels. All of this means that, today, most people in these parts of the world know that those with an 'eating disorder' have some kind of issues with food that make their eating behaviour strange, often leading to severe weight loss, and that treatment involves some kind of psychological therapy and monitored eating to bring back 'normal eating' and 'normal weight'. But if we go back to Carlotta and start looking at what happens behind the orange walls of Il Giardino, we see that things are much more complicated than that.

By the time Carlotta's parents manage to leave, it is lunchtime. Carlotta refuses to eat, and when she is told that she must eat at least part of the meal before she can leave the dining room, she says an unconvinced 'OK'. Then she sneakily hides some of the food in her tissue and some under the plate, and throws some more on the floor. Observing her from the back of the room, standing next to me, Irma looks worried: 'Most patients do this at the beginning, but it's striking that she does it at such a young age. She already knows all the tricks!' Indeed, one of the key skills that I had to learn for my role as volunteer – one that all interns and professionals working here must learn – was 'training my eye' to spot patients' tricks to hide food during mealtimes: 'It is stronger than themselves at this stage, they can't help it. That's why we have to control them from above, like vultures', Irma continues. Three more 'vultures' are walking around the tables in the dining room, stopping when they notice something that should not happen: too much tomato sauce or oil on a napkin, too many breadcrumbs on the tablecloth, too much fruit cut away while peeling it … the list could go on. Patients' aims are apparently always the same – newcomers are taught by Irma and by her colleagues: 'Reducing the number of calories[9] ingested, to reduce weight gain'.

What is here classified as an 'eating disorder' may seem, to an external and untrained observer, to have to do with food, calories and weight. As we will see in this book, however, both the patients and the professionals, although in different ways, seem to agree on one aspect: 'It's not just about food'. If eating disorders are not just about food, then, what are they about? In this book I attempt to provide an ethnographic answer to this question. The answer, we will see, depends on who gives it: patients, their family carers and professionals have different ideas about and theories of what an 'eating disorder' is, and even within these groups different understandings circulate of what is going on. These differences, and the complex effects produced by their circulation and encounter, are at the core of the difficulty of caring for people with eating disorders.

What This Book Is, and What It Is Not

This book is an in-depth ethnographic account of an Italian public treatment centre for people diagnosed with an eating disorder. Based on eighteen months of fieldwork that took place between July 2018 and August 2019, and then from October 2022 to February 2023, the book sits at the intersection between anthropologies of science and biomedicine and anthropologies of ethics, care and kinship, as it examines the practices and the ethics of care that emerge when patients, their families and healthcare professionals meet and clash with one another inside and outside the spaces of treatment. The book, however, is not primarily about whether these care practices 'work' or 'fail'. On the contrary, it situates itself among studies of the failures of eating disorder treatment in other countries by making a case for thinking beyond a binary conception of success or failure. This is because, we will see, even continuous attempts on the part of well-intentioned therapists to do the right thing sometimes are not enough and lead to death, as things turn out to be always more complex. The aim, instead, is to learn, through an analysis of the kind of care that one can find in these spaces, something new about eating disorders and something new about people, which has relevance for eating disorder treatment because it can show where attention and action should be directed for things to get better.

We will see that the kind of care found in the clinic calls for rethinking existing understandings of the relationship between food and kinship. Contributing to both the more specialised literature on eating disorder treatment and to the wider anthropological literature on food and kinship, the central theoretical argument of this book is that it is not only that food is a 'substance of relatedness' which generates kinship (Carsten 1995), but the reverse is also true. What I mean by that is that food can function as a vehicle to make or unmake kinship (by refusing it), and, in turn, kinship itself can become a kind of 'substance' – a medium – that shapes whether and how food is incorporated into persons. This suggests a co-substantiation of food and family, but in a way that differs from existing anthropological accounts. The book thus ultimately argues that it is not only that food makes people into kin but also the other way around – kinship also makes and unmakes people through food, with complicated consequences for both the patients and the work of healthcare professionals. This also seems to suggest that even people in a European country like Italy may not be as 'individual' as one might think. They might be 'dividual' and 'partible' persons, in a way analogous to the Melanesians famously described by the British anthropologist Marilyn Strathern (1988, 2009, 2018): the patients in this treatment centre – their very bodies – we will see are constituted by their social relationships.

The book is relevant for scholars, graduate and undergraduate students from different disciplines. For medical and psychological anthropologists it encourages further thinking about the ethics of care, especially about the complexities of caring for those who need care and yet struggle to see themselves as in need of care. For social anthropologists and other social scientists it enriches the conversation on the relationship between food and kinship, speaking in new ways to classic questions in these fields. For psychologists, psychiatrists and other clinicians it offers a distinctive intervention into debates surrounding eating disorders, being i) the first book-length qualitative study of eating disorder treatment in a European country with a national healthcare system, ii) the first book-length ethnography that brings together the voices of patients, healthcare professionals and families during and *after* treatment (the latter two groups having received considerably less attention compared to the patients) and iii) the first ethnographic book to address the specific difficulties posed by preadolescent patients, a recent and increasingly alarming phenomenon.[10]

Two clarifications are needed here. The first one is that this book does not generalise about eating disorder treatment, nor about eating disorder treatment in Italy. It is a description of the practices and ethics of care in the particular treatment centre where I worked, and yet it highlights issues that are both anthropologically interesting and rich with clinical implications. The book examines care in a treatment centre that mostly admits patients with anorexia and bulimia nervosa. These are typically considered the most severe forms of eating disorders (Gibson, Workman and Mehler 2019; Miskovic-Wheatley et al. 2023) but are not the only ones, and it is being increasingly recognised that other forms, such as 'binge eating disorder', are not less dangerous (American Psychiatry Association 2013). However, the reader will notice that most of the literature that I refer to here is based on research conducted on anorexia nervosa. This is because bulimia nervosa was theorised as a separate illness from anorexia nervosa only in 1979, having existed until then as a 'sub-type' of the latter (Squire 2003: 17). Although it is now clinically recognised that the two conditions share a desire for thinness, body dissatisfaction and fear of weight gain – and that they can often turn into one another during one lifetime (Fairburn, Cooper and Shafran 2003), with between 20% and 61% of people experiencing more than one type of eating disorder (Miskovic-Wheatley et al. 2023) – they are categorised as separate pathologies because their behaviours seem radically opposed: anorexia mostly consists in self-starving, bulimia in binge eating and purging. As pointed out by the feminist psychologist Maree Burns (2004: 269–70), this strict categorisation obscures the relatedness between the two conditions: bingeing is often a consequence of extreme dieting, and many anorexic women practise binge eating and purging.[11] Some (e.g., Squire 2003) have suggested that bulimia is placed lower in the medical hierarchy than anorexia because bulimic practices embody a liminality that disrupts normative values of Western femininity, whereas anorexic practices are read within a continuum of approved feminine behaviour and 'western assumptions about successful selfhood': people with anorexia are supposedly seen by both patients themselves and by professionals as having 'something extra' that distinguishes them from the 'weakness' of those with bulimia (Burns 2004: 276). In this book I do not pay much attention to distinguishing patients according to their specific diagnosis of anorexia or bulimia nervosa, as this was not something that seemed to matter in my field site. Although I occasionally heard comments along those lines, both among professionals and among patients themselves, usually such comments had the aim of criticising simplistic views and did not come to shape differently the issues I examine.

The second necessary clarification is that in this book I will be referring to patients who are 'biologically female' – unless otherwise specified – because virtually all patients in my field site were assigned female at birth. I will not be discussing why eating disorders seem to affect many more girls or women than boys or men, for example. A lot has been written on this already, especially by feminist-cultural scholars in the late 1980s and 1990s (e.g., Bordo 1993; MacSween 1993; Orbach 1986; Weiss 1999). However, it is worth mentioning here that whereas, until recently, it had been taken for granted in the literature that about 90% of eating disorder patients were assigned female at birth, researchers and clinicians have started commenting that these numbers might be incorrect (Halbeisen, Brandt and Paslakis 2022; Raevuori, Keski-Rahkonen and Hoek 2014): many adolescent boys and men seem now to be suffering from what might be called an obsessive relationship with their bodies, physical exercise and food – a relationship that, in addition to manifesting itself in the search for extreme slenderness, may often find expression in the search for an extremely muscled physique, what some call 'bigorexia' (Mosley 2009). It has been suggested that the reason behind such great disparity in numbers is therefore not so much that boys and men 'are not affected', but that i) they are less willing to seek help because of the very idea that eating disorders are 'women's stuff', and ii) eating disorders in boys or men assume not only the forms of anorexia, bulimia or binge eating, but also forms that have not been explored and categorised as illness yet (Dalla Ragione and Giombini 2014: 27–28; Halbeisen, Brandt and Paslakis 2022). Little is known about eating disorders in those who are assigned male at birth, as they have been largely excluded from research despite findings from recent epidemiological studies indicating marked increases in the prevalence of eating disorders among them (Murray et al. 2017). These are all important issues, especially because they result in misrecognition of symptoms, delayed care, increased severity at presentation for treatment and reduced survival compared to women. But they are issues that will not be addressed in this book.

The rest of this introduction turns first to a brief history of the emergence of 'eating disorders' as an object of interest in psychiatry and in the clinical sciences, and subsequently in history and in the social sciences, to show how eating disorders have been puzzling to scholars from very different disciplines. It then focuses on a review of the anthropological literature on eating disorders and eating disorder treatment to show how, in the last three decades, ethnographic studies have called into question much of what has been seen as the 'common sense' regarding these conditions, developing accounts instead of how disordered eating is grounded in social structures and relationships that tend to be obscured in both popular and clinical framings. What eating disorders are, we will see, is a question that sparked long and contested debates within and beyond anthropology, and these debates have direct relevance for treatment. I situate my research within such work and other relevant literature on care, clinical worlds, food and kinship, to outline the key contributions of the book before concluding with an overview of the chapters' content.

From Early Clinical Accounts to Contemporary Treatment Approaches

What is now called 'anorexia nervosa' has been a named clinical entity since the 1870s. Although the British physician Richard Morton is credited as the first to describe a seemingly similar condition as a psychiatric illness in 1694 under the name of 'nervous consumption', it was only in the 1870s that the medical doctors Charles Lasègue (1873) and William Gull (1874) used the modern terminology, in France and England respectively.[12] Following the psychiatric nosology of the time, these clinicians associated anorexia with other 'hysterical affections'[13] and identified its roots in 'suppressed emotional troubles' occurring during maturation (Lasègue 1997 [1873]: 492–93). As the linguistic etymology of anorexia suggests (incorrectly, it would now be held), these scholars saw a 'want of appetite' – not due to any physical disorder, they thought, but to 'a morbid mental state' (ibid.) – to be the crux of the condition. This assumed 'want of appetite' was also observed to be accompanied, notwithstanding the emaciation that resulted, by a 'peculiar restlessness' and hyperactivity (Gull 1997 [1874]: 499–500; Lasègue 1997 [1873]: 494).

From the end of the nineteenth century, the French father of modern neurology, Jean-Martin Charcot, and then his student Pierre Janet became pioneers of what would later be called the 'psychosomatic' view of anorexia nervosa. Both physicians agreed, even if with different theories of the pathogenic mechanisms and therefore of the necessary treatment, that anorexia had something to do with the relationship between mind ('psyche') and body ('soma'). Charcot (1889) gave more prominence to the neurological pathways through which this 'hysterical' condition manifested, taking the body as his primary focus, whereas Janet (1907) gave a more prominent role to the psyche, focusing on processes of what he called 'dissociation' and on the psychosomatic expressions of the traumatic events of one's past that were supposedly stored in what he called the 'subconscious' (Lester 2019: 38–39).

When the Austrian neurologist Sigmund Freud began to study anorexia nervosa in the early twentieth century, the relationship between mind and body became the focus of a new intellectual and therapeutic movement called 'psychoanalysis', as he offered an understanding of anorexia – which was still categorised as a form of hysteria – that combined Charcot's attention to physiology with Janet's on the subconscious. Freud's (1918) explanation of anorexia nervosa, and the post-Freudian developments that followed, provided the basis for most current approaches to eating disorder treatment, as they brought the questions posed by Charcot and Janet into the domains of sexuality and gender: anorexia became, in Freud's framing, mostly an issue of incomplete or improper sexual and gender development, which for him were one and the same. Subsequent psychoanalytic thinkers especially framed food refusal as a rejection of adult sexuality and as an attempt to return to a state of childhood and avoid the responsibilities that come with being an adult woman; so-called 'psychodynamic' approaches focused on the importance of psychotherapy as a way to bring out the 'inner' workings of the mind and study the dynamic relations between the patient's behaviour and its 'unconscious motivations' (see Lester 2019: 40–42).

In the second half of the same century, the German-American doctor and psychoanalyst Hilde Bruch (1962: 188) published an article in *Psychosomatic Medicine* based on her treatment of twelve young patients with anorexia nervosa, describing their condition as being characterised by 'three areas of functionally disordered psychological experience': i) 'a disturbance in body image of delusional proportions' – hence the fear of becoming fat; ii) 'disturbance in the accuracy of perception or cognitive interpretation of stimuli arising in the body', such as hunger, fatigue and weakness; and iii) a 'paralyzing sense of ineffectiveness' (ibid.: 188–91). However, it was Bruch's monograph *The Golden Cage* (1978) that, drawing on conversations with her patients and influenced by social changes later classified as feminist, brought anorexia into broader public consciousness. Here she argued that for young women pressured to satisfy social expectations anorexia was a means of asserting control and power through an extreme practice. At about the same time, the British psychiatrist Arthur Crisp (1980) similarly framed anorexia as an 'adaptive disorder', whereby the prepubertal body size achieved through starvation allowed women to avoid an adult social and sexual life.

As a doctor, Bruch had also noted how starvation likely played a role in influencing 'thinking, feeling and behavior' (Bruch 1978: 4), turning 'formerly sweet, obedient and considerate' girls into 'demanding, obstinate, irritable and arrogant' ones (ibid.: 2) who, 'like other starving people', were now 'eternally preoccupied with food and eating' (ibid.: 8). In recognition of these effects of starvation, Bruch emphasised the importance of 'weight correction' in the first phase of treatment, since one could not expect to do 'meaningful therapeutic work with a patient who is starving' (1978: 129). However, she also remarked that weight correction must occur 'as part of an integrated approach' (ibid.: 98) which might include 'family disengagement' (ibid.: 112) and 'changing the [patient's] mind' (ibid.: 128). She thus warned against treatment that relied simply on 'behavioral modification' to achieve weight gain, as that would generate a 'battle of wills' (ibid.: 99). Individual psychotherapy was her preferred treatment method, through which she aimed to help patients develop a 'capacity for self-directed actions' (ibid.: 130).

In the same year that Bruch's masterpiece was published, two other works later considered 'groundbreaking' in the field of eating disorders came out: Salvador Minuchin, an Argentinian physician who trained in child psychiatry and psychoanalysis in New York, published with his colleagues at the University of Pennsylvania a book titled *Psychosomatic Families: Anorexia Nervosa in Context* (Minuchin, Rosman and Baker 1978). This book placed anorexia, as well as its cure, in the family system: it argued that since anorexia developed within a family context characterised by certain 'dysfunctions', rather than separating the child from their parents – as Bruch seemed to suggest – treatment had to be directed at families to address these problematic aspects. At about the same time, in Italy the psychiatrist Mara Selvini Palazzoli (1978) also called for shifting from 'individual therapy' to 'family therapy' in the treatment of anorexia. These theories informed research work undertaken at the Maudsley Hospital in London during the 1980s, laying the foundation of what became 'family-based treatment' for eating disorders (Russell et al. 1987). As we will see through the chapters, this is now mostly focused on engaging the family as a 'resource' for recovery, through 'empowering' the patient's parents to have an active role in treatment. In the meantime, in the UK the psychiatrist Gerald Russell (1979) first distinguished bulimia nervosa as 'an ominous variant' of anorexia characterised by overwhelming 'urges to overeat' that lead to binges and purging measures. Accordingly, the publication in 1980 of the third edition of the *Diagnostic and Statistical Manual of Mental Disorders* (*DSM-III*), in which a section on 'eating disorders' appeared for the first time,[14] included a separate diagnostic category 'bulimia nervosa'.

In this period, 'cognitive' theories that linked thought patterns learned in specific environments to specific behaviours bypassing the 'unconscious' brought a new model of human behaviour and a new understanding of anorexia nervosa, whereby people would receive positive reinforcement for losing weight up to the point that the patient's self-destructive practices became 'habituated' and very difficult to discard, unless their 'faulty cognition' and 'distorted thinking' were addressed (see Lester 2019: 45). In this context, cognitive behavioural therapy (CBT) started to be a common favoured approach, also because it generated visible and quantifiable improvements (even if only in the short term, many argued) that responded well to the changes in most healthcare systems towards concerns with treatment 'evidence' and 'cost-effectiveness' (ibid.: 46). During this turn towards increasing attention to categorisation and quantification, in the 1980s and 1990s several eating disorder 'diagnostic scales' were also developed. Among these were the Eating Disorder Inventory and the Eating Disorder Examination Questionnaire, the sub-scales of which aimed to quantify issues such as 'drive for thinness' and 'body dissatisfaction' (Marks 2019: 1384).

It is interesting and important to highlight that these various theories and approaches to eating disorders are not mutually exclusive, and most treatment centres in Italy and elsewhere – even most clinicians – combine them in their work, including staff at Il Giardino. We will see that the different ways of conceiving the relationship between body and mind, and the ways in which the 'biological', the 'psychological' and the 'social' dimensions of eating disorders are thought to interact and affect the patient, in treatment turn into practical questions that sometimes demand competing answers.

The Social in the Picture: From 'Culture-Bound Syndromes' to 'Embodied Processes'

From the 1980s, historians and social scientists in the United States and Europe took an interest in the history of anorexia. They traced its origin back to late nineteenth-century Victorian bourgeois families, but they also associated it with self-starvation among medieval Catholic women (see Brumberg 1988; Vandereycken and van Deth 1994). Specifically, the American historian Rudolph Bell (1985) argued that thirteenth- to sixteenth-century Italian ascetics manifested in their 'holy anorexia' dynamics that also characterise contemporary anorexia, and that both conditions reflect a struggle for female autonomy within patriarchal social structures. Bell's colleague Caroline Bynum (1987) argued against reducing the food abstinence of ascetics in the Middle Ages to 'eating disorders', observing that food was the only thing medieval ascetics could control about themselves and their surrounding world. Renouncing food, Bynum argued, allowed women to exercise 'self-determination' – leaving the family, avoiding marriage duties and reaching redemptive leadership roles within the Church.

At the same time, with the rise of feminist psychology, political analyses of this 'feminine pathology' (Orbach 1986) started proliferating. The feminist sociologist Morag MacSween (1993) suggested that anorexic *practices*, rather than women's vulnerabilities, should have been the focus of enquiry. Accordingly, the feminist philosophers Susan Bordo (1993) and Gail Weiss (1999) analysed anorexia as an extreme practice embodying the social denigration of the body and the feminine. Through these literatures, 'anorexia nervosa' emerged as a condition with a multidimensional causation, a seemingly rich history and a peculiar epidemiology. A 'biocultural disorder' for some (Eli and Ulijaszek 2023), it became interesting to anthropologists.

When anthropological work on anorexia was first published in the 1980s, models of 'culture-bound syndromes' were the focus of medical anthropology and transcultural psychiatry. Since these syndromes seemed to be unique to populations in the 'developing world', anorexia was an attractive example because it was felt, at the time, to be one syndrome exclusive to 'the West' (Di Nicola 1990; Prince 1985; Swartz 1985). In the 1990s, the culture-boundedness of anorexia was problematised by calling attention to the religious ascetic dimension that informs self-starvation (Banks 1992) and to the cultural 'ordering' of the disorder performed by Euro-American psychiatry (Gremillion 1992). 'Non-fat-phobic anorexia' was introduced to refer to forms of anorexia now being 'found' in China and Hong Kong (Lee 1996; Lee, Ho and Tsu 1993). Further anthropological work challenged the exclusive association of anorexia to 'Western cultural concerns' with body fat or weight (Littlewood 1995; Ritenbaugh et al. 1996), laying the foundation for analyses of eating disorders in the Eastern hemisphere and the Global South. These were brought together in a *Culture, Medicine and Psychiatry* special issue on 'New Global Perspectives on Eating Disorders' (Becker 2004a), offering a compelling argument against the framing of eating disorders as 'disorders of the West' simply transportable to other contexts via 'Westernisation' (e.g., Becker 2004b).

In recent decades, in fact, shifts of theory and interest in medical anthropology – from culture-bound syndromes and explanatory models of illness to globalisation and ethnographies of 'the body' and 'self', for instance – aligned anthropological studies of anorexia with critical analyses of experience and practice. Anthropological work on eating disorders largely shifted to analyses of the micro-scale of lived experience in European and American contexts, calling attention to the 'cultural logics' (Eli and Warin 2018) that drive eating disordered practices and showing how these practices are embedded within normative social environments. It has been noted that this more recent ethnographic work has analysed anorexia as an embodied process, rather than as a disordered state (Eli and Lavis 2022; Eli and Ulijaszek 2023; Eli and Warin 2018).

In imposing a Cartesian mind–body split, medicalisation had tended to make anorexia a mental disorder – the mind's war on the body – requiring psychological conjectures. But by erasing the Cartesian division and by looking at people with anorexia in their context – a context in which bodies have increasingly become moral arenas wherein eating and exercise test one's strength of character (Niola 2015; O' Connor and Van Esterik 2008: 7–8) – people with anorexia emerged as 'misguided moralists, not cognitive cripples', and their seemingly extraordinary asceticism appeared then to have very ordinary roots in local values and practices (O'Connor and Van Esterik 2008: 7).

The question then became: how exactly do those who suffer from anorexia become 'misguided moralists'? British anthropologist Sue Benson (1997) characterised eating disorders as 'epidemics of the will', as extreme enactments of Euro-American fantasies of self-control. In this framework, the body is experienced as a project of the self: sufferers try to rewrite their self by changing their body through a paradoxical mixture of voluntarism and compulsion. Extreme food restriction, Benson notes, offers the promise of becoming a master of one's body by winning over hunger, but it ends up undermining 'the very autonomy it seeks to establish' (ibid.: 136).

American anthropologist Rebecca Lester (1997) also tried to address this question in her earlier work. She argued that feminist framings of anorexia as 'the crystallization of culture' (Bordo 1993) – as an extreme embodiment of 'Western' ideals about women's bodies and roles – depicted it as an unconscious, self-destructive social protest. Women were conceived as passive bodies and their 'self' was left unexamined, preventing the understanding of its embodied articulation (Lester 1997: 479–81). Drawing on fieldwork in an eating disorder clinic in the United States, Lester proposed to analyse anorexia through Foucault's (1986) notion of 'technologies of the self' – as a deliberate shaping of the self achieved through culturally meaningful bodily practices. She suggested that the body is seen as the material vehicle of the 'internal self'. Restriction of food, invested with meanings about dependency and nurturance, is therefore used to reconstruct the boundaries of the 'body-self', communicating autonomy (Lester 1997: 485–86). As a response to an extreme awareness that our bodies define us, shaping a chosen body becomes the goal. It is essential, Lester thus argued, to first consider the theoretical project of anorexia – 'the self which is being pursued' – and then examine 'its practice' – the behaviours that bring about the self-transformation (ibid.). A slender body is thus the first visible aim because, in what Lester calls 'the West', it reflects a self that can 'rise above' the need to eat – a morally superior self (ibid.).

Carrying on from Lester's approach, Sigal Gooldin (2008), in her ethnographic study of an outpatient eating disorder unit in Israel, suggested that people with anorexia construct their selves as moral selves through the experience of enduring and overcoming hunger, seen as 'an out of the ordinary accomplishment'. Hunger, which involves physical pain and suffering, is experienced by patients as an enjoyable 'hyper' feeling of power and self-efficiency, becoming a 'selfing device' to make themselves 'moral agents', since self-inflicted hunger is experienced 'as a heroic way of being in the world' (ibid.: 290). Going even deeper than Lester into the specific element of the 'technology of the self' that creates such selves, Gooldin suggests that being anorexic is about being hungry and giving meaning to it, no less than it is about 'shaping the body' (ibid.). Her account constructs anorexia in terms of transforming one's self through an existence that may be numbed through active detachment from one's bodily sensations. But, by being active, this existence is also 'fiercely sensed' (Eli 2012: 2).

Lester's and Gooldin's framing of anorexia as an experiment with the self could itself be said to be culturally specific. Anthropologist Anne Becker (1995) has pointed out how the interest in reflexively cultivating one's body depends on the cultural validation of personal agency with respect to the body, which is in turn linked to the experience of self vis-à-vis the community; it presupposes that the body represents a personal resource for expression (ibid.: 37). In her ethnography of bodily aesthetics in Fiji, Becker outlines a relationship between self, body and society which highlights aspects of self and body boundaries, agency and identity that situate both Lester's and Gooldin's accounts. In Fiji, Becker shows, the cultivation of bodily space is a collective rather than a personal enterprise: bodies and the crafting of their form are the responsibility of the community that cares for them (Becker 1995: 5). Therefore, what bodily form communicates is how one has been nurtured or neglected in his or her social universe, not the attitude of one's personal self. One's body in Fiji also encodes one's capacity and propensity to serve one's social universe in return: in an interesting inversion, too-slim bodies are associated with laziness and inability to work, whereas bigger bodies are associated with productivity and willingness to contribute to the community (ibid.: 56–58). The cultivation of the self through personal manipulation of the body therefore emerges as a concept made possible by 'Western' values that encourage autonomy, independence and competitive work to raise oneself above other selves (ibid.: 127–29).

Nevertheless, Lester's and Gooldin's accounts have important implications for clinical practice in offering new explanations as to why patients can be so resistant to treatment. If the eating disorder is experienced by patients as in some sense an ethical project of self-cultivation, treatment will easily be perceived as an external, intrusive attempt to make their personal projects fail. Their work strongly suggests that if eating disorders are addressed as stemming from 'pathological selves', rather than taken seriously as the very practices by which sufferers *form* their 'self' (Tait 1993: 205), biomedical care will continue to fail. The question thus remains of how to approach these issues in a way that takes people's self-projects seriously, without this appearing to result in a neglect of the severe consequences that the same projects can bring.

Ethnographic Studies of Eating Disorder Treatment

We have seen that there has been an extensive anthropological literature on the possible 'causes' and 'nature' of eating disorders. Less attention has been given to treatment – a perfect place for analysing the 'selves' of daily practice. In line with recent ethnographies that have framed eating disorders as 'technologies of the self' (Eli 2018; Gooldin 2008; Lester 1997), several ethnographic works on treatment have focused on patients' perspectives: on their ambivalence towards treatment as a key element of their 'anorexic being-in-the-world' (Warin 2010), including, most recently, on how the materialities of treatment shape patients' ambivalence about illness and their 'resistance' to recovery (Eli and Lavis 2022).

Lester (2014), for instance, highlighted how patients undergoing treatment in the United States restrict their intake of medication – psychotropic drugs that tackle related symptoms such as depression and anxiety, but also vitamins and mineral supplements – in the same way that they restrict food. Drawing on her earlier work (see Lester 1997), she suggested that medication refusal is for these patients a means of 'self-communication' within a larger ethical project. Taking medications presumes someone who strives towards health, but for these patients the optimal state seems to be deprivation (Lester 2014: 249). Lester's study helps clarify why the common practice of presenting food to patients as 'medicine', on the assumption that they will feel less 'guilty' about eating, often does not work: taking medicines is experienced by patients as a way of taking care of one's body; this goes against their self-cultivation project based on overcoming bodily needs (ibid.: 243–49).

Karin Eli (2014), Anna Lavis (2015, 2016) and Connie Musolino and colleagues (2015, 2016) subsequently reinforced Lester's findings with similar ethnographic studies conducted in Israel, England and Australia respectively. Patients, even those who recognise its dangers and negative sides, experience restricting food as a form of caring for themselves, as their only way out of suffering, providing them 'safety'. This is why, even if they feel the eating disorder is harmful, they may want to maintain it (Lavis 2016: 71–72). Looking at these contradictions ultimately means questioning the notion of an individuated, unified self who can give informed consent to treatment (Berliner et al. 2016: 5).

In 2018 a special issue entitled 'Anthropological Perspectives on Eating Disorders: Deciphering Cultural Logics' was published in *Transcultural Psychiatry* (Eli and Warin 2018). This special issue aimed to explore how anthropological approaches to eating disorders had developed in the decade since the 2004 special issue of *Culture, Medicine and Psychiatry* on eating disorders in a global context. The intention was to provide anthropological responses to clinical questions about the low rates of treatment success (Keel and Brown 2010), the high rates of treatment 'dropout' (Fassino et al. 2009) and the modes of managing enduring eating disorders (Touyz and Hay 2015; Treasure, Stein and Maguire 2015). Among the contributions, Musolino, Warin and Gilchrist (2018) have examined ambivalence towards help-seeking in Australia, focusing on narrations of what they call 'triggers', i.e., encounters with food and other social stimuli that prompt women with disordered eating to re-engage in restrictive or binge-purging practices. The authors argue that culturally embedded gendered desires to deny or fulfil certain embodied longings (e.g., for the intensity of the binge or the lightness of the empty body) are fundamental to understanding why people do not seek help or frequently oscillate between recovery and relapse. Lavis' (2018) paper focuses on British inpatients' experiences and examines how patients mobilise practices of eating and not eating to cultivate their relationship with anorexia during treatment. The attractiveness of disordered eating, argues Lavis, lies not in the maintenance of an emaciated body, but in the desire for ongoing illness, with anorexia experienced as a 'safe space' that allows sufferers to 'live through distress' through a 'viscerally felt shield' from the outside world. Similarly Eli (2018), in her analysis of Israeli patients' narratives of their eating experiences, argues that people with eating disorders 'strive for liminality' – actively seeking an ambivalent being through eating disordered practices to survive oppressive familial, institutional and social conditions. Eating disorders, Eli suggests, work as a long-term way of surviving-in-the-world amidst structural vulnerabilities and social suffering.

This body of literature points to the severe limitations of enforced treatment. On the other hand, however, the increasingly celebrated principle of respecting patients' choice seems to be equally detrimental given the intricacies of the conditions in question (cf. Mol 2008). In this context, respecting patients' choice about treatment will not help, as it is likely to lead to chronicisation or death. On this matter, a second strand of ethnographic literature on treatment has usefully drawn attention to how inpatient facilities in the United States (Gremillion 2003; Lester 2007, 2009, 2014, 2018, 2019), Canada, Australia and the UK (Warin 2005) are characterised by settings of care, dynamics of surveillance and treatment practices that unwittingly reproduce the very dynamics that sustain eating disorders, making treatment fail. All these elements – the different authors suggest – are based on a notion of patients' self as lacking in self-discipline, whose problems can be solved by addressing 'the mind'. Still, 'the body' is at the centre of treatment, seen as an uncooperative appendage that needs to be constantly under control.

Helen Gremillion's (2003) ethnography of an eating disorder clinic in the United States contains another interesting and overlooked point. Among other things, she analysed the dynamics between the members of the treatment team – what she calls the 'therapeutic family' (ibid.: 119) – and the patients. 'Affectionate caretaking' was considered a crucial 'natural' feature that professionals had to possess, but at the same time it was perceived as potentially risky, thus requiring staff members to learn to keep a distance through 'minimal mothering' (ibid.: 120). Otherwise, they risked 'overnurturing' patients and generating harmful effects (ibid.: 121–27). Staff members in Gremillion's field site could explain very well how maternal attitudes could lead to over-involvement or punitive behaviours, but less easily what constituted a good nurturing attitude (ibid.: 149–53). A balance between 'involvement' and 'detachment' was seen as necessary, but just where the 'right' balance lay was not clear. Reaching it was known to require time and constant practice. Lavis, Abbots and Attala's (2015) work on the entanglements between eating and caring also invites reflection on this 'slipperiness' of care – on how it is framed both as an innate ability and as something to be learned through training (ibid.: 5–7).

In fact, there has been little attention paid to the professionals in anthropological accounts of eating disorder treatment, other than to point out how well-intended clinicians make sense of their care within systemic failure and end up colluding with the structural limitations of the treatment apparatus within which they work. Lester (2009, 2017, 2018), for example, explored how clinicians strive to provide the best treatment for patients within the constraints of managed care in the United States, which requires quantitively measurable treatment goals. All these works converged into Lester's (2019) monograph – the product of twenty years of ethnographic research in a private eating disorder treatment centre, coupled from a certain point with her own clinical work as a counsellor and informed by her personal struggle with eating disorders from early adolescence into young adulthood. Moving on from her previous framing of eating disorders as 'technologies of the self' (Lester 1997), here she proposes to see eating disorders as ways of extending an ethical demand to others and reframes them as 'technologies of presence' (Lester 2019: 63): as tools that people employ to make themselves seen and responded to in the world. She thus calls for paying attention 'to how professionals care' when facing patients who often do not want to receive treatment, their families in crisis but still resistant to change, and a healthcare system that downplays the kind of clinical expertise that seems to help. She examines how such a situation generates contradictory ideals of recovery and paradoxical notions of the 'healthy subject', thus producing frictions and 'roadblocks' – within a sense of constant precarity due to the system of health insurances requiring quantifiable and predictive evidence of treatment success. Her ethnography is therefore ultimately about how professionals understand practices of care when 'care' and 'harm' are deeply intertwined, and about how they make sense of treatment in the face of such systemic failure – which often leads to more sickness and to death (ibid.: xvii–xviii). She argues that clinicians unwittingly end up assimilating the political-economic logics of US managed care into their understandings of eating disorders, thereby constructing everyday realities of clinical practice that provide ethical space for the withdrawal of care.

This second strand of literature has tended to paint a picture based on a binary conception of success or failure: treatment that should succeed by saving patients' lives and supporting long-lasting recovery clearly fails to do so. This book, instead, takes a step back and examines the difficult care work that is done within the less-than-ideal context of a public treatment centre in Italy, a country with a crumbling but still functioning national healthcare system. This enables the existence of different forms and times of care and makes it possible to see things that are otherwise obscured in managed care contexts, where such care cannot happen in the first place. The book therefore purposefully focuses on the grey areas between 'failure' and 'success' and on how, when difficulties arise and things seem to be failing, professionals – and family carers, too – try other ways to make their interventions work, generating novel forms of care along the way which are not always 'successful' but are still worthy of attention and analysis.

Despite a fixation on the family in the history of eating disorder treatment, and despite attention from some ethnographers to how relatedness is 'reconfigured' in people with anorexia (Warin 2006, 2010), the role of the family tends to be even more overlooked than professionals in ethnographic accounts of treatment facilities (e.g., Eli and Lavis 2022; Lester 2019; Warin 2005). In these accounts the patient's family, when present, features mostly as an additional complication (e.g., Lester 2019).[15] In Gremillion's (2003) notable exception, which examines the production of normalised bodies, subjectivities and families in a hospital-based inpatient programme in the United States, the family features as the realm that offers a template for the anorexigenic power relationships observed within the treatment team and between patients and professionals. Gremillion's analysis of the treatment team as a 'substitute family' focuses on the gendered cultural dynamics that make the mother–child relationship the locus where clinicians locate 'the heart of the problem', and that ultimately make treatment fail (ibid.: 104). In this book I go beyond her focus on what does not work in the 'substitute family' and show how kinship care in this treatment centre highlights something that is interesting to the anthropology of kinship and of medicine more generally – namely, that kinship relations are seen to need remodelling in order to transform patients' eating behaviours, and, through those behaviours, their bodies. By examining what food affords to family and what family affords to food, in this book I bring together some of the issues dealt with in the anthropological literature on kinship, and some of the issues dealt with in medical anthropology, to suggest that kinship and feeding are interestingly aligned in both the production *and* treatment of disease.

On Bodies, Care and Ethics

This book is also a contribution to the literature on the ethics of care. It starts by asking how the multiple 'bodies' and multiple 'eating disorders' of patients and professionals are coordinated during treatment (see Mol 2002): patients and professionals – and within this latter category, different kinds of professionals – each conceive and approach 'the body' and 'the eating disorder' differently. We will see that, for those who become patients, the eating disorder is a way to better cope with life by reshaping their bodies according to their will and control. For the professionals, the eating disorder is a pathology that has to be treated within the realm of medicine – a deviation from how 'normal', 'healthy' bodies and minds should 'function'. But within this second reality, there is more multiplicity. Like 'atherosclerosis' in the outpatient clinic studied by Annemarie Mol

(2002) in the Netherlands, the 'eating disorder' as conceived in this treatment centre is not a natural unity. It might form a unity in contrast to the eating disorder experienced by a patient, but we will see that if one looks at the practicalities of treatment, the treatment centre appears to be full of contrasts.

Mol had pointed out that her study provoked the question of how the body multiple and its diseases 'might be done well' – which is, the question of 'the good' (Mol 2002: 165–66) – but that her purpose was not to answer that question. My book, instead, is an attempt to explore how the multiple dis-eases and bodies that circulate within and outside an eating disorder treatment centre are coordinated with the aim of providing 'good care'. I observe the 'goods' that are sought after, the 'bads' that are fought, and how multiple 'goods' are framed as being good due to the specific limits of what carers can do (ibid.: 176–77). In this sense I follow the approach that Jeannette Pols (2015: 82) calls 'empirical ethics', as I examine the different and sometimes conflicting notions of good care within these specific care practices by analysing the 'goods' that carers and patients strive for, the values and norms they implicitly or explicitly shape and the 'bads' they want to avoid. This places ethics *in* the world of those we study, as a part of everyday practices (ibid.; cf. Brodwin 2013).

From Mol's later work on what she calls 'the logic of care' (2008), I take her approach of avoiding the distinction between 'care' – mostly used to refer to activities, such as washing or feeding, that are done to make daily life more bearable – and 'cure', used for interventions that should ideally heal people from a disease. In an eating disorder treatment centre, especially, things that would be framed as 'care' – feeding, listening – are seen to be the very key to the 'cure'. Therefore, I will use the term 'care' to refer to all kinds of practices going on in the treatment centre, although, we will see, there are different forms of care emerging from different situations. Furthermore, as Mol does in her work on diabetes (ibid.: 7), I take the specificities of care for eating disorders as the focus of why it is important to disentangle care from an immediate assumption of 'kindness', and to be open to including in care also practices that might seem to have more to do with 'force' and 'coercion' but that, upon further scrutiny, reveal themselves as requiring a lot of effort from patients.

A particular kind of affection is in fact expected from staff members of eating disorder treatment units, and yet they are required to perform treatment practices that can also seem antithetical to caring. The necessarily 'harsh' aspects of their job are seen to impede 'connecting' with patients, and vice versa (see Gremillion 2003: 144–45). A complicating factor is that the receivers here of the necessary daily activities of intrusion, surveillance and coercion tend to be high achievers, successful academically and professionally, and apparently capable of making competent decisions in all aspects of their life apart from those regarding their own nutritional intake (Giordano 2005: 1; Kendall 2011: 2). This makes the work of care even more difficult. My book thus explores how the patients' will to remain ill is managed by professionals so that they can go beyond the binaries of 'patient choice' versus 'enforced treatment', and 'cure' versus 'treatment failure' (Lavis 2016: 73). Through what tools do professionals insist and *manage* to insist when patients refuse to eat?

Building on Mol, Moser and Pols' (2010) argument that in care practices the knowledges, technologies, bodies, people and daily lives involved need to be continuously 'tinkered with', here I argue that tinkering with *relationships* of care, and especially tinkering with patients' families, is fundamental to be able to tinker with the food that patients eat, with their daily behaviours and, through all of this tinkering, also with their bodies. The book will indeed show that patients' bodies are a 'border territory' in the healthcare encounter (Hahn 1985: 97–98, cited by Mattingly 2010: 12), as they become the receptacle of 'what is at stake' in daily life for all those involved – patients, families and healthcare professionals (cf. Mattingly 2010: 29). We will also see that the common framing of healing as a 'battle'[16] in this context assumes a very specific meaning, in which not only 'mind' and 'body' often play antagonistic roles but the battlefield is mostly located in 'the mind', with 'the body' being seen as the recipient of the battle's collateral effects. In this I follow Maryon McDonald's (2014) call for making 'the body' the object of ethnography rather than the language of analysis: I note 'the bodies that are acquired' (ibid.) by the professionals, which enable them to see scientifically the bodies of the patients; and I look, too, at how patients *acquire* specific bodies through clinical interactions. In sum, I look at their 'mutual articulation' (ibid.: 130).

The book gives particular attention to the temporality of projects of care (cf. Mattingly 2014a: 39–40), and to the fact that care practices are situated in the specific constraints of practical action and therefore have an experimental and risky character (ibid.: 379–84).[17] The chapters trace the professionals' 'ordinary ethics' as they move between what they feel is 'the ought' and what they can do and therefore 'is' (Lambek 2010: 4–6; Laidlaw 2013): how they speak and act with ethical consequences, how they evaluate actions, how they care and how they are aware of when they fail to do so.[18] But the book also includes storytelling about the activities of family carers – how they perform and experience their caring work, their intentions, their concerns. For both the professionals and the family carers, the aim is to understand the occasions when there are perceived tensions with patients and 'within themselves' – 'moments of moral breakdown' (Zigon 2007: 138) – and to point out the different ways in which they try to act for the best.

On Italy, Food and Kinship

Italy's idealised image as a country where people have an almost 'naturally healthy' relationship with food, thanks to the praised 'Mediterranean diet' and to the care that families supposedly put in cooking and eating together, makes it a particularly interesting country for studying eating disorders. In this romanticised context, more than three million people have received an official diagnosis of eating disorder (Cavanna and Nacinovich 2024). Nevertheless, considering the popular view that, among Europeans, Italians give a specifically strong value to both 'food' and 'family' (Counihan 2004) and that Italy is characterised by a greater 'strength' of family ties (Reher 2004) expressed through reciprocity in providing care for the elderly and children, the anthropological literature on eating disorders and on kinship in Italy is surprisingly scarce. The few ethnographic accounts of eating disorders in Italy are in line with the other anthropological literature reviewed above: Ann Cheney (2012, 2013) conducted a study on disordered eating in Calabria, a region in southern Italy, which describes how women transform gendered relations of kinship and power through practices of not eating, and how such practices allow them to craft locally meaningful moral selves because they mirror the self-sacrificial and morally superior motherly figure 'highly venerated in southern Italian society' (Cheney, Sullivan and Grubbs 2018: 445). Similarly Gisella Orsini (2017, 2021, 2023), in her analysis of compliance and resistance to treatment in a residential facility, suggests that people with eating disorders are actively and deliberately engaged in a project of moral self-transformation that is culturally defined, as it reflects the social expectations of women in these patients' social context and the moral values embodied in thinness, namely the control of bodily needs and pleasure. For this reason, she suggests, patients may accept medical care to achieve objectives other than 'healing': by complying with residential treatment, patients diagnosed with bulimia nervosa, for instance, attempt to '(re)become anorexic' or simply escape from their everyday family environment. These works importantly focus on sufferers' narratives, but they say very little about the specific practices and constraints of treatment as experienced by treatment teams or family carers.

This book aims to start filling this gap, and, by doing so, also to enrich the relatively sparse anthropological literature on Italian kinship.[19] Besides a few dated exceptions that offer a close ethnographic look at the daily lives of families in central and southern Italy (Belmonte 1979; Davis 1973; Galt 1991; Goddard 1996; Moss and Thompson 1959; Pitkin 1985), with a couple highlighting how women's daily food provisioning provides them with a sense of power and fosters a self-sacrificial concept of self (Counihan 1988, 2004; Silverman 1975), the literature on Italian kinship tends to be either more historical and sociological than ethnographic (see e.g., Barbagli and Kertzer 1990; Bell 1979; Bernini 2004; Esposito 1989; Saraceno 2004, 2015) or, when ethnographic, to be mostly focused on race, migration and intimate violence (Krause 2001, 2005; Plesset 2006; Yanagisako 2002, 2018), new reproductive technologies and LGBT parenting (Bonaccorso 2009; Grilli 2018; Guerzoni 2020, 2023, 2024), adoption (Di Silvio 2012), or sexuality and queer activism (Heywood 2018). A relevant exception is the historical and ethnographic work conducted by Barbara Vatta (2012) on kinship in the northern Italian region of Friuli-Venezia Giulia. Her work, although it does not address eating disorders, traces changes in family dynamics including those that regard care through food and argues for a conception of family as 'dependence', showing how 'dependence makes family'.

By expanding on the few works that looked at the interplay between kinship and mental health conditions in Italy (e.g., Giordano 2011, 2018) and at the forms that 'relational labour' takes in the country (Leira and Saraceno 2006; Molé 2008, 2012; Muehlebach 2011, 2012, 2013), my aim is to offer an equivalent, for the anthropology of kinship and medicine, of what Paolo Heywood's (2024) edited collection *New Anthropologies of Italy* has offered for the anthropology of politics, heritage and language. I also want to offer evidence against 'the false assumption that Italian anthropology has nothing to offer to global theory and method' (Herzfeld 2024: 379). Being Italian and having access to the Italian anthropology which has been exclusively published in Italian, but having been trained in the UK and Canada, I second Bonaccorso's (2009: 10) intention to show i) in what ways Italy is a different place from the one depicted by many Anglo-American anthropologists in their earlier as well as in more contemporary studies, and ii) what contemporary 'native anthropologists' trained in the Anglo-American tradition can add when approaching classic questions such as those that have to do with bodies, food and kinship.

Through filling a regional gap, in fact this book also contributes to the wider anthropological literature on the relationship between food and kinship, adding a broader comparative approach to existing ethnographies of eating disorder treatment. After what was seen as a 'crisis of kinship' in the 1970–80s, a new generation of anthropologists suggested that in many sociocultural settings ties of what was now called 'relatedness' were constituted by giving, receiving and sharing food (e.g., Carsten 1995, 1997; Janowski and Kerlogue 2007). Janet Carsten (1995: 223), for example, has famously shown how, among the Malays on the island of Langkawi, feeding (in the sense of both receiving and giving food) is a vital element in the process of becoming a person and participating fully in social relations as kin. In her context, the core substance of kinship is seen to be blood, and the major contribution to blood is seen to be food. Food therefore creates both persons in a physical sense and the substance through which they are related to one another (ibid.: 224). This suggested a processual view of kinship and challenged anthropological definitions that had assumed a universal division between the 'biological' and the 'social', or 'nature' and 'culture'. Similarly, Amazonian ethnographers have shown how commensality is a central means through which indigenous people engage in processes of 'familiarisation' (Fausto and Costa 2013): by eating together and sharing food, people turn into kin (Vilaça 2002) and create intimate relationships.

These authors did not, however, consider much how parental feeding practices intersect with local ideas of what might be called 'good parenting' and 'healthy development'. In her Langkawi work on food as a substance of relatedness, Carsten (1995: 234) mentions that the mother's milk is the source both of shared substance and of 'the strong emotional bond between mother and child', acting as 'the enabling substance of kinship'. She also shows how eating meals in other houses implies a dispersal of 'intimate substance' and is therefore discouraged (ibid.). In her more recent work on blood in clinical labs in Malaysia, Carsten (2019b) suggests how the way food is consumed together by lab technicians during their lunch breaks often works to initiate friendships between colleagues, to signal the thickening and thinning of relations, and, over time, even to generate kinship relations (Carsten 2019b: 175). She argues that food acts as a 'barometer of the warmth and strength of connections', and therefore as a 'kind of moral barometer of social relations' (ibid.: 171). This work parallels her recent call for focusing on what kinship *does*, rather than on what kinship is (Carsten 2019a: 133) – which means also focusing on the *effects* of kinship, especially on the effects of kinship through time. Answering Carsten's call in a way that contributes to examining the implications of 'feeding' for theories of relationship formation, the ethnographic material in this book will offer an example of a world in which feeding is indeed deemed to be not only crucial to the development of 'healthy bonding' and 'healthy development', but also to be something that *stands for* this healthiness: irregularities in feeding, we will see, are here conceived as symptoms, and symbols, of something gone awry in the bonding process, with certain parenting practices being considered detrimental to the creation of 'healthy affective bonds' and therefore of 'healthy eating'.

The few anthropologists who have been exploring how parental feeding practices intersect with local ideas of development and good parenting tend to frame caring through food as a hitherto neglected *alternative* to 'psychological' warmth and 'attention to emotions'.[20] Francesca Mezzenzana (2020, 2021), for example, shows how the Runa of the Ecuadorian Amazon do not tend to verbally speculate about others' 'inner feelings' or 'thoughts', nor to talk about 'emotions' with their children. She argues that care and love are, instead, entirely conceived as being manifested through feeding. She offers her case as an example that contrasts with normative European and North American practices of fostering emotional attachment, which focus on imagination and emotion talk. In my context, on the contrary, we will see that the two domains of 'feeding' and 'psychological warmth' are intimately linked.

At the same time, however, my research contributes to that strand of anthropological literature which, in the face of the current conceptual priority given to 'relationality', reconsiders the potential of 'detachment' and its value in specific settings, recognising that 'engagement' and 'detachment' are interwoven in complex ways (Candea et al. 2015: 1–14).[21] In arguing that treatment practices for eating disorders in my field site turn kinship care into a therapeutic tool for the professionals, the book will draw on and go beyond works that, by looking at kinship in practice, have usefully explored the ambivalent and potentially harmful side of kinship (e.g., Carsten 2019a; Das 1995; Lambek 2011; Pinto 2014), and have highlighted how kinship can be framed as a source of mental distress and at the same time as a resource for remedy (Bradely and Ecks 2018; Buchbinder 2015; Chua 2011). These have variously shown the intricacies between mental health and kinship, and how medical practice engages in kin work by seeking to define the appropriate mechanics of kin care. They have also contributed to challenging the supposed boundaries between a 'domestic' sphere of kinship and a 'public' sphere of work (see McKinnon and Cannell 2013). This book will show how healthcare professionals struggle to build and maintain those boundaries precisely because they need to constantly traverse them in their everyday work.

Outline of Chapters

In Chapter 1, I first situate my field site by tracing a brief history of how 'eating disorders' emerged in medicine and gradually in psychiatry in Italy, and of how their treatment developed accordingly. Second, I zoom in on the treatment centre where I conducted fieldwork, locating its approach within this history and introducing its inhabitants. I then discuss my research methods, my positionality in the field as researcher and volunteer, the implications of this double role and the way I dealt with the ethical issues I encountered.

Chapter 2 introduces the key tensions of the book, by asking: what are 'eating disorders' about? Here I examine the different ways in which patients and professionals construct the causes, manifestations and effects of the eating disorder. Drawing on both previous ethnographic literature on patients' experiences and on my own fieldwork, I suggest that patients frame their eating disorder as a self-care project, but that their self-shaping practices point strongly to relational aspects – i.e., to how these people's self-projects are about selves in relationships. I then examine how, through the patient's assessment preceding admission, what might be experienced by patients as a self-care practice is framed by professionals as pathology, diagnosed and then treated through a careful tracking of the patient's body and mind performed by biomedicine and the psychological sciences. I show that patients' and professionals' diverging constructions, however, have something in common: eating disorders, both parties seem to be saying, *appear* to be about food but are not 'really' about food. Instead, they frame food, the body and weight as the vehicles of a distress that has something to do with relatedness. I also show that in this context of care symptoms are ascribed to an entity that is at the same time external to and within the patient; in this way, professionals construct a partible 'eating disordered self' that helps them make sense not only of the failures of treatment (as in Lester 2007, 2019), but also of the everyday care practices that are seemingly necessary for treatment 'to work'. By framing their somewhat coercive measures as directed 'to the eating disorder, not to the person', professionals try to resolve the tension between care and coercion.

Chapter 3 then traces how patients who are mostly brought to treatment by their family members, and who are seen to be in need of constant surveillance, get to the point of assuming responsibility for doing and avoiding the very things that professionals have forced them to do and avoid at the beginning of treatment. I show how treatment, in its ordering of time, space and therapeutic activities, induces patients to gradually deal with that responsibility by cultivating their 'awareness' – that is, a shift from seeing their condition as a self-care project to seeing it as a form of enslavement to an external force that 'took over their minds' and literally 'blurred their vision', neurologically 'distorting' the way they see their own bodies. I also show that what is conceived as the nutritional aspect of food needs to be momentarily separated from its kinship-making aspect, because problems in the latter are seen to be impeding the former. Treatment, in other words, here means gradually substituting patients' ways of being well with a definition of health that is jointly constituted by the professionals through the use of scientific knowledge and its apparently impartial numbers. Once this shift has occurred, we will see, patients are deemed capable of being responsible for a self-transformation that will enhance their health.

Since eating disorders are seen by professionals as markers of 'things gone awry in family relations', Chapters 4 and 5 show that this work of transformation is felt to succeed only if the patient's family is transformed too. Here, the sociality of patients' bodies is seen to be as important as their physiology. Chapter 4 argues that the treatment team tinkers with kinship care by purposefully functioning as a 'relational laboratory', as the professionals channel what they see as the dangerous aspects of kinship into therapeutic tools. They do so by 'borrowing' from kinship care in their therapeutic work whilst tinkering with its constitutive practices, cleaning it of its perceived dysfunctionality. I thus show how kinship here not only has an ambivalent and potentially harmful side – whereby the patient's family can be framed as a source of distress; kinship can also become a therapeutic tool, in the double sense that i) professionals work to reshape kinship care in patients' families by turning them into resources for recovery, and ii) that professionals simultaneously borrow from kinship practices in their own therapeutic work of 'reparenting' patients. Kinship is thus operationalised into a therapeutic tool, although a risky one to use.

Chapter 5 explores one of the instances in which the transformation sought in patients and their families does not seem to happen. It suggests that treating 'preadolescents' with eating disorders – a recent and increasingly prevalent phenomenon in Italy and elsewhere – puts into question the very paradigm of treatment, because children fail to undergo the desired steps deemed essential for therapeutic transformation. In this chapter I show how children do not become 'aware' of being in need of help and do not reach the point when they want to abandon the eating disorder, failing to assume responsibility for their own treatment. The reasons for this failure are located by the treatment team in patients' 'dysfunctional families' – in their failure to care for their children in a way that provides them with 'boundaries'. These families seem to be so dysfunctional that they cannot even be tinkered with. This makes it more difficult for the professionals to stay clinically detached, because what should be a temporary reparenting role then lacks a foreseeable end. Such an impasse forces professionals (and anthropologists) to rethink treatment and to experiment with other ways of treating children.

Chapter 6 covers another category of cases in which the transformation sought in patients and their families does not happen in the way professionals would expect, as the patients' and the professionals' diverging constructions of the eating disorder keep clashing, generating what the treatment team experiences as 'failure': 'chronic' patients show that the time of treatment and the time of illness intersect in important ways with the kind of care that is seen as key to patients' recovery. The chapter looks at how professional and family carers experience and deal with the limits of their own care, and shows that 'chronicity' and 'comorbidity' put into question two of the pillars that constitute the logic of the treatment model: i) family-based care and ii) framing the eating disorder as a part of the patient's self that can be dispensed with. I suggest that although failure materialises in patients' bodies – which 'fail' to gain weight or to maintain what is seen as a healthy weight gain – it is mostly relationships of kinship care that are seen to be failing, further showing how tinkering with family is difficult work. These cases suggest, however, that even when treatment 'doesn't work' what is perceived as 'failure' becomes productive, because it motivates professionals to try and improve the patient's condition in a different way, generating more attuned attempts of care – which at times seem to work and at others seem to fail too.

The conclusion, finally, brings the chapters together by illustrating how they enable us to think more about the complexity of bodies and diseases and of food and kinship. Here I highlight how, in this treatment centre, patients' bodies are transformed through transforming the relations that constitute them. In doing so, I also look at what happens to patients after discharge from Il Giardino, focusing on whether the family work that is done during residential treatment and that is considered crucial for long-lasting recovery 'travels back' to patients' homes once they are discharged from the facility, and with what kind of short- and long-term effects. Finally, I ask whether 'work with the family' is enough, how it can be improved, and whether perhaps we also need more work with, and more care from, a wider 'social' that keeps harming patients outside the protected environment of treatment facilities.

Notes

1. The name of the treatment centre has been invented by the author, and some of its identifying features omitted, to maintain the anonymity of its inhabitants.

2. The Italian National Health Service (*Servizio Sanitario Nazionale*) was set up in 1978. The central government controls the distribution of tax revenue for publicly financed healthcare and defines the 'essential levels of care' (*livelli essenziali di assistenza*) to be offered to all residents in every Italian *regione* (region). The *regioni* – the first-level administrative divisions of the Italian Republic – are responsible for organising health services through local health units, which deliver primary care, hospital care, outpatient specialist care, public healthcare and healthcare related to social care.
3. The *Diagnostic and Statistical Manual of Mental Disorders* (*DSM-5*) is presented by the American Psychiatric Association as the product of years 'of effort by hundreds of international experts in all aspects of mental health' resulting in 'an authoritative volume that defines and classifies mental disorders in order to improve diagnoses, treatment, and research' (see https://www.psychiatry.org/psychiatrists/practice/dsm).
4. E.g., Green 2013; Hendricks 2003; Hornbacher 1998; Marzano 2011.
5. E.g., for Italy, see Bozzola 2024; Corica 2022; De Bac 2024; for the UK, see Addley 2023; Harris 2024.
6. E.g., the American Netflix movie *To the Bone* (Noxon 2017), in which we also have glimpses of the functioning of a residential clinic in the United States, and, even earlier, the Italian movie *Maledimiele* (Pozzi 2010) and the Rai Fiction movie *Briciole* (Cirino 2005).
7. E.g., the British series *Everything Now* (Parker 2023), the Italian series *SKAM Italia* (season 6, 2024) and the Spanish series *Madres* (Barbero and Gabilondo 2020–22).
8. E.g., in the UK the BBC documentary *I Am a Child Anorexic* (BBC 2006); in Italy the Rai 3 documentary *Fame d'amore* (Casadio 2020–25).
9. The 'calorie' was first defined in 1824 by the French physicist and chemist Nicolas Clément as a unit of heat energy in studies of fuel efficiency for the steam engine. The American chemist Wilbur Atwater introduced the 'kilocalorie' in 1887, to measure the potential energy from food to support human labour (Hargrove 2007). As we will see, in the world of eating disorders food becomes 'calories' and persons become the morally charged numbers of their 'weight': the lower the numbers, the more praised the food/person is.
10. See, for instance, Addley 2023 in the UK; Bozzola 2024 in Italy.
11. In the publications of the *DSM-IV* (American Psychiatric Association 1994) and *DSM-IV-TR* text revision (ibid.: 2000), respectively, diagnostic categories were refined: anorexia nervosa can now be of 'restricting type' OR 'binge-purging type'; and bulimia nervosa is categorised as 'purging type' OR 'non-purging type' (bingeing followed by compensatory exercise or restrictive eating).
12. For more on this historical account, see Pearce 2004.
13. For more on how 'anorexia' was associated with 'hysteria', see Charcot 1889; Freud and Breuer 2004 [1895]; Janet 1907.
14. Before then, the 1952 *DSM-I* had listed anorexia nervosa as a 'psycho-physiologic reaction', and the 1968 *DSM-II* as a 'feeding disturbance' (American Psychiatric Association 1952, 1968).
15. This might arguably be the case because families in the United States still tend to be excluded or sidelined in treatment, and because with patients over eighteen families are not involved in order to protect the ill family member's 'privacy'. Furthermore, as Lester (2019: 44) discusses, standard family-based therapies tend to be based on the idea of the stereotypical adolescent patient with two parents and the luxury of having at least one of them at home to supervise all meals, but this is hardly possible

in single-parent households or in families with trauma, substance abuse, or other mental health issues.

16. This military metaphor in medicine dates to the nineteenth century. It came into wide use in the 1880s when bacteria were identified as the agents of disease (Sontag 1978: 66).
17. See also Kleinman 2010: 23–24.
18. On these matters, see Brodwin 2011, 2013; Davis 2012; Myers 2015.
19. For a helpful tracing of the history of anthropology on Italian kinship, see Bonaccorso 2009: 7–10; Grilli 2019 offers a good mapping of more contemporary literature.
20. See Mezzenzana 2021 and Funk 2021.
21. See also Anderson 2001.

Chapter 1

Into the Field

History, Methods and Research Ethics

We live in Sicily, and my fifteen-year-old daughter was refused admission to the hospital on the grounds that she was 'not undernourished enough.' She was thirty-two kilos. I had to attach my daughter to a drip of forced nutrition at home, with the help of a nurse paid by me. My daughter is doing OK now, thanks to us parents and to those who treated her privately. But who would have been responsible if something went wrong?

—A patient's mother, November 2018

This was one of the concluding comments of an autumn day in 2018 spent talking about 'the state of eating disorder treatment in Italy' – the theme chosen for the Fourth National Meeting on Eating Disorders, held in Florence every year. The meeting was organised by *Consult@noi*, a national nonprofit association founded in 2010 by existing regional associations of patients' families with the aim of creating a network of information and support by bringing together patients' relatives, healthcare professionals and representatives of regional and national institutions – including directors of local health authorities and members of the Ministry of Health and of the Italian National Institute of Health (ISS). This is because in Italy the central government controls the distribution of tax revenue for publicly financed healthcare, but the *regioni* (regions) – the first-level administrative divisions of the Italian Republic – are responsible for organising health services through local health units. The Italian healthcare system, called Servizio Sanitario Nazionale (SSN), is in fact a regionalised national health service that ensures universal coverage for all citizens and legal residents. The central government establishes national policies and allocates funding, while regional authorities are responsible for financing, organising and delivering healthcare services within their areas. Although the SSN is intended to guarantee equal access for everyone, there are notable differences in the quality, performance and availability of care across regions, with some – especially those living in southern regions like Sicily – experiencing greater challenges than others. The comment of this mother was a call for responsibility, a call that was shared by most speakers that day: the lack of facilities offering services with specifically trained professionals – services that are public and accessible to all – seemed to be a problem in almost every Italian region.

The current landscape of eating disorder treatment services in Italy is, in fact, all but rosy. With an epidemiology felt to be the same as in other European countries, Italy has seen a rising prevalence of eating disorders from the 1980s and the 1990s (Garghentini et al. 2003: 168). In 1998, the Italian Health Ministry published the first specific guidelines for the treatment of these conditions (Ministero della Sanità 1998), last updated in 2017 (Ministero della Salute 2017). Since those first guidelines, experts have been calling for an organisational model with four different but integrated levels of treatment that patients can access depending on the severity of their condition, and through which they can move depending on whether they 'improve' or 'worsen': outpatient services as the first level of treatment; day-service or semi-residential treatment as a more intensive intervention, with assisted meals; admission to hospital if the patient's condition is critical; and rehabilitative admission to a nonhospitalised residential facility for a period of three to five months.

However, the SSN has not kept up with the guidelines of the Health Ministry. A number of surveys carried out by the Health Ministry itself since 2008 converged in the creation of an 'online eating disorders map'[1] that traces all existing public services for eating disorders available in the country. These surveys, together with continuous reports of lack of services in the national news (e.g., Corica 2022; De Bac 2024; Palazzo 2020a, 2020b; Ruggiu 2016; Salvatori 2024),[2] show that treatment coverage is patchy throughout the country and can be generally regarded as poor (see also Garghentini et al. 2003: 168). For the more than three million people who have received a diagnosis in Italy, there are few dedicated facilities, causing a continuous migration towards private residential structures, nonspecialised hospitals and psychiatric clinics, not only from the poorest southern regions but also from the centre and the north. One of the results of this situation is that eating disorders reportedly caused 3,200 deaths in Italy by 2022 (Dalla Ragione 2023).

The region where I conducted fieldwork, in central Italy, was among the first ones to develop a complete network of public services for eating disorders, as recommended by national and international guidelines. Today Il Giardino is the reference point for many other treatment centres elsewhere. Its approach was born from the clinical director's view of treatment as 'not only therapy', but also as 'attending to patients with all their experiences and suffering'. This approach is in part the result of the transformations of the Italian healthcare system in the 1970s, which peaked with the closure of psychiatric hospitals in 1978 under the Italian Mental Health Act – called Law 180 or *Legge Basaglia* – thanks to the critical psychiatry movement led by the psychiatrist Franco Basaglia. Basaglia had been calling for a new understanding of 'the sick', and therefore for different spaces of care.[3] But the clinical director's view of 'what works' for treating eating disorders, in addition to her strong Basaglian convictions, was also shaped by a specific history of how eating disorders have been studied, understood and treated in Italy.

Situating the Field Site: A Brief History of Eating Disorder Treatment in Italy

We have seen in the Introduction that the *Diagnostic and Statistical Manual of Mental Disorders* (*DSM*), in all its different versions, seems to create 'eating disorders' as the same object everywhere, within a 'one medicine fits all' project. As some medical anthropologists have suggested (e.g., Kleinman 1988; Kleinman and Good 1985; Martin 2007), such an approach – which frames 'mental illnesses' and each such illness as unrelated to context – is within the optic of a scientific medicine that divests itself of the local, social or cultural (McDonald 2015). But asserting sameness or continuity over time and space for any illness, including 'eating disorders', is problematic.

As noted by some scholars who studied the development of eating disorder treatment (Marks 2019), by the 1990s a considerable multidisciplinary and multinational group of professionals specialised in eating disorders had emerged internationally, resulting in the foundation of the Academy for Eating Disorders in 1993. The year 2001 witnessed the first annual meeting of the International Conference on Eating Disorders in New York City, where the latest research in the disciplines of neurobiology, cognitive neuroscience, genetics and psychopharmacology also started circulating, contributing to shifts in understandings of eating disorders and of their treatment (ibid.).

As will become clear through the chapters, the professionals working at Il Giardino are involved in this 'internationalisation' of eating disorders: many of them read journals, attend and participate in national and international conferences, and collaborate with colleagues working in countries such as the UK and the US. One could therefore say that they enact international theories and treatment, which is why the reader will at times encounter statements that might seem to 'generalise' eating disorders and their therapies. It will therefore be helpful to bear in mind, while reading the chapters, that the 'facts' professionals refer to in their work of diagnosing and treating patients have become international facts through their construction as such in international networks, including publications in journals and conferences. In line with developments elsewhere, recent national guidelines in Italy (ISS 2012; Ministero della Salute 2017) now recommend 'evidence-based treatment' over 'theoretical knowledge', and that treatment should be 'multidisciplinary' – in tune with the 'multifactorial aetiology' of eating disorders – but tackling the 'disordered eating behaviours' first. Nevertheless, we will see that there are some Italian specificities in the way eating disorders are conceived and treated at Il Giardino.

A great deal of biomedical and psychological research on eating disorders has been produced in Italy. Well before the *DSM* framing, several 'pre-psychiatric' conceptualisations (Ruggiero, Prandin and Mantero 2001: 293) can be found of people displaying the eating patterns that are now classified under such a diagnosis. The thirteenth-century physician and philosopher Pietro d'Abano is reported to be the first Italian scholar to frame the restricted eating and excessive thinness of a woman in what we might now see as medical terms. He reported the case of a thirty-year-old woman in Normandy who had allegedly not eaten any food since the age of eighteen (d'Abano 1958). In the sixteenth century, the anatomist and surgeon Alessandro Benedetti (1533) and the physician Simone Porta (1551) described cases of fasting girls, trying to give medical explanations. Porta described the famous case of a German woman in terms of what has since been called 'a true early case of anorexia nervosa' (Ruggiero, Prandin and Mantero 2001: 293): as restricting food from early childhood, having always been very thin, unwilling to eat regularly, often vomiting after meals, and being 'manipulative' – i.e., constantly promising to eat later. Porta explained these characteristics as the consequence of 'dyspepsia', a condition of impaired digestion.

During the Enlightenment period we first see those same behaviours – now categorised as illness – associated with '*voluntary* starvation': the Italian physician Jacopo Bartolomeo Beccari (1745), in his review and discussion of 'the miraculous nature' of starvation, concluded that long periods of starvation could be observed not only in saints, but also in people suffering from what were then called 'melancholia' and 'hysteria'. The first Italian description of anorexia in recognisably modern psychiatric terms was by Giovanni Brugnoli (1875) – considered the father of neuropsychology in Italy (Cubelli and Nichelli 1990) – in the same years that the famous accounts of Lasègue (1873) and Gull (1874) were published in France and England respectively. Brugnoli reportedly ignored their papers, and, differently from them, in his description of the women observed he, for the first time, stressed that the matter was not lack of appetite: in fact, he wrote, those women *did* feel hungry, and yet actively refused food. This, crucially, made their restricted eating not a symptom of another medical disorder, but the central feature of an 'independent neurotic disorder' due to a 'psychological dysfunction' that affected their 'will' to eat (Brugnoli 1875). His work also featured descriptions of 'overactivity', binge-purging behaviours in the night and the effects of the condition on the family (ibid.).

Starting from the 1930s, the psychiatrisation of eating disorders took force with studies that differentiated 'anorexia' from neurological diseases that also resulted in extreme thinness (Accornero 1941; Dotti 1950; Ottonello 1937). At this time Italian studies on eating disorders mainly belonged to the field of neurology. This was because in Italy, until the 1970s, physicians categorised any condition that was seen to have to do with the 'nervous system' in the same category of 'neuropsychiatry', and this happened both for issues 'of the mind' and for issues 'of the body'. As in other countries, 'cachexia' (ongoing loss of skeletal muscle mass) due to Simmonds' disease (a chronic deficiency of function of the pituitary gland that leads to atrophy of the viscera, resulting in emaciation and death if untreated) had been lumped together with the thinness now associated with anorexia nervosa, into what was then called 'young pituitary thinness' (Dogliotti 1936; Galdi et al. 1936).

The psychiatrist Ferdinando Accornero (1941) first introduced a conceptualisation of anorexia nervosa as sharing some features with schizophrenia – such as 'flat mood' and 'lack of reality testing' – but with such features being restricted to body size and eating, as if it were a 'monosymptomatic psychosis'. Studying the 'psychological problems' of the patient thus became key (Basaglia 1959; Martinotti 1953; Rossini 1959). Such an approach can also be found in the first developmental model of the internationally renowned psychiatrist Mara Selvini-Palazzoli (1963, 1965), who described anorexia as a monosymptomatic psychosis with a 'psychotic ego functioning' regressed to the 'oral stage of development'. As we have seen in the Introduction, in a later phase of her career she came to see anorexia as 'a disorder of the whole family' (Selvini-Palazzoli 1978): she described recurrent patterns observed in 'disordered' families and involved them in patients' treatment through interventions aimed at revealing the 'pathogenic links' between the eating behaviours of the patient and the behaviour of her relatives.[4]

An 'eating disorder' was thus moved away from the category of 'organic disease' and closer to that of 'mental illness'. As a consequence, 'psychotherapy' became essential to its treatment. Yet the inescapable fact that this mental illness had severe consequences 'on the body' made inpatient treatment in general medical wards fundamental for people with a life-threatening condition. Until the 1980s, three main kinds of treatment were thus available in Italy for eating disorders: family psychotherapy, individual psychotherapy, and inpatient treatment in general medicine wards for patients with life-threatening conditions (Dalle Grave 1996). Family psychotherapy was offered by a few specialised centres – mostly private – whereas public services offered nonspecialised individual psychotherapy, psychiatric counselling and general medical treatments, with no integration or sequencing of treatments (Ruggiero, Prandin and Mantero 2001: 296).

The fact that this mental illness had severe physical consequences also generated the need to develop a treatment approach whereby intervention 'in the mind' somehow could be transferred 'to the body' through a change in the patient's behaviour. In the 1980s and 1990s, specialised 'multidisciplinary' inpatient units thus started appearing. Cognitive behavioural therapy (CBT) became the preferred psychotherapeutic approach in these units in Italy, drawing on parallel developments in other countries such as the UK and Canada: the British psychiatrist Christopher Fairburn (1981) had developed cognitive behavioural treatment for bulimia nervosa in the UK, while the Canadian psychiatrist David Garner and the American clinical psychologist Kelly Bemis (1982) had proposed a cognitive approach for anorexia nervosa, all of these based on adaptation from cognitive theory as applied to depression. CBT generally included three stages of treatment that lasted for about five months: the first one to 'achieve control over eating' by consistently eating regular meals and snacks; the second one to 'identify and modify dysfunctional thoughts, beliefs and values' related to body size and shape, self-image and mood, which were seen to affect eating behaviour; the third to maintain improvement through 'cognitive restructuring' (ibid.).

Starting as a strictly behavioural programme, CBT as practised in Italy was adjusted to allow for 'more flexibility', by adding 'psychoeducation' and 'nutritional restoration' organised by a nutritionist 'trusted' by the patient, who would provide reassurance about 'weight phobia' and present food as 'medicine' (Dalle Grave et al. 1991, 1993). The emphasis was on establishing 'an alliance' with patients to enhance their capacities, with the aim of fostering 'autonomy' and the greatest practical degree of 'independence' from the eating disorder (Dalle Grave et al. 1991: 297). This approach was the one that the treatment team of Il Giardino was trained into. However, as we will see throughout the book, in practice things are more complicated than that. The care practices involved in treatment must deal with the fact that professionals encounter two kinds of actors who, in different ways, make the process very difficult: patients and their family carers. These actors do not passively and willingly 'receive' the treatment that professionals are trained to offer. On the contrary, they usually resist that.

Il Giardino: How It Came to Be

During fieldwork, I was lucky to get to know Franca, president of *Supportiamoci* (literally: Let's Support Each Other),[5] the centre's association of patients' relatives. Now a sturdy woman in her seventies, in her fifties and sixties Franca had played a key role in the opening of Il Giardino, and had worked there as a coordinator and nurse for some years before retiring. She still comes to the residential facility twice a week, for the weekly staff meetings and for the weekly meetings for patients' relatives. On these occasions, she never fails to show up during patients' lunch, playing the role, she says, of the 'caringly insistent grandma'. She is a living archive of the treatment centre and clearly enjoys telling foundation stories and other anecdotes of 'when things worked properly'.

One hot morning at the end of July 2018, Franca told me the story of how the treatment centre came to be. Back then – it was 2001 – she was working as a head nurse in the children's ward at the local hospital, when an eleven-year-old girl was admitted with a diagnosis of pneumonia. The girl refused to eat and was always crying. She would eat very little and extremely slowly, cutting food in tiny pieces and trying to hide it. The staff called on the now clinical director, who at the time was working in the Psychiatry Department of the main town in the region, for a psychiatric consultation. She concluded that it was 'a severe case of anorexia nervosa'. As soon as the diagnosis was clear, together with a psychologist, a nutritionist and the paediatrician and dietician of the hospital, the psychiatrist organised an 'integrated therapeutic programme' to be carried out within the ward. This was the first case, Franca remarked, of a 'multidisciplinary treatment team' that was based on the recommendations of the national guidelines, which called for 'continuous communication between different experts and for a holistic view of the patient'. Holistic here meant attending 'to the body and the mind of the patient at the same time', Franca explained. In the same year, the Health Department of the region had formed a group of experts to elaborate regional guidelines for those who worked with eating disorders. During the editorial phase of the guidelines, it was noticed that the substantial increase in the demand for care in the region was met with an extremely fragmented and hardly accessible response. Patients and their relatives had to build their therapeutic path on their own, with a lot of effort and confusion, by putting together the different aspects of treatment. The challenge was therefore to build a therapeutic path that was complete, differentiated by the levels of severity of the disorder but at the same time integrated and most of all accessible.

Soon – Franca told me – the staff working in the children's ward realised that the treatment programme, which was giving 'good results', could be applied to other girls. They thus started working in a more structured way at the hospital, creating a day service for evaluating and treating patients. A whole hospital ward was dedicated to this aim. After Franca noticed that a group of cats would regularly gather under the windows of the ward, happy to receive the food that 'rained from the sky' during mealtimes, the newly created treatment team started providing 'assisted meals' – i.e., meals under the surveillance of at least two professionals. The toilets of the ward were closed for two hours after meals to prevent patients from purging. Gradually, protocols and rules were set for each element of the programme, and all the professionals involved started intensive training and supervision with the renowned psychiatrist Riccardo Dalle Grave, who had developed the 'lenient approach' of CBT for eating disorders (Dallé Grave et al. 1993). Thanks to the presence of staff members used to working in a children's ward, it was possible to admit patients as young as ten years old, something unthinkable in most treatment centres at that time and still uncommon today.

By the end of 2002, the hospital where Franca used to work was hosting outpatient services for eating disorders, the day service, and hospitalisation for life-saving interventions. What was missing – the clinical director felt – was a space *outside* the hospital for the implementation of a rehabilitation programme that could offer a continuous form of care without the side effects of long-term hospitalisation. This was eventually made possible by a local charity fund, which administered a sixteenth-century villa in the town centre. The fund enthusiastically embraced the idea of converting the building for this new health need, and in May 2003 the residential facility of Il Giardino opened. In 2011, because of a general centralisation of health services, the local hospital was closed and moved to a new larger hospital in a town nearby. The ex-hospital was converted into a health centre, where the third floor has been dedicated since 2012 to the day service for eating disorders and to out-patient services. Patients requiring hospital admission have, since 2011, been redirected to a specialised ward of a hospital in another town one hour's drive away.

Il Giardino and Its Inhabitants

The first thing that struck me as soon as I entered the residential facility of Il Giardino was the run-down and yet welcoming atmosphere. Upon entering through a big wooden door, one finds oneself in a dark and humid lobby. Walking up some stairs, the smell becomes very different from the mouldy smell typical of most old buildings in the town centre, whose narrow alleys do not let the sun warm them. It is a distinctive smell of fried onions – something that one would not expect in an eating disorder treatment centre. This is because the first floor of the building is inhabited by a *Casa Famiglia* (literally: Family Home) hosting a small community of women with cognitive disabilities, who really like cooking with fried onion as the basis of their meals. Their cat Pepper, who often sneaks out of their apartment into the communal garden, offers occasions for interaction between patients and his owners, who all enjoy running after him. After years of cohabitation, these neighbours have learned well the key rule imparted to everyone new to the treatment centre – including new patients, professionals, interns, volunteers and anthropologists: 'Do not talk about food'.[6] They repeat it like a mantra any time they hear someone breaking it.

On both sides of the entrance to the *Casa Famiglia*, several doors open up to spaces dedicated to receiving the public and to coordinating and administrative activities. The '*front office*'[7] is where volunteers, interns and professionals take calls from prospective patients or their families, organise medical visits, manage waiting lists, and write reports on patients' progress and discharge letters. From the front office one can access the consulting room – where visits with the doctor and the psychiatrist, the daily 'pharmacological therapy' and the much-dreaded weekly weight monitoring happen. Both rooms are surrounded by shelving units that contain the necessary material for compiling patients' files, and where files of discharged patients are kept for records. Another door opens to the 'administration office', which also functions as the office of Il Giardino's coordinator. Here a smaller shelf contains the current patients' files. On the right-hand side of the flight of stairs there is the largest room of the building, reserved for the weekly staff meetings, the monthly supervision meetings with an external psychotherapist, and the weekly support meetings for parents.[8] Equipped with screen and projector, sometimes this room is also used for patients' group activities and for the training of new interns. From this large room, one can access the nursing station on one side and the director's office on the other.

Another flight of stairs leads to the garden entrance: a glassy door overlooking a large green space surrounded by 300-year-old holm oaks and hedges that are seasonally covered with flowers. If one keeps walking up the stairs, one reaches the second floor – the residential space for patients – only accessible to professionals, interns and volunteers. At the top of the stairs, turning left, one finds the door of the toilet reserved for staff, and the opening of a slightly elevated L-shaped corridor along which a series of doors open to patients' bedrooms, with windows overlooking the garden. Laundry services, a locked storage room and two shared bathrooms are also there, with 'shower shifts' written on white sheets attached to the doors. From the end of the corridor, a narrow flight of descending stairs leads to the dieticians' office and to a smaller, back access to the building, reserved for staff and admitted patients. The rest of the floor is where patients spend most of their time. Right across the top of the stairs, after a bright hall decorated with pictures, drawings and letters written by patients who have been discharged, a locked blue door hides the most dreaded space of the building: the '*sala terapia*' (literally 'therapy room'), where patients eat their lunch and dinner. On the right side of the hall, a large living room called 'relaxation room' is enlightened by three large windows and is decorated with colourful paintings. The room features a big table surrounded by chairs – used for drawing, painting, writing, board games and other leisure activities – two large sofas, an armchair, a piano and a TV. At the two opposite sides of the living room, two light-blue wooden doors open to other rooms: on one side, to a second, smaller '*sala terapia*' and to the kitchen, reserved for eating breakfast and snacks but otherwise closed to patients: here it is where professionals eat their meals, before or after patients, depending on their commitments. All the rooms feature high ceilings, terracotta polished floors and antique wooden furniture. On the other side of the living room, another light-blue wooden door leads to the '*palestrina*' (literally 'small gym'), the only room that has been recently refurbished with the aim of hosting '*le attività corporee*' ('body activities'): dance-movement therapy, drama therapy, yoga and meditation. Here one immediately notices a new parquet floor, a large painting depicting a field of sunflowers and the most mysterious feature of the whole building: a locked mirror.[9] On this floor, the air tends to be stuffy and warm and often carries the smell of patients' food, continuously prepared and reheated throughout the day.

The frantic movement is what catches the eye here – or better, the juxtaposition of two different kinds of frantic movement. First: that of the professionals, who spend their days moving up and down the floors, from one task to the next, having to juggle patients' demands, those of the patients' parents and those of the clinical director. They hardly manage to stop for a couple of minutes here and there, in the safe space of the kitchen. The centre employs a multidisciplinary approach that is based on the coordination of about thirty professionals, the vast majority being women[10] in their thirties and forties, except for the clinical director and two others who are in their fifties and sixties. The staff include two psychiatrists (one of whom is also the director), a doctor nutritionist, an endocrinologist,[11] six psychologists (of which two are also psychotherapists), two dieticians, three nutritionists, a dance-movement therapist, two philosophical counsellors,[12] five educators, a social worker who acts as coordinator, two nurses and three healthcare assistants – plus an administrator who deals with bureaucratic matters. On any given shift, there are three professionals and a nurse assigned to the residential part of the building. Their work is supported in a fundamental way by a substantial number of young interns and volunteers whose stay in the centre is organised in morning and afternoon shifts, paralleling those of the professionals, and usually lasts for six or twelve months. For simplicity of expression, in the book I often group together all the carers working at Il Giardino as simply 'the professionals' or 'the treatment team' – as distinct from 'the patients' – unless the persons in question belong to only one of the subcategories just mentioned, in which case I use the name of their specific profession. The professionals are all Italian and the majority were born in the region where they work. The others come from Rome or from southern regions in Italy and, after moving here for training given the reputation of the centre, they decided to stay.

The other kind of frantic movement is that of the patients. About sixteen to eighteen patients – virtually all girls and women[13] – inhabit the residential space on the second floor of the villa. Their frantic movement can often be observed in the garden, and sometimes up and down the stairs between the two floors. During my stay, patients were aged ten to fifty-eight years old, with the vast majority being between fifteen and thirty years old. In line with the relatively recent recognition in the clinical literature that eating disorders do not only affect people from privileged backgrounds (Gard and Freeman 1996; Mitchison et al. 2014), patients' socio-economic situation was quite varied: it ranged from patients whose families owned multiple properties and spent their holidays in fancy hotels around the world to patients whose families could not afford to cover the costs of a trip from a different region to visit them during weekends. Since the treatment centre is public, patients do not have to pay for treatment, but those who are from other regions and therefore live too far away have to pay for rented accommodation once they switch to day-service treatment. For the patients whose family cannot afford that, there are two houses in town composed of about five rooms each that have been donated to the treatment centre by the local charity fund.

Patients' frantic movement is not driven by tasks to do – in fact, as we will see in the next chapter, patients are supposed to be as still as possible. Their movement is instead seen to be driven by 'a compulsive urge' to keep moving in order to 'burn calories' and 'lose weight', professionals explained. Even when they are sitting on the sofa or on a chair, or when they are standing against a radiator to keep themselves warm, patients are rarely completely still: there is always at least one leg frantically moving up and down, or from side to side. Only a very few patients can be observed staying still, but this usually means – professionals say – that they feel extremely unwell and down.

The day-service facility has a very different feel to it. 'It used to be the surgical ward. Each room was an operating room', Franca had told me. Situated in a wing of the third floor of what is now the health centre – where people can access services ranging from vaccinations and blood tests to maternal and child health – the day-service facility consists of a long and wide corridor with light-coloured linoleum floor enlightened by a series of large windows, making the space much brighter but at the same time colder than the residential facility. Windows occupy the right-hand side of the corridor, overlooking an internal courtyard in disuse that patients use to smoke cigarettes. On the other side of the corridors, six lilac doors open onto the different rooms of the facility: the front office, which also works as a weekly staff meeting room and occasionally as a room for individual psychotherapy sessions, when the others are not available; the dining room, from which professionals can also access the kitchen; the relaxation room, where patients spend most of their time between meals and therapeutic activities; the consulting room, reserved for individual sessions with the nutritionist, for visits with the doctor and the psychiatrist, and for the weekly weight monitoring; the group activities room, which is also used for individual psychotherapy sessions; and the 'little gym' room, used for 'body activities' but, as in the residential facility, also for many other group sessions given the general lack of space.

There are fewer people moving around here, partly because there is a smaller number of professionals, partly because patients who reach this stage of treatment – the clinical director tells me – 'have learned, more or less, to keep their compulsive exercise at bay'.[14] Fifteen professionals, plus some interns and volunteers, work in this facility, some of whom also work in the residential facility. However, the bulk of the work and most shifts are carried out by three figures in the 'psy' disciplines (two psychotherapists and one psychologist) and three figures in the 'nutri' disciplines (two nutritionists and one dietician). For every shift, only two or three professionals are present, plus an endocrinologist or a psychiatrist in some morning shifts, although the number of patients admitted is never below twelve. Another difference is that patients here tend to be older: since it is a day service, they need to be at least eighteen years old to live in a rented apartment or in the housing offered by the charity fund. During my stay, most patients here were in their twenties, a few in their late teens and in their thirties, and a handful in their forties and fifties.

Being a Researcher and Volunteer: The Ethics of Doing Clinical Ethnography

My relationship with Il Giardino – which includes both the residential facility and the day-service facility – dates to January 2014. Back then, I was looking for a 'field site' where I could experiment with fieldwork for my master's degree. I was writing a thesis on patients' experience of eating disorder treatment when I came across a video about a treatment centre in Italy. I was caught by the emphasis that the clinical director in the video placed on wanting to create 'a space of care and not just of cure', something that seemed to be lacking in treatment according to both patient memoirs (e.g., Hendricks 2003) and ethnographic studies (Gremillion 2003; Malson 2008; Malson et al. 2004; Moulding 2003; Warin 2005, 2010). I thought that the centre might offer an interesting counternarrative, and I was curious to explore what 'care' meant there. I wrote an email to the clinical director, introducing myself and explaining what I wanted to do. Five months and an ethical approval later, I was there doing my first five weeks of fieldwork. During that brief period I established good relationships with the treatment team and, predictably, I left with more questions than answers. When I contacted the team again asking whether they would be willing to have an anthropologist around them for the much longer period that Ph.D. fieldwork requires, they replied as enthusiastically as the first time. As a result, I spent fourteen months between July 2018 and August 2019 doing doctoral research in the residential and day-service facilities of Il Giardino. I then came back for more postdoctoral fieldwork between October 2022 and February 2023.

As an anthropologist wanting to conduct research in a clinical space I was particularly fortunate, because obtaining access to and taking a role in such settings is usually difficult, even in one's country of origin (Zaman 2004, 2008). This is both because hospital authorities and medical practitioners tend to resist analysis by social scientists – partly due to the latter having often engaged in 'doctor bashing' – and because such settings are only accessible via ethics committees where a clash between medical ethics and ethnographic methods often causes problems (Bell 2019; Oeye, Bjelland and Skorpen 2007; van Ginkel 1998: 260). I was therefore very lucky to find a clinical director who was open to and interested in what an anthropologist could 'reveal' about the implicit working of their treatment practices.

The director quickly authorised my project, assuring me that my presence would not cause any distress to the patients nor to the staff, since they were all 'used to have people around coming and going' – by which she meant interns, volunteers and professionals from other centres who come for training. However, I was aware that my presence would be different from that of the other visitors, because of the key role that 'participant observation' still plays in anthropological research. Moreover, even when access is obtained, the participatory aspect poses special issues in clinical settings. Some anthropologists (e.g., van der Geest and Finkler 2004: 1999; Vermeulen 2004; Wind 2008) argue that unless the researcher is a healthcare professional where s/he conducts research, fieldwork in a clinical setting is not really 'participatory', because the researcher is not allowed to participate in the 'work' around which the social life of the clinical setting is centred – the information circulating being seen as too complex and/or sensitive to be shared with the ethnographer (Vermeulen 2004: 2072). Fieldwork in clinical settings does not fit well with older assumptions of 'participant observer': 'negotiated interactive observation' (Wind 2008) has been proposed as a more appropriate way to describe ethnographic fieldwork in these settings. Anthropologists seem to have found a role in these spaces as analytical commentators, context-givers, or suppliers of 'ethics' – which is one way that the 'social' reappears alongside the 'objectivity' or 'detachment' of medicine (e.g., McDonald 2015, 2017). Indeed, not participating in one of the existing roles is seen by some as desirable (Tanassi 2004: 2055) because not belonging to any of the power groups makes everyone 'feel free to talk' and more willing to do that (Barret 1996: xviii).

One might rightly observe that anthropologists can have problems everywhere with any form of participant observation, and methodologies have changed accordingly. Nevertheless, the additional ethical approval process typically requested by a clinical site can bring these difficulties more into the open. Wind's (2008) description of what ethnographers do in clinical settings as 'negotiated interactive observation' cannot be generalised, however. For my fieldwork, I did not have the role of a patient nor of a healthcare worker, but I still participated in some recognised and useful ways. In both facilities, I had the double role of 'visitor researcher' and 'volunteer'. Volunteering – and the related assumed will to 'give something back' in the form of time, skills and material help – seemed expected in a setting that was constantly understaffed and where going through the 'volunteer stage' was essential for anyone who wanted to access paid employment opportunities in the future. Indeed, most of the other volunteers were not retired people helping in the treatment centre as an 'extra activity' during their free time (cf. Muehlebach 2013). They were mostly students and young professionals for whom 'volunteering' was part and parcel of their training, and an important way of building connections that could enhance their job prospects. It seemed impossible for them to think of being hired without 'having given something' to the treatment centre first. Similarly, for me, entering a world that would typically be foreclosed to social scientists required an exchange in kind. This exchange in kind turned out to be one of the most precious and useful tools for my fieldwork access.

Thanks to my role as a volunteer, I did not simply observe but also helped the staff with several tasks. Still, I had to occupy a position in the available power dynamics of the centre to ensure that I was welcomed. Because the treatment centre was public and part of a teaching institution within the national healthcare system, students in medicine, psychology, nutrition and nursing were carrying out research for their theses and undergoing internships at the time I was doing fieldwork. I thus learnt about the world of the treatment centre from professionals, as they had learnt whilst they themselves were interns. I was placed in the same category as 'interns and volunteers' for the organisation of shifts. During staff meetings, I would sit next to interns on 'their side' of the table. To gain access to the various activities of the treatment facilities, I had to go through their same 'gatekeepers' – the clinical director and the coordinators of the facilities. Although I did not quite fit into their existing categories, I thus gradually learnt to 'dwell' (Ingold 2000) in their community of practice.

I spent most of my days at the residential or day-service facility, helping staff members with supervising meals and with other daily tasks,[15] and participating in patients' various group activities – including psychological group sessions, drama therapy, dance-movement therapy, meditation and nutritional group sessions.[16] My typical day would start at 9 am, when patients were finishing breakfast, and end at around 8 pm, after their dinner. I attended all the weekly staff meetings, during which psychotherapists and nutritionists would present their respective patients and discuss their 'case' with the rest of the treatment team. During these meetings, the staff would sit together, discuss the situation and progress of every patient, and take decisions for next steps as well as for discharges and new admissions. Every Saturday morning I attended the weekly support meetings for families, where patients' parents and other relatives would ask questions, talk of their doubts and difficulties, and share their experiences. Among other things, this allowed me to explore how the skills used by the professionals to manage interactions with patients were 'transferred' to family members, and to what extent they differed (see Treasure 2010: 4). Apart from this, weekends were mostly free from structured activities and were reserved for visits or permits to go home if the conditions of the patient allowed it. I could therefore observe different dynamics from the weekdays, and I had more time to spend informally with both the patients and the staff, chatting, doing puzzles, watching movies and playing board games. The monthly 'supervision meetings' for the treatment team were another precious occasion for learning: during these meetings, one 'case' of a 'particularly difficult' patient is presented by the team to an experienced psychotherapist who does not work in the treatment centre, with the aim of receiving feedback from 'an experienced but fresh, uninvolved eye' (clinical director). One morning per week I managed the front office of the residential facility, performing administrative duties and attending to the needs and worries of patients' relatives. In the last months of fieldwork, I was given permission – with the agreement of patients – to attend first visits and individual nutritional sessions. Attending these was useful for gathering material regarding i) local notions of what it means to be 'ill' or 'healthy', ii) the ways and instruments used to assess this and iii) what kind of action is expected according to the result of the assessment. Finally, outside the treatment centre, I attended several professional conferences on eating disorders and events organised by associations of family carers. These were precious opportunities to gather material on professionals' and families' experiences 'on the ground' in a wide number of treatment centres, to hear more discourses about eating disorders and to enrich the topics that came up in my daily work.

My involvement in all these activities meant that I was seen as a kind of 'hybrid' by my interlocutors – between researcher and volunteer, between volunteer and professional, or in any case a liminal figure floating in the space between patients and professionals. Cleo, an eighteen-year-old patient whom I first met in the residential facility and who later moved to the day-service facility, put it this way: 'I wouldn't know how to classify you. I think of you as someone outside the boxes of this place: you are not a patient, you are not a professional, you are not an intern ... you are just Giulia, you just belong here'. Patients knew that I was an anthropologist doing research and not a professional in their terms, but my role as a volunteer meant that I often had to assume the role of a 'professional': during meals, for example, if patients showed 'dysfunctional behaviours' such as separating food from the seasoning or cutting food into too tiny pieces, I was expected to make them notice what they were doing, and make them eat everything 'in the right way'. Moreover, very early on during fieldwork I was entrusted by the treatment team with the capacity to give patients things that they could only obtain from a professional, such as water or keys for the laundry, and patients would come to me to ask for things as they would do with any other professional. Nevertheless, I was 'closer' to patients and spent more time with them than any of the professionals did. Patients in the day-service facility – who mostly spent their weekends walking around the small town – would sometimes bump into me and invite me to join them for a walk, play board games, or go to the cinema. On these occasions they did not treat me as a professional, but as someone of about their age who was also spending her free time on her own and might want some company. They would often openly complain about one or the other professional, or tell me about 'dysfunctional things' they had done that they would not disclose to the treatment team, confident that I would not do that either as I was not 'one of them'.

On the other hand, professionals seemed to want to protect me from the patients: I was often advised not to spend 'too much time around patients', especially outside the treatment centre, for my own 'mental health'. However, nobody ever told me that I should refuse patients' invitations when patients mentioned my presence in their weekend outings during the usual report at the 'welcome group session' on Monday mornings. It seemed that the boundaries that professionals had to maintain with patients (it would have been inappropriate for a professional to join patients for an outing on the weekend, unless this was framed as a therapeutic activity) did not apply to the anthropologist. On the contrary, I was even thanked by a psychiatrist one day when she learnt that I had offered to spend a Sunday afternoon with Lisa, a patient in day-service treatment who was going through a particularly tough time, and for whom lonely weekends were especially difficult. The psychiatrist told me that it would have been good for Lisa to spend time and talk 'with a girl of her age, but who is not ill'. In that moment, I was stripped of both my professional roles: what counted seemed to be my closeness to the patient as a fellow human being of the same age and gender. Nevertheless, this did not mean that the professionals never saw me as 'one of them' – in fact, they mostly did. Since my presence in the centre went much beyond my shifts as a volunteer, they saw me as someone closer to them than to interns and other volunteers, whose shifts were shorter and whose responsibilities were less onerous.

Sometimes, professionals seemed aware that they were being observed by a potentially judgemental anthropologist. At the beginning, when they would make jokes or 'act silly' – something that I soon realised might be key 'work' to prevent the atmosphere of the centre from becoming 'too heavy' – one of them would suddenly say things like: 'We should stop, there is an anthropologist with us!' and everyone would laugh and compose themselves. Gradually, once the professionals understood that I could be trusted, perhaps because I had seen enough of that world to be understanding of their behaviour, they stopped applying obvious filters with me. If there was something that they were worried about, they would just tell me explicitly: 'But this, don't write it in your book!'

In fact, it did not take long for the treatment team to feel completely at ease with my presence, to invite me to join them for lunch in the centre, and later to invite me for dinner at their place – sometimes even offering me the possibility to stay for the night. They talked about patients or about their personal issues in front of me, or *to* me, as they would do with other colleagues. A few months into my fieldwork, I was added to the WhatsApp group of the professionals working in the day-service facility, and I was invited more than once to events and parties organised by the clinical director or by others. For my birthday, I received a gift from the whole treatment team, something done for other professionals but not for interns or volunteers. The same happened when my fieldwork ended and I had to leave. With some professionals I developed close friendships that last to this day, and that were a precious source of company and support during fieldwork.

My involvement with patients and professionals, and with their practical day-to-day life, meant that at some point during fieldwork I did not simply have multiple roles, but also multiple aims, not always reconcilable. Being caught in the vortex of practical things to do at the centre, sometimes with urgency, and in the welcoming social life of professionals and patients outside the centre, often resulted in doubts about whether I was doing research. Was 'keeping an analytical eye' on everything that happened enough, or indeed possible? Anthropologist Kirsten Bell (2019) has noted how the multiple forms of relationality that characterise ethnographic fieldwork are often presented in terms of the tension between 'participation' and 'observation'. These contradictory qualities of ethnographic research are frequently glossed under the label of 'detached observer and participant-friend' (Rynkiewich and Spradley 1976: 126). As observed by Bell (2019: 11), the concept of the 'dual role' was first designed to address the situation of clinician-researchers conducting a study on their patients, where the dual role was not seen as intrinsically unethical but as a phenomenon to be carefully managed. Similarly, many social and behavioural sciences construct research relations with heavily managed expectations concerning 'contact' with research participants. The 'undesigned relationality' (ibid.) in the research can seem to be 'a noise distorting reliable, objective results' (Lederman 2013: 599–600). The underlying positivism in this conception is evident in that relationality becomes tied to 'truth' and 'trustworthiness', and 'rapport' serves to generate 'data' (Bell 2019: 14). Instead, ethnographic fieldwork is based on the anthropologist learning about an unfamiliar social world by developing practical competence in the aspects of daily life that are enabled by relationships cultivated over time. The multiple roles of 'anthropologist', 'friend', 'student', 'apprentice' etc. are thus all equally 'real' (ibid.).

Conducting fieldwork in a clinical setting problematises participation not only in terms of the roles that one can, as an ethnographer, assume, but also in terms of the extent to which anthropologists can 'understand the other' just because they practise 'participation' (Hastrup 1993: 732; Wind 2008: 85–86). When pain and suffering are involved, one should be particularly cautious about any seemingly participatory achievements (van der Geest 2007: 12), even if one feels 'familiar' with a specific world.

De-familiarising a Familiar Field

Before starting fieldwork, I was aware that my field site would feel familiar: many patients and staff members were of my age, and we shared similar backgrounds. This was not simply because I was a 26-year-old Italian woman, who was born, had grown up and had lived in central Italy for most of her life.[17] It was also because I have a history of having lived with an eating disorder myself – a biographical point that, I later discovered, I shared with some of the professionals. I was diagnosed with anorexia nervosa when I was twelve, but I was young enough and 'caught' early enough that three years later I could say that I had 'recovered'. I was not admitted to any inpatient facility – although at some point I was threatened with it by my doctor as the only feasible option if I did not start eating more – and my treatment was limited to regular outpatient psychotherapy sessions and medical visits. Mine was therefore a 'success story', thanks to the fact that i) my condition was quickly spotted by my family, who brought me to treatment just a few months after my 'disordered eating behaviours' had started; ii) I was young enough that treatment could be more easily 'imposed' on me; iii) I was living in a large town with a good outpatient treatment service; and iv) my family had the means to pay for a private psychotherapist who could see me twice a week in the most acute phase – a level of frequency never provided within public services. All these factors contributed to making my recovery much smoother than the majority of those I encountered during fieldwork.

The fact of having suffered from an eating disorder was at the same time helpful and difficult for my fieldwork. It was helpful because I already had a sense of how to behave with patients in a way that would not harm them or make them feel uncomfortable. I knew the 'typical things' that most people who live with an eating disorder do not need to see or hear, but that people who are not familiar with eating disorders often show and say. It was also helpful because I had myself practised the same 'irrational logics' that patients were enacting in the clinic – the 'manias related to meals, expressions of absurd thoughts regarding the body, weight and eating' (Deiana 2012: 64). So I did not feel overwhelmed by them. On the other hand, the risk of taking things for granted – of not questioning certain logics or notions precisely because they were already familiar to me – was always present. I therefore had to do a constant work of 'de-familiarising' myself from the discourses of my field site. However, I do not think that these issues have been a problem for my 'research outcomes'. As Latour (2004: 19) points out, the distance that one should achieve is not that between the observer and the observed, but 'that between the contents of the world before and after the inquiry'. Nor is it the fact of having suffered from an eating disorder that gives any more 'authority' to my research, as moments of recognition or empathy cannot be proved right or wrong (van der Geest 2007: 9). Nevertheless, as every anthropologist, in carrying out fieldwork I was never neutral nor irrelevant. I spent more time with certain people and in writing I privileged their voices. The 'undesigned relationality' (Bell 2019) that characterises every ethnographic fieldwork thus came to shape the boundaries that I drew for my field site.

A Note on Delimiting the Field Site

Delimiting my field site might have seemed a straightforward task: the physical space of the treatment facilities could be seen to delimit the space of the field itself. However, as with 'the village' (Candea 2007: 175), hospitals and clinics have shifted from being seen as 'cultural islands' in which a global biomedical model keeps 'what happens inside' apart from the social world surrounding it, to being seen as domains that reflect and reinforce dominant notions and values (van der Geest and Finkler 2004: 1996). This position contends that clinical ethnographies can therefore open a window to the social and cultural world (the 'mainland') in which the hospital or clinic is situated (ibid.: 1998). In fact, the longer I spent doing fieldwork, the more I realised that the field spilled outside the physical space of the treatment centre in many directions: to the patients' temporary accommodations in town; to the patients' family homes; to the professionals' houses; to the restaurants, cafes and shops where 'good enough' patients would spend their free time during weekends; to professional conferences around the country. In sum, 'nothing was out of bounds, and no time was off-duty' (Candea 2007: 174). Moreover, the very physical space of the treatment centre was itself less bounded than one might imagine: the residential and day-service facilities were in different parts of the town, and two additional facilities offering hospital beds were located in a different town altogether. Patients and professionals circulated among the four facilities, sometimes even within the same day, and 'ethnographic material' would keep happening simultaneously in all these locations. So how to delimit the field?

Some practical barriers, and the role of volunteer that I inhabited alongside that of researcher, helped me to impose some boundaries to the ever-spilling field. These challenges also worked as a constant reminder that what came to be my delimited field site was not part of a totality that 'awaits to be discovered', but 'a contingent window into complexity' (Candea 2007: 178–79). For example, I had 'arbitrarily and knowingly excluded' (ibid.: 175) the space of hospital wards because of practical and ethical considerations: the hospital was located in a distant town that was nearly impossible to reach by public transport, and patients admitted there were at immediate risk of dying. Making these patients and already overworked professionals spend additional energies interacting with an anthropologist just did not feel right. I thus decided to gather information about what happened in that space through conversations with professionals and patients whom I met in the residential and day-service facilities, but who had spent time in hospital wards. On one occasion, however, I found myself in a hospital ward for two days, when a patient of the residential facility had to be suddenly admitted to hospital and volunteers were needed to supervise her meals. In that case, the physical boundaries I had drawn for my field site did not hold, as my interlocutors asked me to cross them. Their practices made the hospital, and the interaction with the patient in question and her mother, part of my field site.

Similarly, during fieldwork I soon realised that the professionals saw the work *of* and *with* family carers as a key dimension of treatment, so I also introduced my study to the patients' relatives at the beginning of a weekly meeting for families, and then sought oral consent from them to attend every meeting. During those fourteen months of doctoral fieldwork, however, I did not conduct formal interviews with parents, since their time in the treatment centre and in town was very limited and had to be spent with the counsellors and with the patients. I limited myself to talking informally to some of the parents when it happened, as in the case of the patient who had been admitted to hospital. And yet, after concluding my Ph.D., I felt it was important to go back to patients' families and try to interview family members to understand more about their struggles, especially about 'what happens next' – i.e., after patients are discharged and return home.

The aim of the four months of fieldwork (October 2022 to February 2023) I conducted during my postdoctoral research was to explore whether, to what extent and how the work with the families carried out during residential and day-service treatment 'travels back' to the patients' homes once they are discharged from the facilities, and with what medium- and long-term effects. What obstacles do families face after discharge? Which tools learned during the treatment path prove to be most useful? Are there other forms of support that families might need? All these aspects were addressed through further observation of weekly support meetings for families and through interviews with volunteering parents of patients who had been discharged from the treatment centre at different moments in time. Any parent whose son or daughter had been discharged from the residential or day-service programme could participate, as well as any other relative who was at least eighteen years old or had parental consent if a minor (for example, a patient's sibling). It did not matter whether the discharge was recent or not, as it was important that I collected the voices of both families with very recent treatment experiences and those whose treatment experiences had happened several months or even years ago. Willing participants could choose whether they preferred to speak in person in a dedicated room at the treatment centre on a Saturday – before or after the group support meeting for families – or via video call on any other day of the week. I ended up conducting twelve interviews (half of them in person and half of them online, most of them with patients' mothers, three with both parents present, and one with a patient's father). After a preliminary analysis of the material, I organised two three-hour focus groups with all the parents I had interviewed (one online, for those who could not come in person, and one at the treatment centre). Interestingly and luckily, one-third of the parents who volunteered to participate were the parents of patients I had met during my doctoral fieldwork, which made it particularly helpful as I could, in a way, 'follow up' or 'triangulate' what had happened to stories that I already in part knew.

Finally, I conducted participant observation at four two-day workshops organised by the association for patients' families on themes of '*pedagogia genitoriale*' ('parenting pedagogy'). These workshops, which are open not only to parents of current patients but also to those of already discharged patients or of those on waiting lists, can be accessed by paying a small fee that covers the costs of meals and logistics, and are organised by the treatment team twice a year, usually before Christmas and in early June. They are hosted at a nearby friars' convent located a few minutes away from the town centre, where parents can also book a room to stay for the night. The workshops are conceived as a 'special time and space' for the parents to 'listen to themselves', 'work on themselves' and 'learn skills' that will be helpful in their role as family carers, including learning to care about themselves during that caring work (clinical director). They are usually split into two parts: a first part in which the clinical director, the philosophical counsellor of the centre and an invited guest speak of a specific theme in relation to eating disorders – the last ones I attended, for example, were on the themes of 'recognising children as others to ourselves' and 'the gift of care'; and a second part in which parents are split into smaller groups that are each assigned to a member of the treatment team for group activities of the same kind that patients undergo during treatment (including dance-movement therapy, art therapy, etc.). These are meant to help parents 'express themselves' and talk about their 'emotions'.

The location of these workshops might make one wonder about the relationship between the treatment centre and religion. Some might expect religion to feature quite prominently in the book, given that we are in Italy and that eating disorders, as I have mentioned in the Introduction, have been recognised as sharing something with the ascetic practices of Catholic saints and more in general with the denigration of bodily pleasures. But religion did not come up much in my fieldwork. The local charity fund that played a key role in founding Il Giardino and that sustains it *is* Catholic. Workshops for families are hosted in a friars' convent every year, with some friars occasionally giving speeches to the parents and visiting the treatment facilities to talk with patients. But the book does not delve more into these aspects because I never found them to be relevant to the questions I was addressing. There was just one patient, and two patients' mothers, who mentioned 'faith in God' as important in enduring the suffering, doubts and despair that came with the treatment path, but that was it. Similarly, only two professionals, among the older ones, mentioned 'faith' as an important element in their lives. Such instances were rare and did not seem to shape other aspects of these people's experiences of illness and/or treatment differently from those for whom religion did not seem to matter. This might come as surprising to non-Italian readers, because, as Monica Bonaccorso (2009: 12) pointed out in her ethnography of assisted conception in Italy, part of what she calls 'the Mediterranean cultural area construct' rests on the common assumption that Catholicism is a tout court distinctive social and cultural signifier. This assumption fails to recognise that Catholicism, although the main religious denomination in Italy, encounters frictions in Italy too, under the forms of atheism, agnosticism, scepticism and stated belief but lack of practice, especially in the generations starting from the patients' parents. A funny indication of this is that one of the very few reasons accepted by the treatment team to grant permission to patients' requests for leaving the residential facility for one hour on Sunday mornings is '*andare a messa*' (go to Mass), even if 'everybody knows' – Franca once told me – that 'for virtually all the patients it's really just an excuse to go out, walk and stand for a bit. We know that, but it's fine'.

Navigating Research Ethics

The ethics codes and guidelines of the American Anthropological Association and of the Association of Social Anthropologists of the UK have always been my point of reference. But in the complexity of actual fieldwork, conducting ethical research also requires being reflexive and critical of one's own project, and of anthropology itself (Caplan 2003: 2–27). Given the nature of my research, a few points required specific attention: research participants included healthcare professionals, family carers and patients diagnosed with what are classified as mental conditions. However, these conditions do not affect the capacity to take informed and responsible decisions, at least for what does not concern one's nutrition; on the contrary, people with eating disorders are typically described as very 'intelligent', 'mature' and capable of making well-reasoned arguments (Giordano 2005). All participants in my field site were considered capable of deciding whether to take part in my research or not, as confirmed by an authorisation letter that I obtained from the clinical director. That letter also specified that, when patients under eighteen are admitted, the treatment facilities obtain informed consent from their parents regarding the possibility that patients will be involved in research activities, if they themselves also want and consent to that.

The clinical director considered my research project to be in line with the treatment centre's ethical guidelines and did not require approval from a local ethics committee in addition to the ethical clearance that I had already obtained from my department at the University of Cambridge, as the research did not involve the use of invasive procedures.[18] Although the centre had given me formal consent to work there as a researcher, I knew that this was very different from obtaining the consent of every person. Following the director's advice, to ensure participants' 'informed consent' I introduced myself and the research that I intended to conduct on arrival – first to the treatment team, during a weekly staff meeting, right after that to patients at the beginning of a group activity, and later to patients' relatives at the beginning of a weekly support meeting. I distributed the relevant information sheets and made myself available for any questions. I did not approach potential participants individually to invite their participation, since this could have been perceived as a form of coercion. Being Italian and having lived in Italy most of my life, I communicated everything in Italian. I sought oral consent from patients, professionals and family carers to observe and participate in group activities (group therapy sessions, meals, outings, staff meetings, support meetings etc.), and written consent for the 'interviews'. I made explicit the aims of the research to them: a study of professional and family carers' experiences of treating people with eating disorders, that sought to analyse the difficulties encountered and the way carers cope with them.

Participants were recruited for interviews after they expressed interest and showed that they fully understood what their participation involved. At this point, they were given two copies of the informed consent form to sign so that they could keep one for further reference. This form included details about the voluntary nature of the study and the participant's right to withdraw at any point, without being penalised or questioned about their reasons. Finally, I continually renegotiated consent throughout the fieldwork in informal ways.

I conducted only eight formal interviews with patients. Early on I realised that I was gathering a lot of material about patients' stories and experiences by simply listening to them during group activities and by chatting with them informally; more structured interviews seemed to evoke a performative attitude and framings that perhaps they were expecting me to hear. Moreover, many patients were already quite distressed and tired by the work they had to do in the treatment centre, and I did not want to add further stress. Patients' interviews and all other conversations were not recorded.

Instead, all the interviews with the professionals and the parents were recorded; this seemed expected, as interviews themselves seemed to be expected. Interviewees included fifteen parents, the clinical director (a psychiatrist), the coordinator (a social worker), the president of the association for patients' families, two endocrinologists, the second psychiatrist, five psychologists, two psychotherapists, four nutritionists, two dieticians, three educators, two nurses, four interns in psychology and two interns in nutrition. A few other professionals had volunteered, but their tight schedule made it impossible to conduct the interview. However, throughout fieldwork I had the chance to ask questions and engage in extensive discussions with all the professionals through casual conversations over meals or coffee, and while helping them with tasks. Most of the material was gathered in this way.

Any recorded interview has been transcribed, and then the tape wiped clean. All personally identifying information has been removed from the transcripts. Transcribed interviews were coded with recurring themes and analysed together with the other material collected in the form of field notes. I coded the material by myself. All material became 'data' safely stored on the university network and password protected. Data stored on my computer and hard drives have also been anonymised.[19]

Since it was not feasible to obtain formal consent from every person I saw and interacted with without causing major disturbance to the facilities' daily activities, I addressed this issue by i) introducing myself and my research on arrival, and whenever a new patient was admitted or a new staff member was employed; ii) asking permission to observe/participate at the start of each group activity; and iii) not using a tape-recording device except during interviews with the professionals and the family carers, and after having received written informed consent. When introducing myself, I asked those who were not willing to participate in any way in my research to later approach me individually and let me know, but this never happened.

I always relied on the clinical judgement of the staff and the comfort level of patients and family members in determining the appropriateness of participating in any activity and of conducting interviews. Conversations with all the three groups did touch on sensitive topics and might have caused some distress. Whenever I noticed that this happened, I immediately stopped and asked if they preferred to interrupt the interview or switch to another topic.

However, in virtually all cases participants were willing to continue talking. I constantly tried to balance my ethnographic curiosity with the potential consequences of my activities – both for the research participants and for myself. This also implied that I had to be careful about the ways in which I established relationships with participants. Setting 'boundaries', especially with patients' and professionals' requests, was a continuous exercise, which was necessary to define the scope and limits of my role in the field but was also an interesting source of ethnographic enquiry itself.

Notes

1. See https://piattaformadisturbialimentari.iss.it/.
2. One of these newspaper articles denounced the death of a twenty-year-old boy from a town in northern Italy, as having been 'killed by anorexia and by law' because of the 'unacceptable system of care' for eating disorders (see Palazzo 2020a).
3. See Foot 2015.
4. See Selvini-Palazzoli 1978.
5. The name of the association is a pseudonym, too.
6. More on this in Chapter 3.
7. Professionals use the English term 'front office' to refer to this space, which is why it is in italics here.
8. More details on what happens in all these meetings in the following pages.
9. This is the only body-length mirror in the whole building, employed for a specific therapeutic activity that I will introduce in Chapter 3.
10. Of the whole treatment team, only two psychotherapists, one psychologist and one nurse were men.
11. Endocrinology is a branch of medicine that, in the language of biochemistry, studies the role of hormones in regulating bodily functions, and which provides treatment when – as it is often deemed to be the case for people with eating disorders – hormone levels become 'unbalanced'. For a brief history of the emergence of endocrinology as a medical science, see Welbourn 1992.
12. Philosophical counselling is a contemporary movement in practical philosophy. Developing since the 1980s as a profession but since the 1950s as a practice, philosophical counsellors usually have a Ph.D. or at least a master's in philosophy, and offer consultation services to people who look for 'a philosophical understanding' of what are seen as social or mental problems. Philosophical counselling at Il Giardino is offered as a group activity to patients and patients' parents. It fits with and expands the centre's 'holistic approach' – attending to the 'existential aspect' of the eating disorder alongside the medical and the psychological (more on this in Chapter 2).
13. During my doctoral and postdoctoral fieldwork, only three male patients – fourteen, eighteen and twenty years old – were admitted, in different periods of time.
14. We will see how in Chapter 3.
15. These included accompanying patients to medical visits outside the treatment centre, accompanying the youngest ones to school when they were granted permission, and listening/talking to patients in moments of crisis when professionals were busy.
16. More details on these activities in Chapter 3.

17. Since I conducted fieldwork in Italy – and in Italian, my 'mother tongue' – I had to do a significant work of translation when analysing and writing up, with all that this entails for any ethnography.
18. This would not have been the same in the UK.
19. I kept updated with the debates concerning the EU's General Data Protection Regulation that came into force on 25 May 2018, and with concomitant updates to the Data Protection Act in the UK and in Italy, making sure that my research practices conformed to the changes in legislation.

Chapter 2

If Food Is the Symptom, What Is the Problem?

Tensions and Fractures

> *I would wake up at six. I would weigh myself and write down my weight. Then I would do one hour of sit-ups. At eight I would have breakfast of an apple. Then study. At one, lunch of two carrots and a fat-free yogurt. Then one more hour of sit-ups. I would study again until five and go swimming for an hour. Then shower. At eight I would have dinner – some salad and a tomato. I would go to sleep at ten. And then everything would start again. I was making it, I was becoming the master of myself. And here they are ruining everything ... I felt much better when I could see my bones.*
>
> —Sofia, nineteen, interview, April 2019

This is how nineteen-year-old Sofia described to me her 'usual day before admission' to Il Giardino. Weighing 38 kg at the time of admission – which was medically seen as a dangerously low weight for her height of 1.70 m – this young woman had been diagnosed with 'severe anorexia nervosa' and had been brought to the facility by her parents. During treatment her daily behaviours, deemed pathological, were constantly challenged: she had to eat complete meals under close supervision to restore her weight, was prevented from doing physical exercise, and was subjected to psychological therapy to examine her 'internal world' and 'understand the reasons and emotions behind her condition' (clinical director). Professionals would often characterise her as 'unaware' of the severity of her condition, as 'manipulative' and 'resistant to treatment'. In the clinical director's own terms, the aim of treatment was to deconstruct Sofia's 'pathological self' and craft, together with her, an altogether 'new self' for her that would *want* and *choose* to stay healthy.

This brief vignette contains, in a nutshell, one key conundrum of the book. Without questioning the concrete risks and consequences of Sofia's food restriction and physical exercise to the point of exhaustion, we can see that what the healthcare professionals cast as pathological is, for Sofia, a way of 'mastering myself'. Despite their stark differences, both the treatment centre's understanding of the condition and the patient's experience suggest an individuated, internal and autonomous 'self' bounded by the skin and made up of 'reason' and 'emotion', with a 'will' and 'choice' manifested in behaviour (see McDonald 2015: 42–45).[1] This self recurs in this book and figures prominently in treatment, but it takes shape within starkly different constructions of what is going on and what is required to 'be well'. The book seeks to explore some of the assumptions underlying the practices and ethics of care involved at Il Giardino, where these different constructions have to be reconciled for the purpose of treatment. It also highlights how the willingness *to receive* care shapes the extent to which, and the ways in which, carers can *give* care in clinical landscapes, and how complex moralities 'circulate' around suffering, caring and expectations for 'recovery' (Dragojlovic and Broom 2018: 8).

In this chapter, building on existing ethnographic literature on patients' experiences, I explore how patients at Il Giardino frame their eating disorder as a self-care project. We will see that patients' eating disorders can be seen as one of many expressions of contemporary self-tracking practices. Australian sociologist Deborah Lupton (2016) has given an account of the purposes of those who are involved in 'self-tracking' through the use of wearable, implanted and mobile technologies, and has examined the ways in which notions of the self and the body are challenged and negotiated through those practices. The first section of this chapter similarly examines how and why people are interested in self-tracking through what is classified in medicine as an eating disorder, and what purposes they aim to achieve in doing so. Building on Lupton, I further suggest that these self-tracking and self-shaping practices show strongly the *relational* aspect of such projects – i.e., how these people's self-projects are not about 'bounded selves', but about selves in relationships, especially kinship relationships. This, it will become evident through the book, has both interesting implications for anthropological understandings of specific notions of the person and important implications for treatment.

I then shift to how the professionals, on the other hand, construct patients as having a 'disorder of the self' which leads to certain 'dysfunctional symptoms'.[2] By tracing the multiple ways in which professionals conceptualise the 'eating disorder', its causes and manifestations, I suggest that symptoms are ascribed to an entity that is, at the same time, *external to* and *within* 'the person' of the patient. This results in patients being framed as having complicated and fractured 'wills' – the 'will of the real person' and the 'will of the disorder' – and therefore as inevitably ambivalent and resistant to treatment. This framing makes it not only acceptable but also a professional duty to intervene, even if through somewhat coercive measures. We will see how, during the patient's assessment preceding admission, what might be seen by patients as self-improving practices and experiences is framed by professionals as pathology. This pathology is diagnosed and treated through a careful tracking of the patient's body and mind, performed by biomedicine and the psychological sciences respectively.

At the end of the chapter, I examine what kind of therapeutic relationship can be, and often is, generated by this particular encounter between patients and professionals, and what role lies and trust play in the encounter. We will see that there is a key tension in this relationship, a tension between coercion and responsibility. But we will also see that the tension generated by the encounter of patients' and professionals' diverging constructions illuminates what those constructions have in common: eating disorders, both parts seem to be saying, have something to do with relatedness.

Patients' 'Eating Disorder(s)'

The whole disorder is a constant envy for a chimera that can never be reached.
—Lisa, twenty-six, group therapy session, January 2019

In the opening of the book, we saw an eleven-year-old girl being taken to Il Giardino by force. In this chapter, we saw a nineteen-year-old patient recently admitted describing the behaviours that had led to her diagnosis as a way of 'mastering oneself', with treatment apparently 'ruining' all her efforts. Both instances indicate that those accessing the treatment facility may not do so 'spontaneously', out of 'their own will'. Patients, in fact, are often brought to treatment by someone else – mostly by their parents, sometimes by their partners or spouses – and with considerable effort. The father of a fifteen-year-old patient summarised the process vividly during his first weekly support group meeting for families: 'In that moment, I felt like an executioner who, for the good of his daughter, brought her to a place where she didn't want to go, so that she could recover from a condition in which she says she feels totally fine'. But as Lisa's quotation at the beginning of this section suggests, things are more complicated than that.

In the book's Introduction, I traced how anthropologists in recent decades came to take seriously 'patients' experiences' of eating disorders, focusing not only on the practices medically seen to characterise these conditions, but also on the patients' moral reasoning behind them. Lester (1997), as we have seen, proposed to analyse anorexia through Foucault's (1986) notion of 'technologies of the self' – outlining how bodies, in what she calls 'the West', are seen as the material vehicle for an 'internal self', and how restriction of food, invested with meanings about dependency and nurturance, is therefore used to communicate autonomy (Lester 1997: 486). Foucault's scheme of self-formation processes, which Lester draws on, considers four elements: i) the part of oneself that is the object of work – 'ontology'; ii) one's position in relation to one's ideals – 'deontology'; iii) the practical form that the self-forming activity takes, including techniques and activities – 'ascetics'; and iv) the way of being that one aims to achieve – 'teleology'.[3] Following Lester, the ontology in anorexia is thus not simply the body, as it would first seem, but the 'self' *through* the body. The self that is pursued is a self-restraining self, in which 'reason' rules over 'emotion' and the enjoyment of food. This reason/emotion dichotomy, with the emotional and sensuous ranked together, is common in the US and beyond, but perhaps especially so in Europe (McDonald 2018). The 'obsessions' and militaristic regimenting that characterise anorexia thus have more to do with changing the self and communicating its new attitude, rather than with becoming slim. However, Lester argues, at some point the bodily practices take over and lead to 'a compulsively single-minded focus on the body', while the self-project fails (Lester 1997: 485–88). Similarly, we have seen how Gooldin's (2008: 282–90) account of an eating disorder unit in Israel suggests that hunger is experienced by patients as an enjoyable 'hyper' feeling of self-mastery, which becomes an embodied 'medium of selfhood'. In these patients' experiences, the eating disorder is not a problem, but a deliberate attempt to reshape the self as a moral way of living in the world (Eli 2012: 2).

These studies strongly suggest that eating disorders go well beyond issues of body weight and shape: rather, a 'moral practice of deprivation' seems to be part of a complex form of 'self-care' that takes dominant cultural imperatives to their extreme, paradoxically bringing people to self-sabotage (Lester 2014: 249). The fact that people's project 'fails', however, does not seem to reduce the strength with which they hold on to it (ibid.). But to what extent can one contend at this point that their determination is the consequence of an 'autonomous will' stemming from a 'reflective self', as Gooldin (2008) would put it? What is not clear is if and how this perception changes through different phases of the illness and of its treatment. Gooldin does not address this issue, whereas Lester briefly mentions that people with anorexia in later phases of their illness 'realise' that 'obsessive bodily practices' have taken over. Indeed, at this point many do seek treatment (Lester 1997: 487–88).

Most patients admitted to Il Giardino said that 'at some point' they did feel they 'had lost control' over the illness. Even patients diagnosed with 'restrictive anorexia nervosa' – which, among eating disorders, has been reported in the medical literature as the one epitomising pure and total control due to the absence of episodes of 'loss of control' typical of bulimia nervosa and 'binge-purging anorexia' – interestingly framed their restrictive behaviours as belonging to the realm of 'loss of control'. One exchange that happened in the day-service facility, during a psychological group session, is illustrative here: although of very different ages, the two patients involved had both been diagnosed as suffering from anorexia nervosa since adolescence, alternating periods of 'pure restriction' and periods of 'binge-purging anorexia'. They thus claimed to be able to reflect on both 'kinds' of eating disordered behaviour. During the session, 26-year-old Lisa was trying to convince a younger patient, still in her adolescence, that associating her current restrictive anorexic behaviour with 'complete strength and control', and her feared bulimic behaviour with 'loss of control', was unfounded: 'The force of restriction is only an illusion' – she said –'because when you reach the point where someone has to scrape you off the floor with a spoon, you are not very strong. One feels strong only at the beginning'. Loredana, aged fifty-six and now classified as a 'chronic patient', promptly intervened to support Lisa's point: 'Exactly, because even in restriction you lose control, you keep restricting and restricting, losing more and more weight ... and you can't stop'. This retrospective realisation – Lisa and Loredana continued – was what had brought them to treatment.[4] At this point Marzia, a 32-year-old patient who had been diagnosed with bulimia nervosa when she was sixteen, remarked that she had also found herself unable to control the behaviour that until a certain point had had a positive role in her life, leading to ambivalent feelings towards it:

> [The eating disorder] is a protection from the external world, but only at the beginning. At the beginning it's like an escape route, or a mask to call for attention – and then suddenly you find yourself unable to live without it. So you want and don't want to be helped at the same time.

In these cases, it was the patients themselves who had decided to ask for help through treatment. This is typically the case with people who have been dealing with an eating disorder for quite a few years, and who have experienced the negative impact of the condition on their lives. Although worried about what treatment would entail, Lisa, Loredana and Marzia had been keen for the moment of admission to arrive, because they had realised that they could not live with such a disruptive condition anymore. The premise of admission in these cases is different from that of a child or teenager who is dragged to the treatment centre by her parents, or of an adult who is admitted straight after being hospitalised and yet keeps doing everything she can to avoid being fed. The kind of work that needs to be done and can be done in treatment is also very different, as we will see in the next chapters.

The notion of 'technologies of presence' (Lester 2019: 63) resonates well with the way the patients I met talked about their eating disorder. Certain refrains kept coming up, and pointed to the relational function of the eating disorder as opposed to any exclusive focus on a bounded 'self':

> What is the limit between dependence and independence in the disorder? Between visibility and invisibility? Because everything seems very contradictory to me: you want to be invisible, but you want to be seen; you want to be independent, but you need help and you end up asking for help. Why does one want to be independent – not to be dependent on anyone – and then end up being dependent on everybody? (Mara, nineteen, day-service facility, psychological group session)

In her latest monograph, Lester (2019) argues that eating disorders are not simply a way for people to manage what they find too difficult and frightening – as the anthropologist Megan Warin (2010) had put it – but are also 'a means for seeking connection' (Lester 2019: 23). She thus suggests switching from framing eating disorders as 'technologies of the self' to seeing them as 'technologies of presence' (ibid.: 63) – as ways of extending an ethical demand to others by making oneself seen and responded to. But something more seemed to be going on in some of the patients' accounts at Il Giardino. Although many patients framed the eating disorder as a way of 'regressing from having to take responsibility for one's life', and of going back to 'a state of dependence in which the whole family has to act in function of you' (Cristina, twenty), many also framed it as a paradoxical act of family care whereby 'the illness also works to distract other family members from their own problems, which might be even more painful for them to deal with' (Simona, twenty-two). The 'utility' of the illness, as they called it, was seen to be not only for the person who gets ill, but for the whole family. It was, in the words of the psychologist Sara, a 'relational utility'. Another patient confirmed that her parents would probably have divorced by now if it had not been for her illness: 'The utility has been that of keeping them in a coalition to help me fight against my illness' (Marzia, thirty-two). In other cases, the illness had a relational utility in that it freed patients from the burden of caring for other family members without causing major family rifts. This was the case of 56-year-old Loredana, who had to look after her single mother for most of her life: 'In a sense, the illness is a way to be free. I am free not to care for others, because I have the documented justification of the illness'. Here we see how, for these patients, not only is the eating disorder a self-care project that extends beyond their 'individual' and 'bounded' 'self' by placing ethical *demands* on others, as Lester (2019) would put it; sometimes, it is also about *contributing* to keeping the family together by making sure that its attention is focused on the patient's illness, and therefore away from issues that might threaten the family unity.

What we might call patients' notions of the eating disorder – the ways patients understand, experience, construct and 'do' (Mol 2002) their condition – professionals call the 'egosyntonic nature' of eating disorders, a phrase indicating that the behaviours, values and feelings stemming from the disorder are in harmony with the needs and goals of the patient, and therefore are partly 'wanted' and 'desired' by the patient.[5] Whatever the name one gives to it, this necessarily results in a deontological problem for the professionals: Carlotta's nutritionist Irma, whom we met in the book's opening, reported feeling 'in great difficulty' every day that Carlotta had to be taken to Il Giardino by force,[6] and often told me and the rest of the team that she did not know what to do: 'Should I send her back home where she doesn't eat anything? How can I do that? She really doesn't want to stay here ... but it's clearly because we force her to eat'. Ascribing Carlotta's refusal to stay in the facility to 'not wanting to eat' – hence to 'the symptom of her eating disorder' – made Irma decide that keeping Carlotta in treatment, even if against her will, was the right thing to do. In the next section I turn to the different ways in which professionals in this treatment centre talk of the eating disorder and of its relation to the patient's self, and I suggest what ties them together.

Professionals' 'Eating Disorder(s)'

It's in the head that we must eradicate the eating disorder [touching her temple].
—Educator Flavia, interview, June 2019

One Saturday morning in January 2019, I am attending the weekly support meeting for parents, in the big room on the first floor of the residential facility. The mother of a sixteen-year-old patient who has been recently admitted talks of her difficulty in understanding her daughter's problem 'as the expression of mental distress, as you say here'. The father of another patient nods: 'I find it difficult too. I would like to understand … is this disorder a matter of genetics? Or is it more like a cold and a flu, and you get it from a virus, or a bacterium? Does it come from inside or outside? I wonder what bad things I might have done to deserve this punishment'. At this point, the counsellor leading the session – directing her gaze to those who had spoken – answers that the question of 'where the disorder comes from' is an interesting one, as 'there isn't a clearly identified external cause that one could address with an antibiotic'. Unlike for other diseases, the counsellor continues, 'there is nothing that one can see or touch' that could be held responsible for causing it. 'Genetics'[7] – she specifies – 'but also temperament and emotional vulnerability may play a role, but other components are necessary to activate the illness, and this is usually some kind of trauma, something in the environment, often in the family'. 'Nature' and 'culture' seem to be both involved here. 'This isn't an organic disease' – she concludes – 'and yet, unlike other mental illnesses, it has an evident impact on the body. It's a mental illness that speaks through the body, through food. Therefore, it's also about food, but it doesn't end in food'.

During another meeting, a few months later, the same counsellor finds herself having to address a couple of parents' anxieties about 'the very long time' that their daughters seem still to be needing to get better, after two and a half months in residential treatment. The counsellor replies poignantly that she is surprised that they speak of two and a half months as if it were 'a very long time':

> It is a long time, but it's also a very short time if you think that the illness took years to structure itself inside your daughters. Your daughters have taken the road of the disorder with the same determination with which a person whose house is burning sees only the window as an escape route. Even if you show them the door later, it's improbable that they will use it, because they already know where the window leads them. They don't know where they will end up if they go through the door.

From these examples we can start seeing how the 'eating disorder' is constructed in this treatment centre. The treatment team conceptualises the eating disorder as a severe psychopathology, as something within the realm of illness to be treated within the realm of 'Medicine'. The 'seed' of the disorder is seen as being located 'inside ourselves', but the triggers that make someone develop the disorder, that 'activate' the disorder, are seen to come 'from outside ourselves'. 'We can't detach things from their context', summarises the counsellor. This aspect is frequently highlighted during the weekly support meetings for parents, who are generally anxious to know the reason why their daughters are ill, and who would clearly feel better if they only knew there was 'some scientific explanation' – 'faulty genes' is among the favourite – which would lessen their sense of guilt at the thought that something they have done might be at least part of the cause. However, the characterisation of the eating disorder in professionals' discourse reveals a much more complex picture.

The notion of 'complexity' has a long history within eating disorder research, even if popular narratives have often been overly simplified, contributing to stigma and reinforcing misconceptions about who is affected, what causes eating disorders and how recovery works. Within the scientific community, eating disorders are considered among 'the most complex' psychiatric disorders, and there is now broad recognition that they are 'biopsychosocial' conditions (Munro, Randell and Lawrie 2017; Strober and Johnson 2012): their aetiology is considered 'multifactorial', with a combination of predisposing genetic, biological and temperamental vulnerabilities that, interacting with environmental and socio-cultural factors, increase risk in specific developmental contexts and personal histories (Collier and Treasure 2004). This is something that all members of the treatment team at Il Giardino know well, and yet, depending on whom I asked, they framed eating disorders in different, even if intersecting, ways.

First, the eating disorder is conceived – mostly by endocrinologists, nutritionists and dieticians – as a 'disease that has to be treated', with its 'symptoms' mostly linked to 'malnutrition'. Addressing the problem therefore is seen to necessarily imply 'refeeding' the person, without which psychotherapy is pointless. In the most severe cases, patients come to the residential facility straight after a hospital admission. As explained to me by the psychologist Marta – who had previously worked in the hospital ward in the nearby town – hospital admission is needed as a 'life-saving admission' for patients who have virtually stopped eating and drinking and are held to be at immediate risk of dying because their organs have started 'shutting down'. Treatment in the hospital mainly consists of refeeding patients with nutrition bags connected either intravenously or through a nasogastric tube.[8] Even in these extreme conditions, some patients still try to resist treatment, by taking out the tubes or by 'walking compulsively' in their rooms: 'In those conditions you can't work on motivation (*motivazione*) or awareness (*consapevolezza*) ... it is more a matter of support (*supporto*) and containment (*contenimento*)', Marta said.

She continued that treatment in the hospital is therefore supposed to return patients 'to a physical condition away from that immediate risk of death, which would also make them more accessible psychologically'. The idea here is that if a patient's body is too malnourished and depleted, it is impossible to do any psychological work because the mind is possibly not working properly. The endocrinologist of Il Giardino often repeated that one must remember that 'the brain is an organ, which needs nutrients to function'. This pointed to the corporeality of the mind: psychological work cannot take place without nourishment of the body/brain, which seems necessary to allow the will to exist: 'You don't have a mind at all if you don't eat', she kept repeating.

Quite early on in my fieldwork, the same endocrinologist told me about a research project that she was involved in with a clinician from the United States, which aimed to study how explaining to patients the 'Adapted-to-Flee-Famine Hypothesis' (Guisinger 2003) would affect patients' motivation for treatment. This is an evolutionary construction of the condition, whereby the distinctive symptoms of anorexia – restricting food, denial of starvation, and hyperactivity – are seen as 'adaptive' mechanisms that facilitated ancestral nomadic foragers leaving depleted environments. According to this hypothesis, 'genetically susceptible individuals' who lose too much weight may 'trigger' these archaic adaptations. When I asked the endocrinologist how one would explain to patients the presence of their self-reported obsessive thoughts 'telling them' to move and exercise in light of this evolutionary theory, she told me – as a matter of fact – that patients' obsessive thoughts 'are not thoughts that belong to them; those are thoughts generated by a malnourished body that goes into blackout':

> Knowing this is helpful to patients, because it helps them feel less guilty. It also helps us not to ascribe too much responsibility to them for not being able to stay still, for example. If one makes them understand that thoughts come from the brain, which is an organ, they will also understand that if that organ is not nourished properly, it goes into short circuit.

In the endocrinologist's construction, 'hyperactivity' is 'a biological collateral effect of malnutrition not related to patients' will, even if it *starts* as will in the form of wanting to do more physical exercise'. The fact that 'it starts as will' but eventually 'is not related to will anymore' is crucial for the professionals' understanding of the ethical complexity of treating eating disorders.

A similar construction of the eating disorder can also be observed in a recurrent group activity for patients led by the nutritionist Monica, which focuses on the 'Minnesota Study' (see Keys et al. 1950). This was a starvation-rehabilitation experiment that took place in the United States between 1944 and 1946 to understand, the nutritionist explains, 'what happens to the body and the mind in a state of severe malnutrition'. The study reported that healthy people who were (voluntarily) led into semi-starvation displayed changes in eating-related behaviours also found in people with eating disorders – e.g., eating very slowly, becoming obsessed by food, etc. The volunteers also experienced a strong sense of guilt when eating, and in the twelve weeks of refeeding that followed they seemed to have lost a sense of control over their appetite. Finally, what were framed as the emotional and psychological changes that the volunteers experienced during the restriction phase were seemingly 'identical' to those found in people with eating disorders – including marked depression, irritability, intense preoccupation with thoughts of food, decrease in self-initiated activity, loss of sexual drive and social introversion. The content of this research is often presented by the nutritionist Monica to the patients as 'proof that all these behaviours and symptoms are consequences of malnutrition, not of personal matters'. It is these 'biological symptoms' – Monica insists – combined in complex ways with 'psychological aspects', that determine the persistence of an eating disorder: 'This is why we insist so much on nutritional rehabilitation: so that we can eliminate all the stuff that is caused by malnutrition and then access the deep causes of the disorder for that specific person'. Talking about the other changes found in the research participants – and in those with eating disorders – the nutritionist would typically report that among cognitive changes 'there are no alterations of intellectual activities, but we see a reduction of the capacity to focus, of comprehension, critical thought and vigilance'. Scientists of nutrition thereby provide an ethical logic for intervening against patients' apparent will: although patients' intellectual activities may remain untouched, other elements of 'cognition' that are deemed fundamental to making competent decisions regarding their own health – for example, critical thought and vigilance – are framed as being affected.

A second, more psychologically informed, construction is that of the disorder as a 'symptom or symbol of something else', as the external form that 'inner mental distress' takes. Carola, the counsellor leading the weekly support meetings for families, kept reminding parents that 'it's not symptoms that need to be at the centre of our attention; it's the suffering behind the symptoms that needs to be at the centre'. The psychotherapist Mauro, on a similar note, would often repeat during patient group sessions at the day-service facility that, through years of experience, he had concluded that the illness was the result of 'people moving away from things they have known for a long time. What is left unsaid has to get out from somewhere. On a smaller scale, it's the same mechanism whereby when I keep stuff that I would like to say inside, my throat may start hurting'. In fact, one of the most common complaints on the part of patients is that their families do not understand that 'it's not only about eliminating the symptom' – about eating or not eating what they want – but also 'about changing inside'. Parents are reprimanded for not understanding that 'an internal change is inevitable in the fight with the external symptoms'. These complaints are related to the professionals' notion of eating disorders as being the result of a 'mismanagement of emotions' – whereby 'suppressed emotions', especially anger, inevitably 'emerge' in the form of eating disorder symptomatology. For the symptoms to recede, patients need to give voice to their emotions.

Linked to this 'emotion mismanagement', the eating disorder is thirdly framed, especially by professionals of the psy disciplines, as a 'paradoxical act of self-care chosen by patients to deal with problems that they feel they cannot manage' (clinical director): in a situation in which – perhaps due to family issues or traumas – patients feel they are not in control of anything, but are at the mercy of events that keep hurting them, they may 'choose to control the only thing they feel they can control: the food that enters their body and the shape that their body takes. That, at least, has to be perfect' (psychotherapist Teresa). Since this self-care practice ends up harming patients – at least in the eyes of others – this construction also makes the eating disorder 'an almost conscious request for help', whereby 'the disorder might be functional to make things and relationships around us change' (ibid.). This framing is used especially when referring to patients who 'have been parenting their own parents, rather than the other way around' (psychotherapist Valeria).[9] Although the eating disorder is seen by professionals as 'a dysfunctional' request for things to change, there is also the notion that it can be transformed into a more 'constructive protest'. During group sessions, for instance, the psychotherapist Michele often seemed to echo Lester's theory of eating disorders as 'technologies of presence', when he suggested to patients that one could 'read the eating disorder as an act of protest, perhaps due to a perceived lack of empathy on the part of others'. He frequently defined the eating disorder as 'a protest that aims at the well-being of a relationship' and therefore as 'a potentially constructive protest, if one allows it to become an explicit expression of that need for empathy'.

Finally, the eating disorder is commonly framed by the 'psy' professionals and by those who explicitly attend to the 'social' and 'existential' aspects of the eating disorder – namely educators and philosophical counsellors – as a 'disorder of identity': in this framing, the eating disorder gives a person who does not know who s/he is an illusory answer, 'becoming an indivisible part of the patient's self' (counsellor Carola). During a weekly support meeting for parents, for instance, the philosophical counsellor Carola explained that some people are 'more emotionally vulnerable' than others, and that this is necessary, if not sufficient, for someone to develop an eating disorder: 'One is not born with emotional vulnerability, but one can develop it within one's identity'. The counsellor specified that this phrase referred to the possibility of being hurt by the things that happen in the world one inhabits: 'The eating disorder settles where there are these fragile cracks. It's a glue that keeps the pieces of the person together, but that also makes the person rigid, because the glue stiffens and stiffens, until the person breaks into pieces'. Patients themselves often remarked that their greater, 'excessive' sensitivity compared to others had provided a fertile ground for the disorder; that 'people who are not so sensitive' do not develop eating disorders. This kind of discourse would especially come up in the context of group discussions about patients' histories – which they often told as including acts of bullying or heavy criticisms about their body shape and eating habits by schoolmates, siblings or other relatives, and even by sport teachers and doctors. In this sense, the counsellor explained, 'the eating disorder is not a problem for these patients, but a solution. A patient once told me that the illness for her is like a pillow: all the things that used to hurt her, now they hit the disorder'. On another occasion – during a group activity with patients – the same counsellor read a passage from Rilke's *Letters to a Young Poet*, which she presented as perfectly depicting the eating disorder. In her reading of the passage, the disorder is seen as a 'guest' that enters 'inside people' through sadness, and changes them without them noticing it: 'We are alone with that alien thing that has entered into ourselves ... the new thing in us, the added thing, has entered into our heart, has gone into its inmost chamber and is not even there anymore – it is already in our blood' (Rilke 1962: 64). The counsellor's association visualises the eating disorder as an external negative element that slips into people and 'makes a nest inside their identity, by giving the illusion of helping to keep themselves whole, but only to gradually take over their thoughts, desires and behaviours, up to the point of literally destroying them'.

Parents and professionals alike employ this last framing that externalises the disorder. During support meetings, parents commonly express the worry that, when their daughters are at home for weekends, they find themselves 'following the requests of the eating disorder'. It is notable here how parents talk of 'following the requests of the disorder', not of their daughters. Parents with more years of illness experience would routinely point out how they had gradually learnt 'not to give too much space to the disorder' and to keep doing what they liked, especially if they had other children, because otherwise it would be 'like letting the disorder win'. Nutritionists often express their frustration at the fact that whatever addition to the meal plan they propose, some patients always manage to 'twist it according to what the disorder says'. Psychotherapists, during the weekly staff meeting, report that they feel proud when they see that their patients realise that 'the things they say they do "to feel better", they actually do them to make the eating disorder survive' – apparently suggesting 'just how fused and con-fused they were with the disorder'.

In this world, then, eating disorders are not *really* about food, nor about the body. Food, eating and the body are just 'the tools of the illness' (psychotherapist Mauro). But since they are the tools of the illness and deeply affect patients' bodies – which have to be preserved if one hopes to 'work on the mind' – an extensive part of treatment *has to* do with food, eating and bodies. This is highlighted by the amount of time dedicated to 'nutritional therapy', 'nutritional group sessions', 'cooking labs' and 'mirror exposure therapy', as we will see in the next chapter. But also by the fact that the 'psy professionals' and the 'nutri professionals' need to have some training in one another's discipline, and that all of them – no matter their specialisation – are expected to enact multiple roles during their shifts: during lunch a psychotherapist might find herself in the role of 'meal controller'; during a night shift a nutritionist might find herself in the role of 'confidant' and 'psychological supporter'. And so on.

Fractured Selves, Fractured Wills

The professionals' constructions of the eating disorder affect in particular ways how patients and their behaviours are acted upon during treatment. Professionals construct patients with eating disorders – how they think, what they want, how they act – as the result of an external controlling agent 'which took over their mind and body through malnutrition'. Patients are thought to be 'not themselves anymore', even if they feel they are. Common military metaphors characterise the eating disorder as 'an alien monster' who divides and conquers both the patient's self and her family, and patients in treatment become 'ED [eating disorder] warriors'. This is one way in which professionals explain the complexity of dealing with these patients: 'The eating disorder made patients adopt behaviours that don't belong to them' (educator Flavia). Externalising the disorder seems to help professionals and parents avoid assigning full responsibility to the patients for what they do or say, and to legitimate actions of their own that seem to go against the patients' will: 'The disorder takes over your daughters' self ... it takes up half of their brain, so it generates a constant internal battle during treatment' (endocrinologist). In this framework, going against the patients' perceived will is just a way to 'help them win the battle'.

It is not only the professionals who frame patients as being 'invaded by ill thoughts' (nutritionist Irma); patients themselves perceive their wills and selves as 'fractured' and 'multiple', reporting that in many instances they do not know 'who to listen to'. Sometimes this makes patients delegate choices to trusted others, as nineteen-year-old Marina told us one Monday morning during a welcome group session at the day-service facility:

> This weekend I went for pizza with my boyfriend and a couple of friends, and I let my boyfriend choose my pizza. I realised that my brain was starting to race on its own, so I decided to make him choose for me. And he didn't choose an easy one, he chose the pizza with salami! I wanted to strangle him at the beginning, but he told me I was ready for this, and it all went OK.

Marina specified that one useful thing she had learnt in treatment was to rely on others to choose foods when she felt that her brain 'goes nuts, on those automatic thought patterns'. Here, delegating choice becomes a way to fight against 'the eating disorder talking'.

But this strategy does not work for everyone. During a different welcome group session on a Monday morning, Assia – a 21-year-old patient admitted with a diagnosis of binge-purging anorexia – reported being 'afraid of herself' when 'that ill part takes over', since she felt that nothing or nobody could stop her, including her parents' attempts to lock the bathroom door when she was at home: 'I don't recognise me in those moments. I don't understand how that person can be me. Because I also feel pleasure in that moment'. At this point, the psychotherapist Mauro objected, in an interesting turn away from the dominant notion of eating disorders that we have just explored: 'But it's not something *other* than yourself, like in a dissociative personality disorder. It is always *you*, it is a part of yourself that wants to say something'. Mauro continued and explained: 'But if we don't let that part speak to us, if we don't give an emotional representation of what causes us anguish and suffering, we do end up as if we were possessed by something, as if this thing came from the sky, opened our mouth and made us binge and vomit'. In a follow-up conversation on this point, Mauro explained to me that he saw the eating disorder as the result of 'aspects of ourselves that we have always kept silenced and that demand to find space'. With time, he explained, 'these aspects take shape within us in a violent way and make us do whatever they want. When patients say they hear "like an external voice", it is actually an *internal* voice. It is that part of themselves that they don't recognise because they have always refused to be in contact with it!' (original emphasis). Unlike in the case of conditions in which the illness is seen as more clearly 'something that is not you', the fracturing set out by Mauro makes the work of treatment more complicated in that the aim cannot be to 'eliminate completely' the cause of the illness, because part of that is integral to the patient's self (cf. Lester 2017).

Nevertheless, externalising the eating disorder seems to be the prevailing discourse in this treatment centre. Drawing a line between 'the disorder' and 'the person' seems necessary for professionals to do their job effectively by opposing the patient's view of the eating disorder as a self-care project – but also to experience their job as ethical, as the educator Flavia explained to a group of parents:

> Sometimes I am very harsh with your kids. You cannot know how difficult it is to maintain this harshness when they get angry or start crying. But one must think that when one is harsh, one is being harsh with the illness, not with them as persons. And I tell them exactly this, that what I am imposing is against the disorder, not against them.

In her ethnography of eating disorder treatment in the United States, Lester (2009, 2019) suggested that by talking about some patients as having traits of 'borderline personality disorder', clinicians frame subjects whose eating disorder appears impossible to treat. This makes them feel OK when insurance coverage is denied because they cannot provide the required proof of treatment effectiveness. In this way, practitioners reframe unbearable choices by creating 'a blindness to the existence of conflict' (Sturm 2004: 107). Professionals working at Il Giardino seem to be doing something similar, but not necessarily, or at least not only, when they have to make sense of not being able to treat particularly difficult patients. They mostly do it for everyday acts of care that require going against patients' will. Framing the eating disorder as an externalised agent that fractures patients' will justifies seemingly coercive acts. In this way professionals manage to go beyond the binaries of 'patient choice' versus 'enforced treatment'.

The idea that eating disorders are 'disorders of the will' means that someone other than the patient might have to function as a temporary, 'prosthetic' will during treatment (cf. McKearney 2017). In the next chapter we will see that, once patients have been given the tools to become aware that their self has been taken over 'by the will of the eating disorder', they are held responsible, in light of this awareness, to trust their carers and follow what they are told if they want to get better. The expectation is that patients – still ill – could and should actively separate from the ill part of their self. This expectation is reflected in the professionals' frustration at dealing with so-called 'false patients' – false not in the sense that they are not ill, but in the sense that they do not seem 'authentic' (*autentici*) during treatment: 'These patients are apparently very compliant with treatment', I was told by the nutritionist Irma, 'and then magically they don't gain any weight, and it turns out that they stay up all night walking up and down their rooms to burn calories'. These patients are defined as 'manipulative', as they do 'everything they can in order not to gain a gram' (ibid.).

In her account of psychiatric services in Greece, the anthropologist Elizabeth Davis (2012: 65) characterises 'diagnosis' as 'a fundamentally moral activity', especially in that it proceeds 'according to the rules of a game played for truth ... whereby the responsibility to tell the truth weighs on therapist and patients alike, tough in different regards and measures'. In the case of eating disorders, diagnosis and the related ascription of what is called 'focal incompetence' – focal in the sense that it relates only to the 'nutritional' sphere of patients' life – allows the professionals to cope with the moral unease of enforcing a form of care on patients whose behaviour suggests that they do not want it. As will become clear towards the end of this chapter, this problem does not disappear after admission but is always in the background during treatment. We will see how the professionals at Il Giardino navigate it and how, in Davis' terms, 'the game played for truth' also extends beyond the moment of diagnosis to the whole duration of the therapeutic relationship.

Assessment, Diagnosis and Admission: Creating the Eating Disordered Patient

In order to be admitted to Il Giardino, prospective patients need to undergo a '*prima visita*' ('first visit') which consists of an assessment performed by a doctor, a nutritionist and a psychologist. During this initial assessment, the biomedical and psychological sciences create an objective reality of 'eating disorder' and of 'patient with eating disorder' through the use of numbers and specific measurements. First, the patient is asked by a nutritionist and a psychologist what she thinks 'the issue' is, and when the first 'problems with food' started. The patient is asked to give an account of her 'nutritional story', and then an account of the 'family and social aspects' – i.e., what was going on in the patient's life 'at the relational level' before and when symptoms started. The attention on separating, but at the same time correlating, these two sides of 'the eating disorder' is notable, and in the next two chapters we will see how they are addressed in treatment. After this double account, a doctor assesses the physical, nutritional state of the patient by checking her body mass index (BMI), by examining the results of blood tests which patients are required to bring to the first visit, and through a general medical examination.

The BMI is a number obtained by dividing a person's weight in kilograms by the square of her height in metres. It is used in biomedicine to categorise people as 'severely underweight' (under 16 kg/m^2), 'underweight' (under 18.5 kg/m^2), 'normal weight' (18.5 to 25 kg/m^2), 'overweight' (25 to 30 kg/m^2) and 'obese' (over 30 kg/m^2). BMIs under 20 and over 25 have been associated with higher all-causes mortality, the risk increasing with distance from the 20–25 range (Di Angelantonio et al. 2016).[10] Patients' BMI is here a key metric in the monitoring of their health and progress, and is constantly updated in their files after each weekly weigh-in. But the BMI is also one of the factors that determines patients' diagnoses in the *DSM*, which is a reference point for the professionals who work here. It therefore constitutes a patient's very identity as 'anorexic' or 'bulimic' – a metric in what the Canadian philosopher Ian Hacking calls 'making up people' (Hacking 2006) – and their suitability (or lack thereof) for accessing the different levels of treatment. National guidelines (Ministero della Salute 2017: 73) recommend residential treatment for patients whose BMI is not lower than 13.5. Below 13.5 hospital treatment is recommended, as the patient is considered at immediate risk of death. However, in practice the lack of hospital beds for patients with eating disorders means that sometimes patients are admitted to Il Giardino with a BMI of 12 or 13. Similarly, blood tests tell the professionals about the 'hidden' damage that malnutrition has supposedly caused to patients' bodies: they are used to assess the risk that the disorder poses to patients' lives, and which level of treatment is therefore advisable. A physical medical examination complements the tests to assess the 'visible damage done to patients' bodies by malnutrition' (endocrinologist). The doctor looks for 'lanugo' (soft, downy hair on the patients' body, understood as the body's strategy to protect itself from the heat loss associated with extreme thinness), swelling and other 'signs of bad circulation', curvature of the spine, and 'abnormally low' blood pressure and heart rate (endocrinologist).[11]

The apparent diagnostic objectivity of metrics reappears when the patient is then asked to complete several standardised, itemised questionnaires that, together with a psychological assessment done through conversation with a psychologist and/or a psychiatrist, are supposed to measure 'the intensity of the obsessions typical of eating disorder patients'. During this psychological assessment the person is asked to report experiences of distress, and the standardised, itemised questionnaires seek to translate these experiences into quantifiable symptoms. Mental illness is thus imagined as composed of distinct disorders that can be detected through questionnaires and then tackled through tailored treatment. The idea underlying these tests is that, even in the absence of severe visible consequences on the body, the presence of recurrent thoughts and worries about one's body shape and food can predict the insurgence of 'dysfunctional behaviours' which will eventually lead to 'concrete consequences'. The tests are also administered to rule out any other reason behind loss of weight and restrictive behaviour towards food. Obsessive thoughts are thus placed as the 'core psychopathological nucleus' that defines when a patient is 'an eating disorder patient'.

An additional element that needs to be assessed for admission is 'motivation for treatment' (*la motivazione al trattamento*). Patients are asked why they think they need admission, how they feel about it, and what their 'intentions' (*intenzioni*) are. Ambivalence regarding admission is expected and seems to be what defines the 'standard' patient who needs admission. However, complete lack of awareness of having a problem that needs to be addressed with treatment – something that is not uncommon – is viewed as indicating that the patient may not be ready to undergo residential treatment. The numbers constructing and derived from the BMI, the blood tests and the standardised, itemised questionnaires administered on assessment and then again on admission, together with the medical examination and the talk-based session with a professional, all contribute to constituting 'the eating disordered patient', becoming fundamental parts of what are seen to be the patients' very selves (cf. Koopman 2019). Ambivalent motivation becomes one of those fundamental parts. The following and last section of the chapter addresses the first step through which patients' and professionals' views are brought into dialogue in an attempt to engage with the patients' 'inner world': constructing the therapeutic relationship.

Constructing the Therapeutic Relationship: Building Trust through Lies

> *The pleasure of the disorder is the pleasure that you might receive from a secret lover. The problem is that you miss it as you might miss a piece of yourself, even if it brought you very close to death. We need time, we need time to trust and rely on other people.*
>
> —Loredana, fifty-six, group therapy, March 2019

Trust in the professionals is not something that is there or not there, but something that is achieved during treatment. What is interesting in this context is that, as we will see below, the same holds for the other way around – the professionals' trust in the patients – but with different assumptions and implications for how 'trust' develops.

A few months after Carlotta – the very young patient who had been tied in the car and brought to the treatment facility – was admitted, her therapist reported that her parents were alarmed because they did not see 'much progress', especially in terms of weight gain: 'It's true that her progress is slow, but let's remember that she arrived screaming that she didn't want to stay. We didn't give up on her and she is finally starting to trust us'. When someone said that Carlotta was probably making herself vomit after the meals, one nutritionist said that she did not think Carlotta was vomiting. Perhaps she was doing something else, like spitting in the toilet some food that she did not swallow: 'I have been following her outside the toilet with my ear on the door, and I couldn't hear anything'. Others did not seem convinced, so the endocrinologist proposed to do a blood test 'to verify that'. Excessive vomiting over a prolonged period of time, the doctor later explained to me, leads to excessive loss of water and electrolytes from the body, especially sodium, potassium, calcium and magnesium. Expelling the gastric acid contents can also lead to an increased blood pH and a low level of potassium. Medical science is again a tool to 'discover the truth', which is here both corporeal and moral. It is not just a matter of detecting an organic pathological phenomenon – it is about detecting what the patient might be hiding during treatment.

The first thing that a professional must do to be able to work 'in cooperation' with patients is to '*agganciarli*', a term used to indicate the process of 'catching' patients' interest and 'making them realise we can help them' (clinical director). Until this happens – the logic goes – patients will not trust the professionals and will not be honest about how treatment is going, about whether they are managing to follow rules and recommendations, or about what they find difficult. The therapeutic relationship is seen to be based on this trust-building process, which takes time and requires sustained truth-telling from both parties. However, as the discussion about Carlotta's suspected behaviour suggests, even once the patient trusts the professionals, trust is not necessarily mutual. What could be seen as an invasion of privacy – a professional placing her ear on the toilet door – seems to be so necessary at this stage that it does not require explanation. Patients are assumed to lie because, professionals say, 'lying is part of the illness', it is 'almost a symptom of the disorder' (clinical director). Patients (and their relatives) seem to confirm this. Before admission – patients report – they 'had to lie' when asked if they had eaten, when and what. They 'had to lie' when explaining why they were always missing social gatherings involving food, or why they had to run away immediately after eating, to purge in secret: 'During the peak of the disorder, it's all about lies, since the eating disorder can only be sustained through lies' (Loredana, fifty-six).[12] Responsibility for lying, as responsibility for hiding food or for compulsively exercising, is therefore ascribed to the eating disordered part of the patient's self, which makes patients almost 'physically incapable' – in the philosopher Bernard Williams' sense of the term (see Laidlaw 2013: 153) – to do otherwise. Thanks to this framing, patients' lies are not taken personally by the professionals. 'Being lied to' and feeling 'manipulated' is tolerated and accepted as 'a matter of fact' when working with eating disorders. This does not mean that being lied to never feels frustrating to the professionals, especially when it makes them feel they have to act 'as the police' (educator Flavia). The moment when a patient starts 'opening up' and 'being honest' about her difficulties is marked as a conquest: it is taken as a sign that the patient is 'really willing to recover' and that the therapist has done a good job.

Professionals not only maintain a sceptical stance towards patients' truth-telling. They themselves occasionally lie to patients, on the grounds that 'when treating people with eating disorders, especially the most difficult cases, you *have to* lie sometimes' (nutritionist Irma). This typically includes the extent of patients' weight gain, or what is inside their meals, or the quantity of what they eat: 'Otherwise, they risk disintegrating. It is not really lying, because you will eventually tell them the truth when they are ready' (ibid.). As suggested by anthropologist Ignacia Arteaga (2018: 206) in her ethnography of colorectal cancer treatments in London, what for some is a lie, for others is better understood as 'the pacing of information': 'breaking news step by step' is seen by the professionals at Il Giardino as necessary for what they frame as patients' 'emotional well-being'. Although at Il Giardino lying to patients is not standard practice, when it happens it is 'for the best, because the patient could not have handled the truth' (nutritionist Irma). Some professionals strongly disagree with this way of working, arguing that it risks destroying the relationship of trust on which everything is built: 'If they find out that you lied to them, that is when you lose them for good' (psychotherapist Mauro). This last position is usually that of psychotherapists, who – nutritionists point out – 'are not those who have to tell patients how much weight they have gained every week and increase the composition of their meals'. Psychotherapists, nutritionists seem to imply, do not understand how delicate and difficult their task is, and how easy it is 'to generate a crisis and risk a dropout'. Here the professionals' lies are justified by the idea that certain truths sometimes might not be appropriate for a patient (cf. Fainzang 2002: 129).

In the world of this treatment centre, it seems, both parties start from the premise that the other may be lying at some point. Patients too are often suspicious of what they are told by the professionals, especially at the beginning. As noted by Davis (2012: 65–110) about the patient–professional relationship in psychiatric services in Greece, when both parties suspect that the other party may be lying, mutual suspicion transforms the 'distancing manoeuvres' of patients' self-presentation and of professionals' assessment and control 'into a more intimate, if antagonistic, relation', because the desire to know the truth helps secure mutual dependencies. Lying therefore helps *constitute* the professional–patient relationship. Patients and professionals in the eating disorder treatment centre endlessly try to ascertain 'what is in the mind' of one another, trying to transform the motives, emotions and actions of the other (cf. Mattingly 2010: 47). Ultimately, then, what happens after a lie is told and uncovered brings together patients' and professionals' competing views of the eating disorder and of health – an inevitable clash that can subsequently generate confrontation and more intimacy.

Drawing on ethnographic material from a psychiatric ward in the Netherlands, Els van Dongen (2002: 143) has defined lying as a 'ritual of affliction': the lie signifies suffering and can turn into more care. Lies for patients at Il Giardino similarly seem to be paradoxically necessary to 'open up' a space for receiving help. On the other hand, the lies of the professionals are expressions of a struggle against an uncomfortable situation in which they do not know how to act for the best of the patient while being fully honest at the same time. Professionals' lies are framed as 'temporary lies' that are only necessary in particularly delicate phases of treatment, and that function to prevent patients' self-discharge. Lies are thus seen as essential to maintain the existence of a therapeutic relationship in which, eventually, lying will not be necessary.

Conclusion

In the same way that Davis (2012: 16) claims to understand the patients in her ethnography as 'theorists of the psyche and theorists of relations', here I took both patients *and* professionals in my field site as theorists of the 'mind', the 'body', 'relations' and 'ethics'. I have suggested that the professionals working at Il Giardino construct a specific 'eating disordered self' as a way of making sense of and making bearable not only the impossibility of treating some patients, and therefore the *failures* of treatment (as in Lester 2009, 2019), but also their everyday tasks that contribute to the *working of* treatment. This is because, as we have seen, treatment brings together multiple and diverging 'eating disorders', which can be simplified as: for the patients, a relational self-care project;

for the professionals, a mental illness that by 'working through the body' takes over the patient's identity.

But there is more. Framing everyday acts of care as ethical would not be possible for the professionals at Il Giardino without a notion of the self as not only 'multiple' (see Lester 2017) but also 'partible'. Only a partible conception of the self allows the professionals to reconcile the tensions inherent in their job: between the stated aim of treatment – bringing patients back to an 'independent', 'autonomous' and 'responsible' state[13] – and the demands of clinical work, which include everyday activities of intrusion, surveillance and coercion directed at people who are mostly capable of making competent decisions in all aspects of their life other than their food intake. We have seen that patients with eating disorders do not present a unified will as assumed by principles of consent at the heart of medical ethics. As Patrick McKearney (2021: 159) has noted while writing about the complexities that professionals face when caring for patients with 'cognitive disability' in a Christian community in the UK, without a unified self to relate to, care will inevitably coerce and neglect at least part of the patient. McKearney (2017, 2018) argued that when it comes to respecting patients' independence and to assigning responsibility for acts of resistance to care, the carers 'distribute' responsibility 'across selves' (Laidlaw 2013), including 'the ill self' of cognitive disability. This distribution, which allows the carers to stay 'detached' from the patients' frustrating behaviours, seems to occur with eating disorders too, when professionals blame treatment resistance on 'the eating disorder talking' (see Lester 2017). In a similar way, by framing their coercion as directed 'to the eating disorder, not to the person', professionals at Il Giardino attempt to resolve the tension between care and coercion. However, whereas in McKearney's case the carers act ethically on the assumption that they cannot know what goes on in the patients' mind, embracing that very 'opacity' (Robbins 2008: 426), here we have seen that professionals seem to manage to act ethically on the assumption that they *do know* what is in patients' mind: which is, thoughts and desires 'determined by the illness'. The notion of an externalised mental disorder that 'takes over the real self' of the patient is employed by the treatment team to interpret non-compliance as the result of 'vulnerable invalids' (Lester 2009: 376) and to justify care practices that seem to go against a patient's will. This difference may be related to the difference between a reversible 'illness', whose mechanisms can be understood through psychotherapy and 'shown' by science, and a permanent 'disability', the bearers of which are deemed incapable of articulating. Moreover, the reversibility of the illness in eating disorders means that there is a 'normal state of health' that patients can return to.

This difference in the case of eating disorders seems to suggest that responsibility is not only distributed 'across selves', as McKearney (2017) put it, but also across *parts* of the self. In a way that reminds of Strathern's (1988, 2018) notion of 'partible persons' as 'potentially partible minds and bodies', patients' actions are here conceived as the way they select – or are incapable of selecting – one of their 'multiple compositions'. The notion of a 'partible self' anticipates the possibility of 'partition' of one or more of its parts (ibid.). As we will see in the next chapter, the aim of treatment is the departure of 'the disordered part of the self', which can happen only once it is recognised by the patient as an external agent. Ethnographically, seeing patients' selves as partible allows professionals to frame the 'internal battle' that patients feel they undergo during treatment, and the suffering that comes with it, as something temporary that can be overcome and is therefore worth enduring.

Notes

1. See also Lock 1993: 138; Rose 1996.
2. For an account of how patients in the UK and Australia report being constructed as 'eating disordered patients' by professionals, see Malson et al. 2004.
3. See Foucault 1986 [1984]; Laidlaw 2013: 103–4.
4. As in Saba Mahmood's (2005) study of pious women's self-cultivation in Egypt, the ethnographic material presented by Lester and Gooldin, together with the views of those patients whom I have cited here, suggests that reflective projects of self-cultivation can paradoxically end in their own curtailment (Laidlaw 2013: 150–67). In a similar way, the result is the elimination of the very capacity for reflective decision-making that allows the self-cultivation path in the first place. And yet patients here are often reflectively aware of the problem with their self-project, but they still cannot act differently without feeling a moral failure (cf. Lester 2014: 245).
5. See Lavis 2016: 69.
6. The youngest patients are admitted to the residential facility with the difference that – at least for the first weeks of treatment – they return to their family house to sleep, so that admission is not 'too traumatic' (educator Flavia).
7. For more on the 'genetics' of eating disorders, see Trace et al. 2013; Watson et al. 2021.
8. Nasogastric intubation is a medical process involving the insertion of a plastic tube through the nose, past the throat, and down into the stomach.
9. More on this in Chapters 4 and 5.
10. Efforts to define a practical index of 'relative body weight' began in the US soon after actuaries started reporting increased mortality among overweight insurance policyholders. In 1903, the Society of Actuaries and the Association of Life Insurance Medical Directors of America defined being 'overweight' as weighing more than the average for insured people of one's own age, height and sex (see Hacking 2006). These efforts culminated after the Second World War, when the relationship between weight and cardiovascular disease became the object of epidemiological studies (see Eknoyan 2008). From these studies it was concluded that the best index was the ratio of the weight in kilograms divided by the square of the height in metres – an index that had been described in 1832 by the Belgian mathematician, statistician and sociologist Adolphe Quetelet. Studying human growth, he had concluded that besides the peaks occurring after birth and during puberty, people's weight increased as the square of their height. This was thus known as the Quetelet Index until 1972, when the US physiologist Ancel Keys renamed it Body Mass Index (see Keys et al. 1972). In 1998 the World Health Organization defined

being overweight as having a BMI of more than 25. 'Underweight' was defined as below 18.5. Ian Hacking (2006) takes the invention of the BMI as an example of how statistics scientise bodies: he suggests that sciences 'make up people' through their 'engines of discovery', such as statistical analyses, that are thought of as having to do with 'finding the facts'. In this sense, before the invention of the BMI, 'underweight' or 'overweight' persons did not exist, as people could not experience themselves in that way.

11. Lock and Nguyen (2010: 32–54) have noted how the notion of risk in medicine emerged as a result of statistical metrics introduced in the nineteenth century by the new disciplines of epidemiology and public health. Drawing on historical and ethnographic works, they have suggested how deviation from the norm became disease, but also how risk stratifications emerged. As they note, it was only when an investigative approach to the interior of the body based on anatomy took hold in the early nineteenth century that arguments about the relationship between normal and abnormal biological states were debated. A fundamental development, they suggest, came about when bodily variation started being defined in terms of deviation from a statistical 'average': once the material characteristics of individual bodies were described and quantified, they were then assessed against 'normal values' established by statistical surveys of 'healthy' populations. On the other hand, statistical metrics made the notion of risk fundamental to discern factors external to the body that contribute to disease, revealing a tension that, they say, has been present from classical times in European medicine: that between an internalising discourse in which disease is socially decontextualised, and an externalising discourse that emphasises familial, social and environmental influences. We will see in Chapter 3 how the tools and measurements of biomedicine and the related notion of risk are employed not only to construct the eating disordered patient, but also as a key treatment strategy.
12. See Warin 2005.
13. More on this in Chapter 3.

Chapter 3

From Coercion to Responsibility

Transforming Bodies, Transforming Minds, Transforming Selves

It is lunchtime on a Wednesday at the end of September 2018. I am 'on shift' as a volunteer in the day-service facility. Patients are already waiting behind the closed door of the dining room – the so-called 'therapy room' – when I open it after I have finished helping Rosa, the social worker on shift that day, to set the table and arrange the food trays. The nutritionist Irma is already inside, next to the table where the tray containing the first course of the meal is ready to be served. Patients take the bowl from their assigned seat and start queuing towards the food, in tense silence. The soft music in the background and Irma's encouragements are the only audible sounds, although there are eighteen people in the room. One after the other, the fifteen patients take the big scoop placed in one of the trays and serve themselves. 'A bit more', Irma reminds most patients, making sure that each scoop is a level spoonful by pushing the food down in the scoop with a spoon. Once patients are all served and back to their seats, they are allowed to start eating. Most of them start chatting with one another or with Irma, who is now eating with them, sitting halfway along the long table. The newly admitted patients are quieter and more inquisitive towards the food on their plate. Those who have been admitted for longer eat slowly and carefully, but they seem more interested in the conversation than in the food.

As every Wednesday, the afternoon is centred around 'group therapy', led by the psychotherapist Mauro. By this time I have learnt how to arrange the uncomfortable orange plastic chairs for group therapy sessions into a perfect circle in the dedicated room at the end of the corridor, so that no patient stays hidden from Mauro's gaze or from that of fellow patients – a panopticon-like structure (Foucault 1991 [1975]), one might say, but with no central hidden observer. Instead, the observer analyst sits in the circle together with the patients, as exposed to their gaze as they are to his. I have also learnt that I should place two different chairs, one for me and one for the psychology intern on shift that day, outside the circle in two opposite corners of the room, marking us as external observers of the group dynamic.

Today Azzurra is invited to start talking, because this is her last group session. After six months of semi-residential treatment, she will be discharged on Friday and will continue her treatment path here through weekly appointments as an outpatient.[1] Azzurra is a thirty-year-old woman who was diagnosed with anorexia nervosa ten years ago. During this last group session, she voices her fear of having soon to respect the quantities of her meal plan 'on her own', that is, without the constant watchful eye of the nutritionists. At this point Lisa, twenty-six years old and sharing the same diagnosis, suggests that perhaps Azzurra is scared of 'taking responsibility' for her eating: 'As long as you were here you were forced to, and therefore you were given the permission, to eat. But when it has to be you who gives yourself permission, then you are scared'. Azzurra seems to agree with Lisa's explanation: 'Yes, now I will have to take care of myself. Even if I have the tools to fight these thoughts, I still have the thoughts. One part of me knows what I have to do, but another part still thinks that this food is too much, and that I need someone external to take this responsibility'.

At this point of the conversation Marzia, a patient usually seen as of radiant personality, looks visibly upset. Marzia is thirty-two and was diagnosed with bulimia nervosa when she was sixteen. Her treatment until recently consisted of irregular outpatient sessions with several psychotherapists, psychiatrists and dieticians. She had asked to be admitted to the day-service facility after going into a coma caused – the doctors had explained – by the 'electrolytes imbalance' due to her frequent binge-purging behaviour. After that frightening episode, in which her boyfriend at the time had found her lying unconscious in the toilet and had to rush her to the hospital, she promised herself that she would try 'to get out of bulimia once and for all' with a more intensive treatment.

Mauro notices Marzia's distressed look and asks what troubles her. She reveals that during her last weekend visit at home her parents told her that she had better recover this time, because one of her uncles had just been diagnosed with stomach cancer 'without doing anything to provoke it', they had said. This had really upset Marzia, because she felt as if her parents were telling her that she had actively chosen to develop an eating disorder. Many other patients become visibly outraged and say that those who think that someone can choose to have an eating disorder are either ignorant or very silly: 'Nobody would do that. One doesn't go to a shop and "buy" this illness. It just happens'. At this point Josy, thirty years old, points out that although she agrees, there *is* a difference between them and someone with cancer:

> We can choose to recover, they can't. Their recovery doesn't depend on their internal strength, will, or motivation, but on medicine and other external things. I am not saying that motivation and will alone are enough for us, but the solution is still in

> our hands: with treatment, we can understand ourselves and the function that the eating disorder has in our life. Even if it's difficult, we have the possibility to choose to get better; people with cancer don't.

Mauro smiles and nods in agreement, saying something that strikes me for the audacity of the image proposed to a group of girls struggling with their bodies getting bigger during treatment: 'Yes, you are like pregnant women, in a way: you will give birth to something at the end of this treatment path'. Patients look startled. Mauro explains what he means: treatment, he says, generates 'something new' in patients, just as pregnancy generates something new 'starting from your own self, through the encounter with someone else'. The 'someone else' here is the treatment team, and the intended result of the pregnancy is an 'aware, motivated, and responsible self' for patients. In this chapter I trace the course of these patients' metaphorical pregnancy, examining their self as an 'enactment' in Mol's (2002) sense of the term – that is, as constituted and reconstituted through dialogical, imaginative, interpersonal and institutional practices.

What I observed in the group session suggests a world in which people are conceived as persons with 'selves' that can become 'autonomous' through psychotherapeutic work. Nikolas Rose (1990) has traced the development of psychotherapy as a set of techniques within which the modern self has been formed, suggesting how the world of psychotherapy precedes the person. He has shown how, during the Second World War, 'interpersonal relationships' first became recognised as a site of intervention through 'group work'. Rose has also traced how nineteenth-century philanthropy laid the foundation for the expectation of 'self-regulation' by the individual. This 'regulated freedom' required techniques for introspection and self-government. Human subjects became susceptible to 'reshaping': through psychotherapeutic techniques, individuals could now learn 'self-awareness', which provided them with a way of changing how they operated in relation to themselves and others. This also brought an 'obligation to be free', entailing the right to a sense of 'autonomy' as the capacity to make informed, uncoerced decisions (ibid.). In the world of this treatment centre, a moral responsibility to get better follows from the possibility to autonomously choose to recover. Once change towards recovery is underway – as the examples cited seem to suggest – it is the patients' responsibility to keep going in that direction. It seems that, from the moment of discharge, the responsibility to 'eat properly' must shift from being shared with the treatment team to being entirely managed by the recovering patient. But how does this happen? How do patients who are brought to residential treatment by force, and who 'can't help' hiding food unless under constant surveillance, get to the point of assuming responsibility for doing – or avoiding – the very things that they were forced to do or avoid at the beginning of treatment? This chapter will explore how patients 'get there', by examining how responsibility travels through the network of care.

In her compelling ethnography of what she calls 'failed care' for eating disorders in the United States, Lester (2019) argues that the managed care view of eating disorders as 'self-inflicted illnesses' – for which patients are blamed and deemed responsible – makes it impossible for patients to receive adequate care. Framing eating disorders in this way, by assigning responsibility to patients for their conditions, seems to prevent health improvement. Here I look at how professionals in a treatment centre in Italy, where there is a very different healthcare system, try to navigate these 'double binds' (ibid.) and make patients 'treatable'. We will see that shifting responsibility away from patients allows professionals to treat them, even if it means 'coercing' them in some instances, and then *subsequently* to reassign responsibility to them for recovery.

Anthropologist Else Vogel (2018a) has similarly traced how what she calls 'agency' is configured and redistributed throughout post bariatric surgery treatment for people with obesity in the Netherlands. She shows that in the clinic's complex care – consisting of dieticians, exercise coaches and psychologists – the qualities and abilities of the patient's self, and the socio-material conditions through which these emerge, are rearranged. This rearranging, she notes, is in her case to an important extent done by the patients, who 'willingly submit themselves' to surgeons and psychologists in order to craft themselves differently: 'Patients make things act on them that in turn make them act in certain ways, and that transform them in the process' (ibid.: 509). In this chapter we will see that at Il Giardino something similar happens, although starting from a very different premise, and in a different sequence: here patients do not actively subject themselves to becoming 'the subject of intervention' (ibid.: 511). Rather, the transformation of patients' minds and bodies is the necessary *starting* point for patients to reach a state in which they will start 'actively' subjecting themselves to treatment.

Throughout the chapter, I will trace how patients who are defined by professionals as 'resistant', 'ambivalent' and 'manipulating' are turned into 'aware', 'authentic', 'motivated' and 'responsible' ones. I will describe how the structure, rules, knowledges and everyday practices of treatment function as tools to foster such a development, and show what kind of bodies – and therein minds – patients 'acquire' through clinical interaction (see McDonald 2015: 40). This is a process in which, ethnographically, mind and body are two entities: 'bodies' and 'minds' here are an ethnographic matter, not an analytical device imposed by the ethnographer (ibid.). We will see how the professionals work on patients' minds to create new, 'healthier' bodies for them, and how in turn, with a healthier body, patients are seen to be able to acquire new, 'more autonomous' minds.

Anthropologists Karin Eli and Anna Lavis (2022) have recently offered a powerful and important 'materialist account' of treatment resistance in eating disorder facilities in Israel and the UK, calling for a reconceptualisation of 'the body in treatment' and showing how objects and spaces shape, maintain and 'trigger' anorexia. Their work suggests an absolute opposition between patients' experiences and what they call 'the clinical perspective', as if the latter did not take into account the former in any way. Here, instead, I show that at Il Giardino things are more complex than such a binary account, as the treatment team constantly engages with and 'works on' patients' views and experiences, in recognition that 'change must come from within'. Nevertheless, in what follows I embrace the authors' call for understanding bodies as part of a network in which both human and nonhuman others come to shape eating disorders (ibid.), as I look at how the ordering of time, space and objects in the facilities of Il Giardino contributes to patients acquiring specific minds and bodies. I focus on the therapeutic activities that cultivate patients' 'awareness' – that is, a new way to 'see' the condition they find themselves in, not as something that protects them and makes them feel powerful but as a form of enslavement from an external force that 'took over their minds' and 'blurred their vision', both metaphorically and literally. We will see that this external force, as it is conceived by the professionals, neurologically 'distorts' the way patients see their bodies, with thin bodies made fat. This apparent distortion is reconfigured by teaching patients an alternative way of seeing their bodies and the food that nourishes them – a new view of the body as composed of parts that are all equally important, with food providing the necessary building blocks for its functioning.

The Therapeutic Contract

In Chapter 2 we have seen that patients are often admitted to Il Giardino 'against their will'. I suggested that assigning 'incapacity to choose' to the patient's 'authentic' self, subsumed to the will of the eating disorder, is one way in which the professionals deal with the problem of applying care where it is not wanted. Another way in which they seem to cope with this problem is by requiring patients to sign a 'therapeutic contract' on admission.[2] The contract contains information regarding the organisation of the residential facility and establishes 'the rights and responsibilities' of patients during treatment, including respecting a long list of rules – e.g., compulsory participation in the weekly group activities; being 'collaborative' with 'nutritional therapy'; avoiding purging and other 'compensatory behaviours'; avoiding self-harming behaviours; avoiding alcohol, drugs, laxatives and diuretics. In the last section of the therapeutic contract, patients agree to employ four 'basic techniques of self-control' to 'counteract' their symptoms. These are i) 'writing a diary'; ii) 'doing alternative activities'; iii) 'asking professionals for help'; and iv) 'employing reattribution techniques (by attributing one's obsessive thoughts to the fact that one is affected by an eating disorder)'. Noteworthy is how the last point is expressed with the use of the passive form – pointing to the notion of the eating disorder as an external force 'taking over' the person.

The therapeutic contract functions to give the impression that treatment is 'voluntary'. However, patients are not expected to observe all the rules from the first day of admission: 'That would be impossible, or else they would not need admission. Rules function as an ideal to which patients must strive' (clinical director). The 'voluntary' ideal seems to contradict the framing of patients as incapable of choosing to undergo treatment, because a contract signed without capacity would have no legal force. One might wonder why patients are asked to sign at the beginning if they are not expected to keep to the code of conduct immediately – i.e., if the idea in the contract is only applied at a point when patients are considered to be regaining their capacity. It is interesting that the complete list of thirty-three rules is given to patients only *after* they have signed the contract and 'agreed' to what it entails. In fact, the clinical director tells me in one of our first conversations, the contract has mostly a 'symbolic' function. It seems that although the contract has no legal force, it is signed so that if a patient keeps resisting treatment, professionals can use it to argue that s/he is not respecting it and can decide to discharge that patient and give their place to someone who could 'benefit more'. This is why the contract has to be signed at the beginning, not when the patient's competence is considered to have 'returned': it is a kind of hedging against the possibility that a patient will never reach the stage where the professionals consider them 'competent', but will keep refusing treatment. In fact, sustained dismissal of the rules over time results in the treatment team questioning the patient's 'motivation' for recovery and often imposing a 'pause for reflection', during which the patient is sent home. This could later lead to discharge if the patient does not change behaviour upon returning to the treatment centre. The waiting list for this public service is known to be long and if a patient is not motivated enough, it is reasoned, that spot could be better used for someone else.

There appears to be something else going on, however – something that has to do with instilling in patients, from the beginning, the idea that they are responsible for how treatment goes, and that, without their collaboration, treatment will not work. In her ethnography of psychiatric treatment in Greece, Davis (2012: 217) suggests that, where behaviour modification is at the basis of treatment, the contract has the explicit therapeutic aim to 'inculcate self-control and personal responsibility in the patient', whose efforts to meet the terms of the contract are evaluated and reinforced by the treatment team. Working towards the behavioural goals set by the contract together with the therapist becomes a matter of 'self-control' and 'personal responsibility', with responsibility becoming a therapeutic tool (ibid.: 218). In the treatment of eating disorders, the eradication of the 'self-control' deemed typical of the eating disorder is as much a therapeutic aim as the inculcation of a new self-control for recovery. Within the world of these therapists, the aim is to move from a particular 'external' control of the self by the eating disorder towards a new 'internal' self-control by the patient.

Restructuring Time and Space

New patients are admitted to the residential facility in the morning. One nutritionist and one psychologist take care of '*accogliere*' ('welcoming') the new patient – meaning that, after signing the contract and doing the medical visit, there is a brief session with them. Here the patient is introduced to how days are organised into group activities, is given a tour of the facility and the complete list of rules. The patient is then brought to her bedroom, and by then it is usually lunchtime.

Lunch, or 'nutritional therapy' as it is called here, is the first encounter that new patients have with treatment: suddenly, the patient finds herself in a large dining room. At the centre of the room there is a big oval table where up to eight patients can sit; at the back of the room there are two square tables, for four patients each; on the opposite side, a single table facing the wall is reserved for 'particularly difficult patients'. Patients are assigned a different seat for every meal, but always trying to keep a configuration such that 'the most problematic patients do not affect the more vulnerable ones' (nutritionist Irma). There is always music on during meals, to disguise the otherwise 'unbearable silence' (clinical director) and facilitate the creation of a cheerful atmosphere with small talk and occasional jokes, while professionals carry out their 'controllers' role.

Lunch, like dinner, is followed by a 'rest period' of one hour, during which patients are required to stay all together in the 'relaxation room' so that the treatment team can make sure nobody is purging in the toilet or exercising in their bedroom. During this time, only activities that can be done while sitting are allowed: watching TV, reading, studying, drawing, writing a journal. In the relaxation room, chairs, armchairs and sofas are thus transformed from pieces of furniture into clinical objects and become central actors in the fight against the eating disorder (see Eli and Lavis 2022): they become the tools of the fight against patients' 'compulsive' urge to move and burn calories, a fight that is hard to win. Most patients, in fact, can be seen keeping at least one leg constantly moving, even if almost imperceptibly to the observer.

Rules of this kind, as noted by Eli and Lavis (ibid.: 353), foreground 'the optimisation of nutrient absorption as paramount to patients' temporal, spatial and bodily routines'. The authors argue that rules function to 'designate food as *the* treatment for anorexia, thereby framing anorexia primarily as being both *in* and *about* the body' (ibid., original emphasis). This clinical perspective, they point out, fails to see that anorexia is not really about the body, but is only enacted *with* the body. In Chapter 2 we have seen how at Il Giardino, instead, if there is one thing in common between the diverging constructions of the patients and those of the professionals, it is precisely the notion that eating disorders are not *really* about food and the body, but about issues of relatedness enacted *through* food and the body. The treatment team here is well aware of what they call the 'relational baggage' (*bagaglio relazionale*) of food for the patients, and of how distressing 'nutritional therapy' is to them precisely because of that 'baggage'. In fact, if you ask the professionals why it is necessary to make patients rest all together in the same room after a meal, they will tell you, in addition to the 'obvious' reasons that have to do with controlling their behaviours, that it is a way to prevent patients from 'being alone in the most difficult moments of their day' (educator Flavia). Staying surrounded by others, distracted by TV or a book or knitting, is supposed to 'tone down the obsessive thoughts' about the meal just eaten and the need to move to 'burn it off', which is how they would 'respond to the distress they feel' (ibid.). It also allows the professionals to see if someone is going into 'a crisis' and to intervene by bringing her to a separate room to talk. This rule, therefore, is not only about surveillance and making sure that nutrients are absorbed, but also about care for the patients' distress that comes with letting their bodies absorb nourishment.

After the first meal, the new patient is officially part of the treatment facility and will follow the stream of activities that constitute 'therapy'. 'Therapy' in the residential facility can be imagined as a carousel onto which patients jump while it is turning. Here I am thinking of one of those modern carousels which, instead of being populated only with horse-shaped mounts, include a variety of mounts with different animal and non-animal shapes. Several group activities structured around the five compulsory meals per day constitute the rotating circular platform of the carousel. Individual weekly sessions with one's assigned psychotherapist and nutritionist define the shape and motion of each patient's 'mount': each patient, in fact, has a personalised path in terms of 'the psychological work' they do and the 'meal plan' that they have to follow, with adjustments made in the course of treatment depending on 'progress'. Whereas the rotating circular platform keeps spinning in the same direction and at the same speed, each mount on the rotating platform has its own different motion: a horse might move up and down, a giant teacup might spin in the opposite direction.

Time is structured and categorised in a particular way in this facility. Patients shift from a situation in which – before admission – their days 'revolved around the endless and meticulous process of preparing and consuming and expelling food, with all the rest receding into the background and time losing its shape' (Lisa, twenty-six), into a situation in which half-hours, hours, days and weeks are categorised into different 'therapeutic activities', including mealtimes. Individual weekly sessions with one's assigned therapists can happen at any time, depending on the professionals' shifts and duties. But aside from this, days in the residential facility are heavily structured. Every Monday morning patients receive a 'weekly planner', which lists the group activities that will happen every day and always follows this structure:

8.00–8.30: psychopharmacological therapy
8.30–9.00: breakfast
9.00–10.00: individual sessions
10.00–11.00: first group activity

11.00–11.30: mid-morning snack
11.30–12.30: second group activity
12.30–13.30: lunch
13.30–15.30: time for resting/studying/reading
15.30–16.30: third group activity
16.30–17.00: afternoon snack
17.00–18.00: fourth group activity
18.30–19.00: psychopharmacological therapy
19.00–20.00: dinner

After dinner, patients are 'free to do what they want', which typically includes making phone calls, watching a movie with the educator on the night shift, or playing board games. All the patients are ideally supposed to be in their bedrooms at 11 pm, regardless of age. Saturdays and Sundays have a less structured schedule, with group activities ending by lunchtime on Saturday and the rest of the weekend left 'free' for patients to receive visits from relatives and friends, or to go out for their weekly permits.

Not only time, but also space is ordered for patients in a specific way. This ordering of space has to do with what are seen to be the specificities of eating disorders. In her ethnographic research on eating disorder treatment in Canada, the UK and Australia, Megan Warin (2005) has shown how for people who live in shared houses the bedroom becomes the single space for storing, preparing, eating and expelling food. These reconfigurations of space allow people to avoid the surveillance of others, eat what they choose, hide food and purge. Inpatient treatment – Warin suggests – tries to prevent these behaviours, but the single bedrooms at the basis of most hospital programmes unwittingly reproduce the very configurations of space that support them, as eating, sleeping and expelling food happens in one conflated space (ibid.: 104). In her conclusion, Warin (ibid.: 109) calls for more attention to residential contexts that position themselves in contrast to hospital-based treatment. Il Giardino is certainly one such context.

In the residential facility, rooms and areas that might have a role in 'reinforcing the symptoms' of eating disorders are either forbidden to patients or their use is strictly regulated. The kitchen, where food is stored and prepared, is a 'red zone' for patients. One of the first things that professionals told me when I started fieldwork was that, every time I left the kitchen and nobody else was there, I had to close the door and lock it, always hiding the key in a cupboard where every member of the treatment team, but not the patients, would be able to find it. The dining room is also a red zone outside mealtimes, and its door is carefully locked at the end of every meal. Toilets and bathrooms are another space of risk: in life before admission, patients would access them to purge what they had just eaten, exercise in secret, 'obsessively check' their bodies in the mirror and weigh themselves. For the same reason, there are no scales in the treatment centre, besides the one in the doctor's office where medical examinations and the weekly weight monitoring happen. Equally, no mirrors are to be found in the facility, except from small mirrors fixed high on the walls of toilets and bathrooms so that the only part of their bodies that patients can see reflected is their faces. For a while, the professionals told me, toilets were indeed kept locked for one hour after every meal. At some point, however, the treatment team decided to try and keep them open, 'trusting patients' that they would respect the rule of staying in the common room for one hour after meals. Keeping toilets unlocked mostly meant, I was told, shifting the responsibility for avoiding compensatory behaviours onto patients: 'If they make themselves vomit, it will come out in their weight monitoring' (nutritionist Irma). Patients' bedrooms are not locked, but patients are not supposed to spend much time there during weekdays. This is meant to prevent them 'from exercising compulsively', but also 'from isolating themselves in vulnerable moments' (educator Flavia). Similarly, access to the garden is not prevented by any physical barrier, but the limited time for its use – which patients employ for 'legitimate things' like smoking, reading and sunbathing, but also for 'dysfunctional ones' like 'rounds of compulsive walking' (ibid.) – is specified in the list of rules that patients must follow. Patients deemed to be 'in a particularly severe physical state' are often told they cannot access the garden until they have reached a safer weight. Nevertheless, many patients routinely retreat into their rooms or disappear, to then be found walking in the garden.

One might wonder why an understaffed treatment team spends so much time running after patients, risking that they do things that seem to counteract their treatment and knowing that that indeed often happens. I would suggest that this loose ordering of space functions not only to 'fight' the symptoms of the eating disorder, as in recognition of the iatrogenic effects that Warin (2005) has noticed in hospital inpatient settings. It also has to do, again, with an instillation of responsibility in patients, seen as a key ingredient for a long-lasting recovery. It is as if the treatment team were preparing patients, from the start, 'to deal with a world in which toilets, bedrooms and gardens will not be locked' and in which 'self-control will have to come from within themselves' (educator Teresa). The kitchen and the dining room are exempt from this work of '*responsabilizzazione*' (fostering responsibility) because they are conceived as having a different quality: they are seen less as a source of 'temptation' for patients to engage in 'dysfunctional behaviours' – i.e., bingeing on the food stored in the kitchen or prepared in the dining room – and more as a source of potential 'exposure to phobic elements' (nutritionist Irma). Most patients, the professionals hold, would not dare eat the food in the kitchen, as they would be too scared to be caught. The danger, instead, is mostly perceived to be in patients '*seeing* all that food', and possibly the calorific content written on the packages that are always carefully removed before serving it to patients. This would inevitably lead to 'crises of anxiety' which could compromise treatment and result in self-discharge.

'Tuning It Down': Trusting Drugs, Trusting Therapy

When 'dysfunctional thoughts' are felt to be 'out of control' – and seem to make it impossible for patients to think about anything else, causing severe anxiety and lack of sleep – psychopharmaceuticals such as antidepressants, mood stabilisers and tranquillisers come in to literally transform what is in patients' minds. Around half of the patients are prescribed one, but often more than one, psychotropic medication. Twice a day the nurse on shift rings a bell and the patients who have a prescription go to the room dedicated to medical visits. Here, psychopharmaceuticals are given to patients one by one, under the watchful eye of the nurse, who checks that pills and drops are swallowed.

Convincing patients to accept psychotropic drugs is not easy work, because of the popular association of these drugs with their side effect of 'weight gain'. The psychiatrist ascribes this difficulty to 'lack of information', since many new psychopharmaceuticals do not have that effect anymore. 'With bulimic patients it is a bit easier' – she tells me – 'because they hate their symptom so much and would do anything to stop it'. Those suffering from anorexia seem more resistant: 'The biggest obstacle is their idea that all these drugs will make them gain weight. Which is not true. There are many new drugs now that don't have that collateral effect, and it is up to us to prescribe those'. The problem – the psychiatrist continues – is that some psychiatrists keep prescribing drugs that make patients gain weight on purpose, this way 'mining the therapeutic alliance'. The same psychiatrist told me that many patients also express the worry that, when they start taking medications, the thoughts and behaviours they would have during treatment would be 'due to the drug' they are taking, that they would not be 'in control' of their thoughts and actions anymore. In the face of these patients' fears, the psychiatrist responds to them by pointing out that their thoughts and actions are '*already* out of their control', because they are controlled by the eating disorder. Drugs are thus framed as external but benevolent agents that can help patients regain *real* control of their thoughts and actions:

> Of course patients are still themselves: drugs can't eliminate dysfunctional thoughts or make patients take decisions; they can only 'lower the volume', the intensity and frequency, of obsessive thoughts, so as to make space for *other* thoughts and make patients capable of accepting help by respecting the rules – exercising less, eating properly.

Here again we are in a world in which an intervention that is external and somewhat imposed on the patient is deemed necessary to counteract the effect of another external and coercive agent – the eating disorder. Contrary to what has been observed in the United States (cf. Lester 2014), patients seem to accept this external intervention endowed with therapeutic power surprisingly readily once their fears are deconstructed by a trusted professional: most patients happily queue to receive their pills or drops, and many look forward to those two moments of the day. A few members of the treatment team suggested that this might also have to do with the fact that taking medications is a powerful and tangible 'proof' that patients are recognised as ill and are legitimately receiving help – an additional tool in their technology of presence, to use Lester's expression.

On the other hand, the psychiatrists working at Il Giardino, although very efficacious in communicating to patients the reassuring 'certainty' about the effect that specific drugs would have on them, were uncomfortably aware that there was always an element of 'trial and error' in their prescribing psychopharmaceuticals to patients. This is because, both explained to me, there are no psychopharmaceuticals 'proven to work for the core symptoms of eating disorders'[3] – i.e., wanting to lose weight, 'body misperception', obsession with calories etc. This means that they can only use various kinds of psychopharmaceuticals to tackle the 'side symptoms' of eating disorders: depression, mood swings, anxiety, the frequency of obsessive thoughts. A further complicating factor, the psychiatrists concurred, is the issue of dosage: 'Our patients are so distant from the prototypical patients that most of these drugs and their side effects are tested on … you know, we don't treat many 70 kg adult males here!' In fact, the vast majority of patients are young girls with half that weight: 'It's all about experimenting with different kinds and dosages, very gradually and carefully', they remarked.

Coercion, Awareness and Responsibility

The four group activities that happen during the day vary depending on the professionals on shift and have different aims: facilitating patients' understanding of the 'meaning' and 'function' of the eating disorder in their lives (psychological group therapy); stimulating patients' 'expression of emotions' and 'connection with others' (dance-movement therapy, drama therapy, poetry); 'informing patients' (nutritional groups); 'cultivating awareness and motivation' (motivational group, objectives group); facilitating patients' 'reconnection with their body' (yoga, meditation, 'body relaxation'); or simply keeping patients 'busy' and 'away from their obsessive thoughts' (knitting, gardening, literature). All group activities have a strong didactic aspect, also expressed by the term 'educators' that is used to qualify the professionals who lead them. In many of those activities, the resemblance to educational settings is noticeable. Most patients have notebooks and take detailed notes, asking for clarifications when they do not understand. Educators often leave patients 'homework' for the next session. As if marking the resemblance to school, the beginning of every therapeutic activity, including meals and the administration of medications, is signalled by the ringing of a bell placed in the living room.

Awareness and motivation for treatment are cultivated through all these activities, but most explicitly during 'psychomotivational group sessions'. During these sessions, psychologists and educators 'make patients see' all the disadvantages of living with an eating disorder, and what patients are missing and losing by 'sticking to it'. These sessions are typically structured around a patient who volunteers to explain the reasons behind her desire to interrupt treatment and go back home. Most patients ascribe their desire to go home to the fact that at home 'one is free to do what one wants' and has 'control over one's life', whereas in treatment 'one feels constantly coerced'. The educator monitoring the session then starts asking the patient what she was free to do at home, 'concretely'. This typically pushes patients to 'recognise' that the freedom they felt they had was actually very limited, often consisting only of deciding what one would or would not eat. Patients are thus put in front of what these professionals see as the 'illusion of freedom that the eating disorder gave them'.

Special group sessions are organised by nutritionists to further 'unmask' this illusion. These sessions are meant to show patients that the nutritional rules imposed by the treatment centre, experienced by patients as coercive, are nothing compared to the 'imprisonment of the internal tyranny that they have imposed on themselves through the eating disorder' – and that these new rules function as a way to gradually break the rules imposed by the illness, with the aim of regaining some 'true freedom'. The idea is to make patients understand the rationale behind the rules of the treatment centre by making them more aware of the rules 'imposed by the eating disorder'. The clinic is thus constructed as a world in which the 'rules of the eating disorder' and the 'rules of the treatment centre' fight against each other. In this picture, the coercion imposed by the treatment team is framed not as something against freedom, but as an unpleasant necessary step *towards* freedom, and therefore as a feature of care.

Most rules are in fact related to the symptoms of eating disorders: avoid talking about food, calories and weight at any time; avoid tight clothes and clothes that expose one's skinniness; avoid exercising; avoid comments on food during meals; avoid hiding food and cutting food into tiny pieces, and so on. Through these rules – aimed at stopping 'feeding the eating disorder' – the nutritionists encourage patients' 'normal self' to emerge. As part of this effort, the first and most evident aim of nutritional rules is to 're-teach' patients 'what and how to eat in a normal way' (nutritionist Monica). This can range from how one properly sits at a table, to how much one cuts different foods before bringing them to the mouth, to how one chews food or peels fruit. The resemblance to parents teaching the same things to young children is stark.[4] But there is more going on. At an 'individual' level, the aim of many of these rules is not simply to correct 'abnormal' behaviour because it makes patients 'absorb less food' and therefore not gain weight. As anticipated above, the professionals see in the ritualistic behaviour of the eating disorder another negative function, expressed by the adjective 'dysfunctional' that is usually associated with it: it is 'the only way' that patients have found 'to manage their deep anxieties and unresolved issues'. Accessing that 'depth' is framed as key to recovery, but this can only happen if the dysfunctional behaviours are reduced and 'crises' can emerge and can be talked about.

Finally, respecting nutritional rules is framed as a matter of responsibility towards other patients. A constant refrain from nutritionists to patients is that they should not be cutting pasta during meals because they risk 'contaminating' others who perhaps are doing their best to avoid the same behaviour, thus undermining their recovery. One might note here the dominance of corporeal medicine and of the language of infectious diseases seeping into other realms: behaviours are depicted like viruses, and the eating disorder is framed as not only 'affecting' but also 'infecting' patients' thoughts and behaviours. A sort of collective responsibility to heal seems to be present, perhaps not too different from the one most typically found in discourses about infectious diseases. With infectious diseases, the imposition of care – be it prophylaxis, isolation, treatment of the symptoms – is justified and legitimised by a 'disease' that threatens the social body, placing a collective responsibility on affected individuals. I would argue that patients in treatment for eating disorders are constructed as having a collective duty to heal, even if their conditions are not 'infectious' in the strict sense of the term. Professionals are always very explicit that 'you don't get an eating disorder like you would get a flu' when they reassure concerned parents that they do not have to worry about their daughters 'passing' the eating disorder on to their other children.[5] And yet the language that the professionals use is exactly the language of infectious diseases when it comes to patients 'contaminating one another with their dysfunctional thoughts and behaviours' (educator Flavia). The kind of collective responsibility cultivated in these patients, then, is not – as in the case of infectious diseases – directed so much towards 'healthy people', but towards fellow patients, those who are already ill. Patients are rendered responsible towards one another as if the struggle against the eating disorder were a collective struggle that required unity in the face of a common, external enemy which is now 'inside themselves'.

'Nutritional Rehabilitation': Turning Food into Medicine

Mealtimes become times of 'nutritional rehabilitation' here because, in the world of normality that the treatment team seeks to reassert, patients' pathological control over food needs to be 'deactivated'. Doctors and nutritionists constantly remind and reassure patients that 'the composition of meals' is balanced and proportionate to the needs of their 'severely compromised organism'. Here we see that food becomes scientised, as patients are given 'what is required for their body to function' (endocrinologist) – the 'nutrition' that one needs to stay alive. Underlying this notion is the idea that there is a correct amount of 'nutrients' needed by the human body to maintain health (Cuj, Grabinsky and Yates-Doerr 2021: 3). By framing food as 'nutrition', in a scientific discourse, professionals try to detach food from the (supposedly problematic) relationality in which it was enmeshed before admission: this detachment is a process of abstracting food from the social – a process that allows professional attention to physiology and turning persons into 'patients'.

At mealtimes, patients find on the table a sealed plastic package with their name, containing their specific portion of food prepared by an external supplier. Completing the meal means facing four of such packages one after the other: a first course mainly composed of 'carbohydrates' – pasta or rice; a second course composed of 'proteins' – meat, fish or legumes; a 'side' of vegetables coming with a slice of bread; and a portion of fruit. For a patient on a first day of admission this amount of food is usually unsurmountable, and professionals prove themselves flexible after a few attempts. Gradually, however, patients are pressured and expected to eat everything that is put in front of them.

In 'nutritional rehabilitation' the constant refrain is that 'food is medicine'. Eating food in sealed packages rather than having 'normal plates' – as patients say – contributes to the feeling of 'taking a medicine' rather than 'having lunch or dinner'. Since food is conceived as 'nutrition', as something that works as 'fuel' providing the 'building blocks' necessary for a depleted organism that would otherwise die, then food *is* medicine. In the same way in which paracetamol would be ingested to be able to think about things other than a headache, one has to eat food to act on the symptoms that are due to malnutrition, including the worsening of obsessive thoughts, which prevent one from thinking about anything else. The purpose of this framing, common in eating disorder treatment, is to strip away the 'pleasure' and 'enjoyment' connected to food and its associations with family commensality, and make it appear as if it were a drug to be taken because the doctor prescribed it. In this way, it is held, patients should ideally 'feel less guilty about indulging in eating', and 'less affected by negative emotions related to their family dynamics' (nutritionist Viola). This rationale was presented to me by all the professionals when I enquired about whether they did not find it problematic that most food given to patients tasted – everyone agreed – 'really bad'. I found it disconcerting that in a treatment centre where patients had to 'regain familiarity with food', food was evidently of poor quality and badly cooked. Instead – the professionals explained to me – patients either 'do not even notice' as a result of years of food restriction during which they had excluded most foods from their diet or, if they notice, they 'actually prefer it that way' as it feels more like 'a bitter medicine that they are forced to take' (nutritionist Viola). With time, however, and especially once they shift to day-service treatment, patients start complaining about the taste of the food they are given, which professionals take as a sign of 'progress'. Here we see how in 'normal bodies' there is a discrimination of taste: outside the facility, people have 'acquired' bodies in which they have learned to be affected by taste; they have acquired taste that would make that food awful (see McDonald 2014). Patients who end up in this treatment centre seem to have lost that. Their body-selves no longer make those discriminations in taste, and part of their recovery is about relearning to be affected by it (see Latour 2004). But in the immediate urgency of residential treatment, in which 'bodies are at risk' (endocrinologist), that is not seen as a priority.

What is seen as a priority, instead, is to work on making patients embrace 'nutrition science', but 'the healthy one' (nutritionist Irma). This 'healthy' nutrition science is used by nutritionists and dieticians to deconstruct the 'dysfunctional nutritional knowledge' focused on dieting and 'accelerating metabolism' that most patients are experts in when they reach admission. For example: since food, in the world of eating disorders, is categorised in the language of calories, in treatment the language of calories is forbidden, and food is categorised – and taught to be seen – in terms of 'first courses', 'second courses', 'sides' and 'fruit'. If a patient really wants to know 'how much' food she is given, quantity is expressed in 'grams', never in calories. 'Nutritional group sessions' with the aim of 'deconstructing the myth of the calorie' are regularly held by nutritionists, who teach patients that 'calories don't exist "out there" in food, but are a social convention that doesn't accurately represent what goes on when we eat' (nutritionist Irma). Instead, nutritionists present to patients a more complex picture of food in which different 'nutrients' (carbohydrates, proteins, fats) are all fundamental to health and interact with each other and with a person's specific situation and environment. In this framing, not only is the 'quality' of food as important as 'quantity', but complete control of the processes of balancing intake and output of energy is impossible to achieve (cf. Vogel 2018b: 394). The nutritionists seem to embrace postindustrial scientific understandings of food and bodies, which complicate industrial models of metabolism centred around the calorie and focus, instead, on 'feedback loops' between the body and the environment (Landecker 2011).[6] Nevertheless, industrial framings of food as 'building blocks' are also constant refrains in their work with patients, showing how biomedicine is not a monolithic set of practices and discourses.

In her account of treatment for obesity in the Netherlands, Vogel (2018b: 397–98) has highlighted how, in the language of calories, bodies are portrayed as machines storing or using energy, and metabolism is black-boxed as the mechanism through which energy is processed and neutralised. Movement is framed as what allows this process, and therefore as the key to reduce one's 'weight'. In this framework, movement and food need to be carefully calculated to know what one is allowed to eat, or whether one undid the 'damage' caused by eating. Both food and movement are to be counted: what matters is the ability to stay in control (ibid.). This kind of reasoning, which patients with eating disorders are seen to have embraced 'at its extremes', is the object of constant 'deconstruction' at Il Giardino. The alternative model proposed by nutritionists, endocrinologists and dieticians, very much as in Vogel's account, is a notion of metabolism as a process that ensures the release of energy in the body, as a fire that can intensify or diminish. In this framing, food is not only described as 'building blocks', but also as fuel that can feed the 'fire of metabolism': to make one's metabolism 'work better' and 'accelerate' – something that most patients are deeply concerned about – patients are taught that they should eat *more*, not less. Food, in this logic, is potentially a facilitator and activator of metabolism, and therefore of the possibility to eat more without 'storing fat'. This is because – patients are told – 'the body is smart and interprets food scarcity as famine', going into 'energy-saving mode' by slowing down its metabolism 'to protect itself' (endocrinologist).

The patients' eating practices before admission, then, seen through this 'healthy nutrition science', emerge as harmful 'excesses of will' that fail to adequately respond to their bodies' needs. Whereas counting 'input and output' is completely in the hands of the person, relating to bodies as complex systems implies having to be responsive to and trusting something other than oneself. This is considered key in the path towards recovery, as we will see below.

Food, in this treatment centre, is thus 'tinkered with' (Mol, Moser and Pols 2010) not only in the sense that it is scientised and abstracted from the messiness of family commensality, but also in the sense that it is framed in a specific way – supported by a specific form of nutrition science – to achieve what for the professionals is a desirable end: to make patients eat. Patients are also taught that, although they have 'damaged' their metabolism through months or years of disordered eating, they can still 'tinker with' their metabolism by 'eating properly' and regularly, and by making sure that 'all the necessary building blocks' are there. Patients here do not simply have to learn how to make better decisions for their bodies, but also 'how to be, and act as, a different eating body altogether' (Vogel 2018a: 517).

Patients are weighed every week on the same day. Nutritionists then make adjustments to their patients' meal plan depending on whether the weekly 'weight gain' is considered enough or not. They refer to these changes as 'a battle to be fought slowly, by tiny victories' (nutritionist Viola), as they are the object of long negotiations with the patient during individual sessions. These sessions are also the moment when the two parties have to agree on the weekly permits to 'experiment with food' outside the facility. There is a gradual progression of such 'experiments'. Patients typically start by having the afternoon snack outside, and if these first experiments 'go well' – i.e., if patients eat everything and do not have any 'crisis' – further and more complex experiments await them: 'free breakfasts', 'packed lunches', and 'free meals' at home or at a restaurant with relatives or friends during weekends. These experiments are meant to test patients' readiness to be discharged and move to the day-service facility, where there will be less external control regarding food. In the day-service facility, in fact, patients are asked and expected to 'put more effort' towards their recovery and to gradually shift from 'mechanical eating' – i.e., 'eating because someone forces you to' – to 'true motivation in eating' (nutritionist Irma).

However, recovering bodies do not automatically turn into recovering minds. After some weeks of treatment, patients often report feeling 'as if the body keeps going on the treatment path on its own, and the mind is left behind' – i.e., 'not accepting the weight gain' and 'stuck with obsessive thoughts' (Elena, eighteen). The underlying notion here is that the body and the mind can proceed at different rhythms in the path towards recovery, but that this 'split' feels alienating, revealing an assumption of a coherent and aligned body–mind axis in a situation of health.

Numbers to Trust: Scientific Knowledge as a Tool of Treatment

One way in which the treatment team tries to make 'the mind keep up with the body' in the process of patients' self-transformation is to use 'scientific evidence' as 'a tool to bring patients back to the level of reality' (endocrinologist). Scientific facts are conceived by the professional specialists as a powerful instrument that can be employed 'to debunk the dysfunctional obsessive thoughts of the eating disorder' (ibid.) and trusted as reliable reference points to orientate oneself when feeling anxious. The science historian Theodore Porter (1995) has traced how decisions based on 'impersonal numbers' came to occupy a prominent place in democratic societies as people sought numbers to guarantee 'objectivity'. Porter describes quantification, and the trust in what are seen as objective numbers, as a 'social technology of distance' (ibid.: ix, 49) which is also a sign of weakness of the community of practice that promotes it. Weak groups, he argues, turn to quantitative methods to gain strength, because to succeed in standardising methods, measurements and calculations is to succeed in stabilising a community of practitioners within which it is then possible to exercise judgement (ibid.). In a slightly different sense, professionals in the treatment centre gain strength over the strength of the eating disorder to the degree that they are able to establish their numbers.

Findings of scientific articles reporting the details of how 'the risk of death for underweight people is comparable to that for overweight people' are routinely discussed with patients during nutritional group sessions. If patients appear 'distant' – as if those statistics did not apply to them – nutritionists quickly remind them that they do not perceive that risk because the eating disorder is 'affecting' and 'infecting' their mind:

> I know that you think this can't happen to you, that you feel invincible. But it's the eating disorder that makes you feel invincible. Malnutrition affects your cognition, and it makes you unable to recognise this and take the necessary course of action, because your mental space is completely taken over by the thoughts about what to

> eat, how to eat, how to burn it after you eat ... But with your BMIs, *you are* at risk – you *can see* the data here. (nutritionist Isabella, my emphasis)

Clinical tests are another powerful tool used by the nutritionists to offer patients a 'reality check'. The BIA – Bioelectrical Impedance Analysis – is an inexpensive method for measuring 'body composition'. The instrument, the nutritionist Viola explained, uses electrodes to send an imperceptible and harmless level of electric current through patients' bodies, which is conducted differently by 'fatty tissue' (low in water) and lean 'muscle tissue' (more than 70% water). The BIA thereby 'measures' the proportion of 'body fat' versus that of 'lean body mass'. Patients undergo this test at the time of admission and then regularly every two months to monitor changes in their body composition in relation to parameters that define thresholds of 'health' versus 'malnutrition'. As the professionals explain to the patients while showing them the results of the test, in situations of semi-starvation underweight bodies are actually 'left with body fat' (since muscle mass is the first type of mass to be consumed). When patients start regaining weight during treatment, the test thus shows them that they are primarily regaining muscle mass, which tends to reassure and motivate them to continue treatment. Similarly, the Bone Mineral Density test 'measures', immediately after admission and then once or twice before discharge, the amount of calcium and minerals present in the patients' bones, 'showing' patients how dysfunctional eating behaviours lead to osteoporosis, with potential irreversible damage which may compromise the ability to do physical exercise in the future. Nutritionists agree that the main role of all these tests, beyond the actual monitoring of the patients' physical condition, lies in their 'awareness potential': in their capacity to 'scare patients by *revealing* and *making them see* the damage that their disordered behaviours are causing to their bodies', even 'internally', beyond the extreme thinness that they may desire and yet not see when they look at themselves in the mirror (nutritionist Viola, my emphasis).

Learning to See One's Body

This matter of the illness preventing one from 'seeing how one really is' is perhaps the most widespread and popular 'belief' about eating disorders, typified by images and videos featuring skinny girls, but lately also boys, looking at themselves in a mirror and seeing their bodies as fat. In professional terms, this effect is called 'body image distortion' or 'body image disturbance'.[7] It refers to the supposed mechanism whereby people with eating disorders, when looking at themselves in a mirror, would not see their bodies 'as they really are', but much larger and fatter – especially in the abdomen, buttocks and thighs, deemed to be 'phobic parts'. This 'disturbance', the scientific literature reports, causes significant distress, often persists after otherwise successful treatment and is a reliable predictor of relapse (Button 1986; Glashouwer et al. 2019; Keel et al. 2005). The dance-movement therapist Serena explained to me at length how one's body image is affected 'by cognitive, social and emotional aspects, with different parts of the body potentially being affected differently'. She continued that if someone tends to be very rigid in their thinking, has a particularly low self-esteem, and is therefore especially vulnerable to the social pressure that praises thin and perfect-looking bodies – which is deemed to be the case with most patients diagnosed with eating disorders – then their body image will reflect all those elements and result in a 'distorted image'. The 'dysfunctional behaviours' of eating disorders are therefore also understood as 'coping mechanisms' that patients employ to 'correct the presumed defects they see in their body' (dance-movement therapist Serena).

Starting from the 1960s and 1970s, extensive research[8] has been produced on the 'body image' of patients diagnosed with eating disorders, especially anorexia nervosa. A range of tests have been subsequently developed in the field of psychology to 'measure' the extent of patients' body image distortion – which is 'how much' the way they see their bodies differs from 'reality'.[9] These works all assume a 'real body' that can be the object of a more or less correct sensory perception, potentially influenced and distorted by what are seen as cognitive, social and emotional factors, but measurable and quantifiable by science, whose numbers are always to be trusted.

A more recent and increasingly expanding field of research, highly praised by the endocrinologist working at Il Giardino, is that of neuropsychology, which 'looks at what happens to the patients' nervous system' through Magnetic Resonance Imaging (MRI) studies. One of these studies (Sachdev et al. 2008) is the object of regular group discussions with patients. During group sessions, the endocrinologist explains to patients that in the brain of 'healthy individuals' several regions appear 'activated' when they are exposed to images of themselves and others – with images of themselves causing a greater activation of a region in the brain called 'insula'. Patients appear to process images of others in the same way that healthy people do, suggesting that there is no fundamental disturbance in their so-called 'functional architecture of body image processing' (ibid.: 2167). However, when exposed to images of themselves, patients' brains do not appear to activate the insula, which is thought to suppress the emotional and perceptual processing of the information. This inactivity is supposed to be at the basis of the failure 'to correct their self-image disturbance' and is believed to explain why patients have a 'distorted view' of their bodies (ibid.). The article is regularly presented to patients coupled with an illustration of the MRI scans described in the study (see Figure 3.1), which – the endocrinologist points out – 'really show what goes on in patients' brains'. Patients are told that the disturbance is reversible with weight gain and treatment, as it is more likely to be a consequence, rather than a cause, of the eating disorder (ibid.).

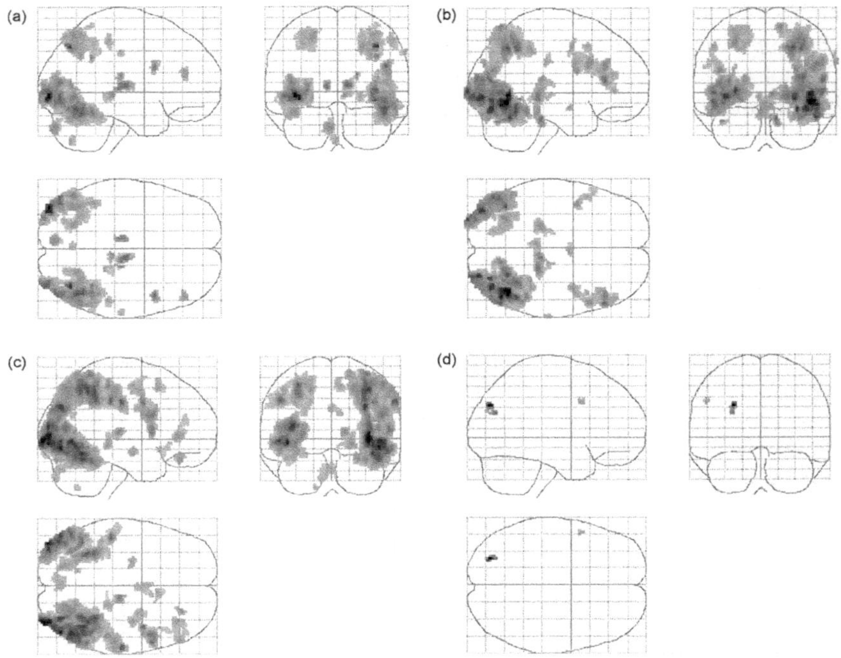

Figure 3.1. 'What goes on in patients' brains.' Image reprinted from Sachdev et al. (2008), showing that similar activation patterns were observed for control subjects (a) and anorexia nervosa patients (b) viewing non-self-images, but that very different patterns were observed for control subjects (c) and patients (d) when viewing self-images. © Elsevier, used with permission.

Specific therapies aimed at treating this 'symptom' of eating disorders have been developed since the end of the 1980s under the name of 'body-oriented therapies' (Vandereycken, Depreitere and Probst 1987), which include 'systematic mirror exposure'.[10] 'Mirror exposure therapy' is one of the specific techniques employed at Il Giardino. It is based on seven weekly one-to-one sessions with a therapist, who guides the patient through a gradual 'exposure of the body' – fully clothed in the first two sessions, then gradually exposing arms and legs by wearing sleeveless shirts and form-fitting trousers, and eventually wearing only underwear in the last two sessions. Before starting the sessions, the patient is given two tests to fill in: the Body Shape Questionnaire (see Cooper et al. 1986) – which measures the intensity and frequency of 'feelings of fatness' – and the Body Uneasiness Test (see Cuzzolaro et al. 2000), which evaluates 'the discomfort with one's own body image' (clinical director). These same tests are administered to the patient again in the final phase of treatment, to evaluate and quantify the change 'obtained' through the therapeutic technique.

The sessions, patients are told, are designed to help them shift from 'a dysfunctional mindset' that focuses on self-criticism to a 'more holistic perspective of their unique body' (dance-movement therapist Serena). It is interesting that this is supposed to happen not only through 'systematic and protected exposure' guided by the therapist, but also through 'a change in the language' that patients use to describe their bodies – 'from negative, subjective terminology, to nonjudgemental, fact-based terminology' (ibid.). Learning to describe objectively here implies learning to *see* themselves in a different way. During each session, the patient is placed in front of an otherwise locked, full-length, tri-fold mirror in the room dedicated to 'body activities'. She is asked to look in the mirror and assign a level of anxiety from 0 to 10 to every part of her body – from head to feet – while the therapist writes the answers in the first column of a table that has a box for each of those parts (see Figure 3.2). The patient is then asked to describe 'the functions' of each of those body parts, again from head to feet. These functions are sometimes discussed with the therapist, who sits out of view. During the sessions, the patient's body is thus visually 'dissected', in a way, 'as if the patient was describing it to someone coming from another planet who had never seen a human body' (psychotherapist Sara). The patient is asked to refrain from using critical or

Mirror exposure	Anxiety level – before	Anxiety level – after	Comments
Head			
Forehead			
Face			
Neck			
Arms			
Torso			
Abdomen			
Hips			
Buttocks			
Thighs			
Legs			
Feet			

Figure 3.2. Mirror exposure therapy template used by therapists. Sketch by the author, 2019. © Giulia Sciolli.

unkind language and any positive or negative judgement, and is encouraged instead to use terms related to colour, texture, shape and, most importantly, 'function'. At the end of each session, the patient is asked again about the level of anxiety she feels for each body part, with the therapist writing it down in the second column of the form. She is then asked to draw her body on a piece of paper, 'as she sees and feels it'. This has the aim of tracing the 'cognitive-emotional change' in the way she perceives her body through the sessions (psychotherapist Sara).

Mirror exposure therapy is illustrative of how patients are taught that they 'cannot trust their mind' nor 'the signals sent to them by their bodies' (psychotherapist Sara), and of how treatment attempts to literally change the way patients see their bodies. Patients are taught that the way in which they see and experience their bodies is a consequence of a disorder that makes their brains function differently, but that this 'distorted view' can be treated and 'removed' by both renourishing their bodies and retraining their minds. The testimony of 24-year-old Gloria about her experience with mirror exposure therapy is telling of this change:

> I experienced [mirror exposure therapy] as a path towards the discovery of my *objective* body image, of my body image *cleaned* from all the *misperceptions* caused by the illness. I was really scared ... and instead I eventually *discovered* my body as the external part of myself that allows me to relate to the world. A body composed of many parts – each of them with a specific function, *which is there even without my critical judgement on it.* It was an important step towards learning how to love my body and how to take care of it; towards accepting it as it is and committing to keeping it healthy, so that it can perform all its functions. (my emphasis)

The Day-Service Facility: A Step towards Autonomy

> *We all work with the aim of becoming superfluous, of eventually meeting patients outside as strangers. When I meet an ex-patient, I never say 'hi' nor wave at her unless she does it first. Because patients have the right not to recognise me, because they don't need me anymore.*
>
> —Philosophical counsellor Carola, interview, June 2019

One Saturday in September 2018, during a weekly support meeting for parents, Lisa's mother was complaining about the absence of 'family counsellors' in the day-service facility. The family counsellor, as we will see in the next chapter, works in residential treatment as the main channel of communication between the treatment team and the patient's family. Lisa's mother could not understand why this figure was absent in day-service treatment, considering that patients were 'left much more on their own' there, with 'more risks to worry about'. The counsellor replied that the two facilities intentionally offer different modalities of care, and that in day-service treatment parents 'have to bear the space of autonomy' that their daughters are slowly reacquiring: 'In the same way that you taught them how to walk, you have to stand the fear that they might fall'.

Day-service treatment is still an intensive stage of care: patients are required to arrive by 9.30 am, after having had breakfast at home, and spend the whole day in the facility. Days consist of four group activities separated by the mid-morning snack, lunch, afternoon snack and dinner. Right after dinner, patients are free to leave and go home. The facility is open from Monday morning to Saturday after lunch, which means that patients spend half of their weekends 'on their own', having to 'manage free time' and their meals for one day and a half. The last group therapy session each Saturday – 'the check group' – and the first one each Monday morning – 'the welcoming group' – are meant for patients to reflect on how they 'experience and manage these spaces of autonomy', which are supposed to gradually prepare them for 'life outside' once they will be discharged and continue with outpatient treatment.

The 'autonomy' sought in treatment is therefore of two kinds: first, it amounts to an ever increasing freedom from the disorder, conceived like an external intruder that has invaded the patient; second, it amounts to an ever increasing independence from carers – both from the professionals and, as we will see in Chapters 4 and 5, from family carers. Nevertheless, as those chapters will make clear, there is not a search for 'absolute independence' from other human beings. Dependence and independence are fuzzy concepts. Just as one can be 'in a relationship' with someone or something in many different ways (Piasere 1998: 155), so too can one be dependent on someone or something in many different ways. Dependence can be physical, economic, emotional. It can be reciprocal, asymmetric, temporary, reversible, occasional, alternating. It can concern a one-to-one, one-to-many, or many-to-many relationship. And it can be considered on a scale of values: from the most negative end, seen as a situation incompatible with the ideal of the free, adult and whole person; to the most positive end, seen as intrinsic to the realisation of the individual and the achievement of their freedom (Vatta 2012: 93–94). Patients in semi-residential treatment are recommended not to spend weekends completely alone, but to seek the support of their family members, friends or even fellow patients. This highlights how day-service treatment gradually shifts the responsibility to follow the professionals' directions onto patients themselves, but not on them as beings that are completely independent from others. By spending part of their free time with other patients – and particularly by spending meals together, sometimes even buying the groceries and cooking together – patients create a network that functions at the same time as 'emotional support' and 'mutual control' (psychotherapist Mauro). As we have seen in the opening of the chapter, meals also work differently in day-service treatment. Patients can choose what to eat from two options for every course of the meal, and serve themselves by using 'the volume' of common kitchen utensils to know 'how much food they need to take', rather than having food already weighed and individually packaged. Patients eat all together at the same large table, and two staff members only supervise the portioning phase of the meal, with one nutritionist then eating with patients while sitting at the centre of the table. This is supposed to recreate a more 'normal' and 'family-like' meal, while still allowing support and a less evident 'control' on the part of the nutritionist.

The didactic aspect in the day-service facility is similarly more dispersed, as if patients indeed start, as the psychotherapist Mauro put it, to '*responsabilizzarsi a vicenda*' ('make themselves responsible for one another'). This is evident during meals, in patients' mutual support during weekends and in the dynamics of group activities. In residential treatment, communication during group activities tends to be dyadic: from professional to patients and back. Here, instead, dyadic communication is often paralleled or even substituted by a more circular communication: patients mostly interact among themselves, with the therapist receding into the background and only intervening if necessary. During one group session on a Wednesday afternoon at the end of April 2019, for instance, 29-year-old Alessandra reported that she was upset because her request to travel home for a long weekend had been denied. She had been losing weight to the point that the treatment team were considering moving her to hospital, which made a long trip by bus on her own out of the question. Alessandra said she expected other patients to sympathise with her, and to cast her therapists' refusal as an unjust 'lack of trust'. Instead, several patients told her that although it was understandable that she felt angry and did not feel in danger, she had to trust the treatment team, because it was 'scientifically proven' that 'the illness prevents one from seeing how one really is'. Professionals had a more 'complete' and 'objective' view of the situation, another patient told her. Most patients seemed to be accepting, at this point, that they were 'wrong' when they first resisted treatment, and to be gradually embracing the view of the treatment team.

Conclusion

When patients are admitted to residential treatment, the way they see their bodies and experience their condition is in stark opposition to the way professionals see them. In this chapter, we have seen that treatment works by gradually substituting patients' self-care projects with a definition of health that is jointly constituted by the treatment team, partly through the use of numbers offered by the natural sciences. In the progress from residential to day-service and then outpatient treatment, patients are thus required to gradually assume responsibility for a kind of well-being that is determined elsewhere than in their self. For this to happen, a 'collaborative mode of ethics' (Davis 2012: 14) allows someone other than the patient to function as a temporary 'prosthetic will' at the beginning, supplying the responsibility that patients are deemed to lack during the first phase of treatment. Some coercion is thus considered necessary to first deconstruct patients' 'pathological' self-control. A specific ordering of time and space, psychotropic medications, strict rules and supervised 'nutritional therapy' are framed as allowing patients to reach a point in treatment when their partly renourished 'bodies' will allow their 'minds' to be open to listening to the professionals. Only then can the patients acquire the tools for a self-transformation that will enhance their health. This happens by exposing patients – through one-to-one and group therapeutic activities – to information and experiences that teach them to see their bodies and condition in the way professionals see them, and therefore to reach a point when they themselves want to 'abandon the eating disorder'. Once patients are deemed capable of 'seeing how things really are' and of choosing to get better, they are given more and more responsibility to do that, while the coercive role of the treatment team proportionally decreases, shifting into guidance. Patients are thus seen to become capable of healthy self-care only after a long and difficult work through which their minds and bodies are transformed.

Notes

1. Outpatient treatment consists of only coming to the facility for weekly individual sessions with one's assigned therapists – one week with the nutritionist, then one with the psychotherapist. If everything goes well, after about six months therapists and patient agree to meet less frequently for 'check-ups', until, if the patient consistently does well for a year or so, she is discharged from outpatient treatment too.
2. Therapeutic contracts have been used to define therapeutic relationships in many psychiatric settings since the deinstitutionalisation movement that took place in Europe and North America in the 1970s (Davis 2012: 217; see also Castel 1981).
3. See Milano and Capasso 2019; Preston, O'Neal and Talaga 2013.
4. More on this in Chapter 4.
5. When patients' siblings are also diagnosed with an eating disorder, the 'cause' is never ascribed to the already ill sibling, but to the fact that 'there is something wrong in the family system'. More on this in Chapter 4.
6. The notion of dietary management and of food as 'nutrition' emerged out of nineteenth-century concerns in Europe with productivity and labour: for governments and employers, the measurement of the calorie presented scientific 'standards of living' that contained wage levels while maintaining a productive workforce (Cullather 2007). Science historian Hannah Landecker (2013) has pointed out how the industrial metabolism of nineteenth-century biology, concerned with labour efficiency, modelled the body after the factory (see also Rabinbach 1992), in which raw materials are converted into manufactured goods and pathology is framed as disruption due to broken parts in the machinery. Postindustrial nutrition science, instead, has focused on 'feedback loops' between the body and the environment: pathological states are seen as 'regulatory crises' of a complex system, whereby the 'inside' and the 'outside' are deeply intertwined, suggesting that 'people eat foods, not nutrients', and that they do so in relational contexts (Cuj, Grabinksy

and Yates-Doerr 2021: 14). This brief and simplified history highlights how, through the development of nutrition science, food has become and keeps becoming a different object ontologically. The science of 'nutrition' is influenced by historically and culturally specific aspects that give coherence to its practices. For more on the history of 'metabolism', see Landecker 2017.

7. The Austrian psychiatrist and psychoanalyst Paul Schilder (1935) is considered the father of theories of 'body image development', thanks to his work *The Image and Appearance of the Human Body.*
8. E.g., Bruch 1962; Garfinkel and Garner 1984.
9. See Harari et al. 2001; Probst et al. 1995, 1998; Slade and Russel 1973.
10. See Delinsky and Wilson 2005; Key et al. 2002; Wilson 1999.

Chapter 4

'We Are a Relational Laboratory'

Kinship as a Therapeutic Tool

The family is completely shaken by the eating disorder, as if at sea, at the mercy of ten-meter-high waves, and we are trying to bring ourselves to safety.

—Paola, a patient's mother, interview, November 2022

It is a Saturday morning in early September 2018. I am sitting on one of the thirty green plastic chairs at the back of the large meeting room in the residential facility of Il Giardino. Every Saturday morning, this room is reserved for the weekly support meeting for families, open not only to the relatives of patients who are currently in residential treatment, but also of those in day-service and outpatient treatment, and to the relatives of prospective and discharged patients. Although the meeting is open to 'any relative who is more or less involved in the care of the patient', the room is mostly filled with parents, which is why the professionals refer to these meetings as '*le riunioni dei genitori*' ('the parents' meetings'). Partners, spouses, sisters and brothers, daughters and sons,[1] grandparents, aunts and uncles also attend, albeit in small numbers. Parents are in fact the main family carers in most cases, including for patients who are already in their thirties. This is due both to the specificity of the Italian context – with its renowned long-term cohabitation in the parental house and economic dependence on parents (Ghezzi 2012; Rusconi 2004; Saraceno 2004, 2015) – and to patients' social life having shrunk after years of suffering from a condition that substantially limits social interactions, let alone intimate relationships.

Today, the meeting is run by the psychotherapist Carlotta and by the nutritionist Viola. They open the conversation by explaining how the meetings work: this is 'a collective space', and 'personal questions' regarding specific family situations should therefore be directed, instead, to the assigned family counsellor during individual meetings. Any other question or comment regarding the disorder, the treatment path and daily difficulties is welcome. This introduction opens the way for a wave of questions on 'how to deal with meals' at home. Most parents depict mealtimes as the most feared times of the day – characterised by continuous arguments and 'battles on every little thing': a teaspoon of oil, a slice of bread, a spoon of grated cheese. The parents of a prospective patient report that they cannot wait for the moment their daughter will finally be admitted to residential treatment, and for 'the magic of Il Giardino' to reduce their daughter's resistance to eating. This prompts the psychotherapist Carlotta to clarify what she sees as a problematic misunderstanding on the part of the parents:

> It's not the 'magic' of Il Giardino that can change the negotiations about food between you and your daughters, in the same way that it's not the 'magic' of any pill that your daughters might be given. What is key is the introduction, within a dual relationship, of a third element – of something *like* Il Giardino. Who has the possibility of really opening a dialogue between you and your daughters in the fight about meals? It's the famous meal plan, which contains the so-called 'right amount of calories' for your daughters' daily needs. This, at the nutritional level. But at the relational level the meal plan is a deal – it's something that opens up a space for dialogue within the arm-wrestling between you and your daughters. This third relational element here, with the nutritionist and the psychologist who stand behind the meal plan, helps to prevent the negotiation from becoming a battle about demonstrating something to one another. (original emphasis)

The treatment team – embodied by 'the nutritionist and the psychologist' mentioned by Carlotta – is here depicted as a third, neutral element that needs to be added to an already existing (and supposedly fraught) patient–parents relationship. In the previous chapters I started setting the stage for an understanding of treatment by introducing the two key parties involved – patients and professionals – and their opposing stances. But the interaction between patients and professionals emerges here as inserting itself into a previously existing relationship of family care. Professional carers are brought in when family carers realise that their care 'doesn't work'. This chapter therefore introduces the patient's family as another key actor in the network of treatment – one whose care precedes that of the professionals but that, we shall see, is temporarily 'put to one side' by professional care, as the latter reframes and reshapes the parent–offspring relationship within this residential context.

Carlotta's words seem to carry an assumption about the need for neutrality in medicine, and about the negative consequences that the absence of such neutrality could cause for treatment. If professional care at Il Giardino is defined as 'magic' by parents, that 'magic' is framed by Carlotta as the opposite of the nefarious power struggle that she associates with the family. In an interesting parallel, in his account of witchcraft as 'the dark side of kinship', anthropologist Peter Geschiere (2003: 46) suggests that for his interlocutors in Southeast Cameroon the most dangerous witchcraft attacks are framed as coming 'from inside the house', because witches are supposed to have 'a special hold' over their relatives. Geschiere argues that, although kinship is seen as the basis of trust and solidarity, the way people talk about and act on witchcraft highlights that 'this very intimacy is at the same time a deadly danger' (ibid.). For this reason, the healers who can save people subject to witchcraft cannot be from within the family. Importantly for the argument of this chapter, healers are thought to be able to heal only because they are involved with witchcraft themselves: they are described as 'super-witches' who have been *trained* to 'use their powers only to heal and never to kill' (ibid.). Healers are thus considered able to channel what is seen as the dangerous side of kinship and use it instead 'in a constructive way' (ibid.). In this chapter we will see that something similar happens at Il Giardino, as the professionals are trained to channel the dangerous aspects of kinship into supportive tools towards recovery. I will suggest that they do so by 'borrowing' from kinship care in their therapeutic work, whilst tinkering with its constitutive practices.

Since early clinical accounts of 'anorexia' in the late nineteenth century, family members have been described as 'the worst attendants' (Gull 1874: 26) – as having a 'particularly pernicious' influence on patients' treatment (Charcot 1889: 2010). Until the 1970s, the academic literature of the psy sciences framed the family not only as responsible for the development of the illness, but also as a 'toxic' element detrimental to recovery. Patients – the clinicians held – thus required a 'parentectomy', i.e., exclusion of the parents from the treatment plan and work with therapists to 'extricate' themselves from their families (Murray and Anderson 2015: 279).[2] As mentioned in the Introduction, starting from the 1970s, however, what were subsequently considered 'family therapists' challenged this idea: since anorexia seemed to develop within families characterised by 'dysfunctions' such as 'rigidity', 'enmeshment'[3] and 'conflict avoidance', rather than separating the child from their parents, these therapists held, treatment should be directed *at* the family to address those aspects (see Minuchin, Rosman and Baker 1978). In Italy, Mara Selvini Palazzoli (1978) launched what came to be known as 'the Milan approach', which called for focusing on 'family therapy'. These theories laid the foundation of 'family-based treatment' for eating disorders, which is now the international gold standard for treating young patients. Families then shifted from being viewed simply as the main responsible agents for the development and maintenance of the illness to being seen as the main 'resource' to be marshalled for a successful recovery (Russell et al. 1987). As a result, although the specific configuration of family therapies varies across and within countries, most treatment approaches today 'work with the family'.

In her ethnography of a hospital-based inpatient programme in the United States, Gremillion (2003) notes how the gendered power dynamics within the treatment team mirror those of the typical 'American family', reproducing its hierarchies and dysfunctions with negative consequences for the patients. Here, however, I will not be focusing on the gendered dynamics of treatment and on what is characteristically Italian about the gendered kinship care at Il Giardino. If I had to focus on that, I could highlight that the treatment team is mostly composed of women; that the clinical director has, as many members of the treatment team often repeat, 'a male, paternal role in the treatment centre' (with this, meaning that she is the one with authority, power and 'harsher' manners); and I could certainly say that the gender dynamics occurring in treatment, which do partly mirror those of the typical 'Italian family',[4] are instead seen by the professionals as mostly *conducive* to recovery. But here I do not focus on these aspects, not only because they have already been generally addressed in the literature, but especially because they did not emerge as central to the questions I was asking.[5] My interlocutors seemed to deal with the nexus of kinship and food much more. This is why here I want to focus on how care practices at Il Giardino suggest something that is relevant to the anthropology of kinship and of medicine more generally – namely that kinship relations are seen to need remodelling in order to transform patients' eating behaviours, and, through those behaviours, their bodies. This chapter therefore differs from existing anthropological accounts of eating disorders in that it examines a situation that places aspects of kinship care at the core of treatment. By looking at what happens when families manage to bring their daughters to Il Giardino, and at the extent and ways in which family care is incorporated into treatment, I examine care at the intersection of professional and family care practices, and how these shape one another for the sake of what the treatment team calls 'therapeutic efficacy'.

The chapter draws on and goes beyond anthropological literature that, by looking at kinship in practice, has usefully highlighted the potentially harmful side of kinship (e.g., Carsten 2019a; Das 1995; Pinto 2014) – including those works that have explored how kinship can be framed as a source of mental distress and at the same time as a source of remedy (e.g., Buchbinder 2015; Chua 2011). In addition to all of these aspects, kinship here becomes a therapeutic tool – albeit a difficult one to use – in the sense that professionals employ kinship care in their own reparenting work with patients, by borrowing from family care practices but cleaning them of the 'dysfunctionality' that is seen to characterise patients' families.

After seeing in Chapter 3 the already enormous difficulty of using food as a therapeutic tool, this chapter will highlight the even greater difficulty of using family as a therapeutic tool. In their work with the family, professionals need a different kind of language from the one they use when they work with food. The complication here is that what we might call 'the science of kinship relations' is not readily available with a language that clearly guides professionals as is the case with nutrition, 'the science of food'. Work with the family is thus even more about tinkering and experimenting. Professionals do not have an objective model of kinship to follow in the same way that they have an objective model of food. We will see how, through the more difficult language of family, they 'do' (Mol 2002) a particular kind of family: family as a therapeutic tool, which is 'caring' because it is intended to make up for what patients 'lacked' in their own families.

Returning for a moment to Carlotta's words, we might note the distinction she draws between what she calls the 'nutritional level' and the 'relational level' that the meal plan and the feeding process that follows seem to encapsulate. 'Nutrition' here separates food from 'relations' (or nurturance). Whereas in many anthropological accounts food acts as 'a substance of relatedness' that creates kinship through care as nurturance (e.g., Carsten 1995), we have seen in the previous chapter how in the world of this treatment facility, due to the urgency of patients' malnourished bodies, nutritionists scientise food by turning it into 'nutrition' (cf. Cuj et al. 2021) – that is, food detached from kinship-making commensality. Since it is problems in 'nurturance' through relations that are seen to be impeding 'nutrition', the pairing nutrition–nurturance is temporarily broken in this facility: nourishing (to feed) is food necessarily detached from nurturing (to care for).

By framing food as 'nutrition', these professionals try to detach food from the problematic relationality in which it is enmeshed: this detachment is a process of temporarily 'eradicating the social' (McDonald 2015: 35). But since, as we have seen in Chapter 2, the development of an eating disorder is understood to have something to do with things gone awry in family relations, professionals also need to *rely* on the social: they need to reintroduce it but as part of treatment, as a reshaped family turned into a therapeutic tool. Professionals are indeed adamant that the separation between food from its relationality – which takes shape in the anonymised, packaged meals provided to patients in the residential facility – is only necessary in the acute phase of treatment. As the nutritionist Viola put it, the long-term aim for day-service and outpatient treatment is to 'put the social back on the plate' (*'rimettere il sociale nel piatto'*). This chapter therefore focuses on 'nurturance', on what Carlotta called 'the relational level' of treatment, to show how the sociality of patients' bodies is as important here as their physiology, and how the treatment team deems the work of transforming the patient possible only if the patient's family is transformed too.

In the same way that professionals need to abstract food from the social and make it 'nutrition', they need to abstract kinship and remodel it. Kinship needs to become a scientific matter too – the social needs to be wrung out and remodelled. We will see that the aim is to end up with a co-substantiality of food and family that are then resocialised together, in a 'simultaneity' (see Ardener 1989). This is important since simply 'giving food' to patients without addressing family issues is seen as risky, especially upon discharge from the facility.

The objects that the therapists are dealing with – food and kinship – need to be momentarily 'detached' from their previous social context, in the sense just outlined. This is the first kind of detachment that we will observe here. The second kind of detachment is that of the therapists themselves: they need to be 'detached' too. Professionals know that family care is a risky therapeutic tool, because the family is, in a way, the opposite of clinical detachment. They have to transform it into something that is therapeutic, but to do this they need to be able to 'stand back' – 'distancing themselves as part of their technology' (McDonald 2015: 45). Scientising the family is much more difficult because family *is* attachment – it is hard to 'stand back'. The therapists only manage to do it if they are constantly on their guard, because they are aware that they are 'professionals'. This clinical detachment, like the one achieved by surgeons, for example, is therefore a peculiarly difficult 'social accomplishment' (ibid.: 50), one whereby professionals are ideally able to talk about patients as 'cases' and to construct case histories that are not just personal narratives. There is also, therefore, a certain scientisation of the person that has already turned persons into patients – a first step seen as necessary to help them.

The rest of the chapter first situates what happens in the residential facility through a description of the specific form of kinship care that can be found in the families of those diagnosed with an eating disorder, as a result of the lack of care on the part of the Italian State. Against this background, I then zoom in on the cases of two patients whose families did manage to get their daughters admitted to Il Giardino, to shed light on the kind of 'family work' that treatment for these conditions is seen to require. We will see how, in this facility, kinship is framed as a source of harm as well as of good, as it can do both 'too little' and 'too much'. In the final part of the chapter I show how the professionals then tinker with family care in response to those 'excesses' of kinship – i.e., as a remedy for the harm that both 'too much' and 'too little' family care generate in patients.

When the State Does Not Care: Delegating Responsibility to Families

We have seen in Chapter 1 that lack of specialised facilities for eating disorders causes long waiting lists and continuous migration between regions towards the few facilities available. Parents are often forced to care for their daughters at home for months while waiting for admission, and may then need to travel for hours and spend considerable time and money to make sure that their daughters receive adequate treatment. As already mentioned, the Italian region where I conducted fieldwork is one of the very few that have all the four levels of treatment recommended by national and international guidelines, making Il Giardino one of the key destinations for these 'therapeutic migrations'. Descriptions of such migrations were a common refrain during fieldwork. Patients' parents call them 'trips of hope'. Their stories, however, also tended to mention a further complication. Parents do not 'simply' have to travel miles to obtain treatment for their daughters. First, they have to obtain an '*autorizzazione*' ('authorisation') from their local health authority, which has to pay for the extra-regional treatment. This is because in the Italian national health service each region manages its own regional health service. Some local health authorities grant these authorisations more easily and for longer periods of time, but others do not – especially those in regions where 'on paper' all the levels of treatment are present. However, most of the time such facilities do not actually provide the services that they claim to provide, and the professionals who work there are often not specialised in eating disorders. Lack of specialised training is deemed to be another consequence of the general lack of attention given to eating disorders: not only do many psychiatrists, psychotherapists and nutritionists not receive adequate training on eating disorders in their standard university path, but nor do medical doctors. The latter include those who work in emergency departments, general practitioners and paediatricians, who are precisely the ones who could spot the problem early and then refer patients to specialised professionals.

The context of a shrinking Italian welfare state, increasingly characterised by cuts to public funding and healthcare expenditures, places the burden of care entirely on the family (Minelli and Redini 2015; Saraceno 2011). These cuts only worsen the already difficult conditions in which families find themselves as part of a Mediterranean welfare state model. This is characterised by social spending being largely directed towards the older generations (the only universalistic transfers being old-age pensions and healthcare) and by very limited services for families with children and the elderly (Vatta 2012: 74–75). As a result, families themselves often act as a social safety net for their more vulnerable family members, importantly shaping the kind of family care that professionals 'see arriving' with patients on admission. In this scant clinical and social landscape, before admission to a facility there is already substantial family labour put into treatment, a labour that families need to do because the State does not. In what follows I show how, after admission to Il Giardino, much of this family work must (ideally) be suspended, if only temporarily. Families that have done so much work are asked to back down and change their care.

Katia: When Kin Care 'Too Much'

Katia was a nineteen-year-old girl from a large city in central Italy, who had been diagnosed with anorexia nervosa when she was thirteen. She was admitted to Il Giardino at the end of January. The clinical director had presented her case at the weekly staff meeting, defining her as 'a very difficult patient' who would have to be constantly monitored because of her 'extremely severe condition'. 'Severity' was defined in terms of her BMI, which on admission was 13 – a number that placed her in the category of 'severely underweight'. Katia was emaciated, with only a little dyed-blonde hair left. On admission, it was evident that she did not want to stay. She was brought to the residential facility by her mother, a woman in her fifties whose face carried the signs of years of difficult care work and – professionals suspected – of either self-harming behaviours or scratching from Katia, in the form of uncountable little scars. Katia was seen to behave 'abusively' and at the same time 'very dependently' towards her mother. She would be alternately screaming and crying – shifting from heavily attacking her mother for 'being mean' and 'betraying' her, to acting as a child desperate for affection. Katia's mother was visibly distressed, and appeared relieved when the professionals on shift asked her to leave Katia and go home, reassuring Katia that she would see her mother soon.

The following Tuesday, during the weekly staff meeting, the clinical director explained that Katia had been referred by a psychiatrist in Katia's city, who had been in charge of her outpatient treatment for a long time. He had informed the director that Katia was an extremely difficult case, whom nobody else had 'managed to treat': after several failed attempts with outpatient treatment, countless hospital admissions and three inpatient treatments in other parts of Italy, Katia's main problem was located by the professionals in a 'highly symbiotic relationship with her mother'. This 'unhealthy relationship' was reported to have developed during years of illness and was traced back to her 'disastrous family history': Katia and her twin sister had lost their father due to sudden death when they were nine years old, and the children had since then been raised by their single mother and maternal grandmother. This had generated, in the view of professionals, 'pathologically dependent relationships' among them.

Two days after admission, Katia had a big crisis and tried to escape, a clear sign to the clinical director that she could not stay without her mother. The clinical director agreed to the mother renting a flat close to Il Giardino and visiting Katia every day. Katia was therefore reserved special treatment, with the possibility of spending time with her mother. Other patients took little time to notice this, and soon started complaining that it was not fair. Most professionals agreed that this arrangement was not sustainable, and quite pointless: Katia's constant contact with her mother – they kept saying – did not help and made treatment 'more difficult'. Meals were characterised as 'a lost battle', and Katia's sessions with the psychologist and the nutritionist became 'disarming' because she was 'exclusively and unrealistically focused on not wanting to gain weight but wanting to be discharged' (nutritionist Irma). At some point, Katia became so resistant to treatment that the only way the clinical director could convince her to continue was to allow her to stay in the residential facility from 11 am to 3 pm only, when she would go home with her mother. At 4 pm, an intern or a volunteer from the treatment centre would go to her house and stay with her until 9 pm, making sure that she ate her afternoon snack and dinner, and that she did not spend time walking around.

I was among the 'volunteers' recruited. Katia's mother had been advised to leave the house while volunteers were there for the assisted meals, but she almost never did because Katia would start crying. When my turn came, with difficulty I managed to send the mother away for a walk at the time of the afternoon snack. I was sitting and chatting with Katia after she had finally finished her snack, when her mobile phone rang. It was her mother telling her that she was in the square two minutes away from the house. Predictably, Katia wanted to join her mother and there was no way of keeping her at home. I could only follow Katia, and we ended up with her mother in a small grocery shop. Katia bought her usual 'zero-fat' foods, which she was not supposed to buy because she should have eaten the meals sent by the residential facility. She was not even supposed to enter grocery stores in the first place. That evening for dinner – which started one hour later than planned because Katia refused to eat earlier – Katia only ate the salad sent by the facility, substituting the first course with some chickpeas and the second course with a few slices of turkey breast. The mother ended up eating the meal sent by the treatment centre, and I could only make sure that Katia ate at least all the things she had chosen.

Eventually, what was characterised as the 'counterproductive' behaviour of Katia's mother, plus the difficulty for insufficiently trained volunteers to assist with meals in her house, led the clinical director to decide that Katia should be left at home with her mother every day from 5 pm, after eating the afternoon snack in the facility. The professionals told me that this whole arrangement was unprecedented, and beyond all the rules: 'It runs against the very principle of making parents delegate their feeding role to us. It's clear that the mother can't do it anymore, that the two together don't work'. The reasons for things 'not working' was ascribed to the fact that Katia's mother let her do whatever she wanted: 'she has a neurotic interlock with Katia: she is completely dedicated to her ill daughter. Once Katia recovers, she will lose her aim in life'. The implication here was that this was the reason why – 'unconsciously' – the mother was counteracting treatment with her presence. There was a professional awareness here that bending the rules of treatment in this new arrangement prevented the separation between food as 'nutrition' and food as 'nurturance', seen as necessary for patients treated in the facility: the mother's nurturance, characterised as 'excessive', prevented Katia's nutrition. Professionals used the psychological term '*invischiamento*' ('enmeshment') to denote Katia's and her mother's 'unhealthy' interdependency, suggesting that it is possible to 'care too much'. However, equally frequent are cases in which the main obstacle to recovery is traced back to an opposite situation. I now turn to one of such cases, where parents are deemed 'too absent'.

Maia: When Kin Care 'Too Little'

Maia was a 33-year-old patient from a small town not far away from Il Giardino, in the same region. She had been diagnosed with anorexia nervosa when she was fifteen, and had been in and out of the residential facility (the time 'out' spent mostly in hospital wards and other residential facilities across the country) for the last ten years. During fieldwork, Maia's parents never attended the support meetings for families and I managed to see them only a couple of times, in situations of emergency. There were of course important differences from Katia's case: Katia was still considered a 'kid', whereas Maia was classified as a full 'adult'; Katia's mother was in her fifties, whereas Maia's parents were in their seventies; Katia had been ill for a long time already – for six years – but Maia had been ill for more than half of her lifetime, reaching eighteen years of illness. These aspects made professionals somehow 'make sense' of Maia's parents' absence: they were 'understandably exhausted' after eighteen years of their daughter's illness, and their old age now meant they did not have 'the energy' to be much involved in treatment anymore. Still, most professionals depicted Maia's parents' behaviour as unacceptable: they were not only completely absent in her care, but did not even follow the professionals' recommendations when these required a little effort on their part. When Maia's conditions worsened to the point that the treatment team decided to admit her to hospital, for instance, they strongly advised Maia's parents to hire a professional that could have the role of 'meal controller', because hospital staff are not trained nor paid to monitor patients' meals. But because that would have been at the family's own expense, Maia's parents refused to hire someone, although Maia had proposed to use money from her own disability pension – which had been virtually untouched until then given that she had been living in the residential facility for most of the last four years. Maia's mother eventually took the role of 'meal controller' for the two weeks of hospital stay, with professionals claiming that they were sure Maia would be able to deceive her. The problem came up again when, upon discharge from the hospital, Maia's parents were told that she would have to stay at home for a while before being readmitted to residential treatment: her condition was still precarious enough to require the intravenous feeding that she had been receiving in the hospital on top of regular meals, and that was not possible in the residential facility – so the treatment team had arranged for a nurse (to be paid by Maia's parents) to be present at home for her. The coordinator of Il Giardino was the one who called Maia's parents to inform them of this decision. She reported to the rest of the team that the parents had reluctantly said: 'We will see what we can do. Then, it will be what the Lord wants'. She said she had felt she 'wanted to get hands on them' when she heard them say that. She continued: 'But *we* can't abandon her. We have to keep trying to help her' (original emphasis). Professionals were very critical of the 'delegation of parenthood' that Maia's family was gradually pushing for, but it seemed that they themselves had already 'internalised' it in a way. Some proposed that when the moment of discharge from Il Giardino eventually came, it might be better for Maia to live in a group home such as those for people suffering from addictions, rather than returning to live with parents with whom she did not 'share anything anymore'.

It is worth noticing that, in both Katia's and Maia's stories, the attempt to involve parents in treatment ended up suggesting that the only way for these patients to get better was to remove their parents' care (excessive or insufficient) from the picture – as if the move away from 'parentectomy' towards treating parents as a 'resource' in treatment hardly works for some cases. Nevertheless, it seems that there is something about kinship care that cannot be taken away: Maia's exclusion from family care resulted in the treatment team stepping in and taking that role. What happens when shifts like this occur? We will see in Chapter 6 how these shifts can have deleterious consequences for treatment. For now, let us turn to how the professionals work to tinker with kinship practices to preserve, if in some modified form, what they see as fundamental in kinship care. We will see that kinship relationships are here the object and simultaneously the tool of the transformation that should ideally occur in treatment. But how does this transformation happen? In the two final sections that follow I provide a few examples of how the treatment team reshapes kinship care, first, by teaching parents how to be 'good parents' to their children, and, second, by themselves enacting appropriate kin-like relations with patients.

Reshaping Kinship Care

> *The parents of children who suffer from an eating disorder find themselves in the uncommon situation whereby their daughter is at the same time a victim to be protected from a threat and the very agent of that threat. This situation generates confusion in the otherwise natural behaviour of parents, which would make them protect their children by attacking the external threat. This confusion leads parents to oscillate between protecting and attacking, and this cannot but generate fear, anger, guilt and shame.*
>
> —Clinical director, interview, May 2019

This quotation from the clinical director suggests some of the reasons why parents might often respond to their daughters' needs in ways that the treatment team might see as unhelpful, as in the two cases just discussed. The eating disorder is seen as putting into question the 'natural' care response of parents towards their child, 'as if she were suddenly split in two – victim and perpetrator' (clinical director). During a meeting for patients' parents, the counsellor moderating the meeting intervened by saying that, for that reason, the only way for parents to protect their children was to 'put some distance' between themselves and their daughters, and 'temporarily delegate' parts of their role as parents to the treatment team. The counsellor was here pointing to the limits of parental care: treating the eating disorder was something that 'parental love' could not do. This brings us back to the professional view of the eating disorder as an agent that 'takes over' the self of the patient, and that needs to be seen as the target of the coercive measures that treatment might require.[6] The idea is that it is very difficult for parents to understand this – hence their difficulty in managing their daughters' conditions at home, and the need to bring them to a facility where they can temporarily delegate their care to someone else.

Observing what happens on admission to Il Giardino, at first sight it might indeed seem that parents' responsibility for care completely shifts in the hands of the professionals. Parents are asked to 'delegate completely' their responsibility for feeding their daughters to the treatment team, which should act as 'a more skilled second family'. The team is supposed to stop patients' 'dysfunctional behaviours' by forcing them to eat 'normal meals' and by preventing them from purging and 'over-exercising', while working to understand 'the reason why they developed an eating disorder' in the first place. Parents are told that they are incapable of doing this because they are 'too emotionally involved'. On the contrary, professionals are supposed to be able to 'stay detached' from the personal dynamics underlying 'dysfunctional behaviours' (counsellor Carola).

A very specific form of parenthood is therefore desired from parents at Il Giardino: being able to entrust professionals with the 'immediate care' of their daughters – i.e., feeding them, monitoring their weight and health, being there in moments of crisis – here becomes a fundamental part of being 'a good parent' and 'a good carer'. Notwithstanding the relief that this in part brings to parents, entrusting strangers – 'professionals, but still strangers' – with the care of their daughters is not something that parents do easily. A designated 'family counsellor' has the role of updating parents and is ready to answer their questions and worries, but parents are not told all the details of what happens in treatment – what their daughters will be fed, or how much weight they gradually gain. Parents who do not 'trust' the treatment team are characterised by the latter as 'very demanding' and 'polemical', and are seen as 'inadequate' and 'counterproductive'.

In her ethnography of an eating disorder inpatient unit in the United States, Gremillion (2003: 101) describes how parents are excluded from participation in patients' treatment and are not given advice about how to help their daughters at home, on the assumption that 'a natural maternal feeling will perform invisible healing work' (ibid.: 110). At Il Giardino, instead, parents are very much involved in treatment, so that they can gather all the 'tools' (*'strumenti'*) necessary for when patients will return home. Moreover, there is no assumption of, let alone confidence in, any kind of 'natural' parental healing. Here 'proper' healing work is the result of effort and training by professionals. At Il Giardino, therefore, the delegation of immediate care comes with the expectation of other forms of care. Spotting the problem and bringing one's daughter to treatment is only the beginning of parents' responsibilities, as the family counsellor often pointed out during support meetings for families:

> We can substitute your feeding role, but there are no substitutes for parents. You entrust us with their care, but there is no way of delegating your being their parents. Your parenting role should be made even more explicit while your daughters are here. It's just a different way of parenting from the one you are used to.

After admission, parents are in fact expected to make patients feel that 'they are present' by visiting as much as possible, by 'working on their ways of parenting' and by finding 'alternative ways of doing things'. This includes different ways of managing arguments with their daughters, and – a key point – learning how to manage food-related issues at home differently, 'in a way that can be supportive'. Parents are required and expected to have a very specific behaviour during mealtimes when patients are at home for weekends: the golden rule is that they should never make any kind of comment on what and how patients eat – nutrition is not their responsibility. Especially at the beginning, parents are told to cook specifically measured meals without letting patients do it. On top of this, it is preferable that during the meal other members of the family eat more or less the same things – and, in any case, never less than the patients, to avoid making patients feel even worse. When parents behave differently, they become the object of complaints on the part of patients and professionals alike, and are seen to be showing either that 'they haven't understood anything' or, worse, that 'they don't care'. When reporting on their 'weekend experiments' at home, patients are adamant that it is very difficult to 'stick to the rules' if their family members ignore professional advice – as they reportedly often do – and start commenting on what their daughters eat, eat 'light' foods in front of them and go to the gym or running for hours. These are all behaviours that patients are 'struggling to battle against' and that family members should therefore avoid. Parents are supposed to learn 'how to behave' in these situations by coming to the weekly support meetings for parents and to the appointments with the assigned family counsellor. They are also expected to 'work on themselves', preferably by starting their own psychotherapy. Many parents are reluctant to do this, for lack of time, money, or – in the words of the psychotherapist Michele – 'because starting to question oneself and one's family dynamics is scary'.

Meetings for parents therefore have a strong didactive function. The counsellor Carola often depicted treatment as a parallel path in which daughters and parents gradually learn to 'manage emotions'. 'Mismanaged emotions', as we have seen in Chapter 2, are here conceptualised as key to the 'psychopathology' of eating disorders, and to the 'dysfunctional family dynamics' that can perpetuate it:

> To be a parent means to protect your daughters, in this case from your unelaborated emotions. The eating disorder works as a modulator of emotions. This means that when you ask your daughters to recover, you are asking them to learn to stay in their emotions and manage them without the disorder. Therefore, you must be the first ones to do it.

The counsellor is here asking patients' parents to do what sociologist Arlie Hochschild (2003) calls 'emotion work' by 'surface acting' – i.e., the adjustment of one's outward countenance to induce a desirable state in the other. However, this can only be successful if parents also engage in psychotherapeutic work, what Hochschild would call 'deep acting' – i.e., the effort one makes to change one's overall 'emotional experience' by drawing from one's prior experiences. When emotion work as a kind of 'care work' is absent, professionals often attribute the lack of progress in a patient's treatment to the lack of involvement from the family, as in Maia's case. This is one of the greatest causes of frustration for professionals, who often joke about the idea of setting up 'a parallel residential facility for the parents'. 'Emotion work' here becomes part and parcel of kinship care and care for illness, as therapy for the patient extends to therapy for the whole 'dysfunctional' family unit.

Unlike in other clinical contexts in which anthropologists have looked at the role of family carers (e.g., Clemente 2015; Mattingly 2010, 2014a), here recovery is seen as inherently possible. This aspect sets up the possibility of blame: if treatment seems to be failing, it is 'people' that are to blame, not 'biology' or 'the disease'. This means that the stakes in the relations of care are even higher, as parents are placed in the position of being at the same time 'targets of intervention' and 'therapeutic agents' (Buchbinder 2015: 139). As we have seen in the cases of both Katia and Maia, one further complication is that this care work is supposed to last for years. For those who are lucky, two to five years are considered necessary for 'complete recovery' from an eating disorder; but for many others relapses are common, and a considerable number of people end up living with the condition through the rest of their lives.

For now, we have seen how at Il Giardino kinship care practices are turned into an object of treatment, so that the family can be turned into a resource that helps patients' recovery. Similar dynamics have been noted by Mara Buchbinder (2015) in her account of the work with the family in a pain clinic for children in the United States; and by Jocelyn Chua (2011) in her analysis of how parenting practices in South India – especially in relation to how parents (fail to) teach children to 'wait' – are framed by state psychiatric institutions as responsible for and simultaneously as the vehicle of 'therapy' for a 'suicide epidemic' in children. In the next and final section of the chapter, I will suggest that something more is going on at Il Giardino, as kinship care is not only a 'tool' in the sense that patients' families are turned into resources for recovery; here, professionals also employ kinship care as a tool in their *own* work with patients, borrowing from kinship care practices but cleaning them of the dysfunctionality that is seen to characterise patients' families.

Turning Kinship into a Therapeutic Tool

> *Our job* consists of *becoming emotionally involved. You establish some rules of course, a distance. This distance doesn't mean separation, or being far away, but*

is the space within which the therapeutic relationship can develop. I wouldn't give patients my address, I wouldn't tell them what I do at home. There are some areas in which they must not enter, and one needs to keep them very clear. In other areas, they can enter, and those are the areas that have to do with the therapeutic relationship. One needs to know that they are not friends, nor daughters: they are guests, patients of this treatment centre, and it's this distance that allows us both to speak to one another.

—Psychotherapist Mauro (original emphasis), interview, June 2019

In her ethnography of hospital care for children with incurable conditions in the United States, Cheryl Mattingly (2010: 12) shows how 'border encounters' between families and clinicians can lead to 'imaginative borrowing, syncretic inventiveness, the creation of common ground'. At Il Giardino, not only 'imaginative borrowing', but also a kind of 'practical borrowing' occurs, as the treatment team borrows attitudes and practices seen to pertain to the realm of the family and employs them in the therapeutic work with patients. I have often heard professionals, patients and parents alike say that Il Giardino '*sembra una casa e sa di casa*' ('looks like and tastes like a house'). In this 'house' a lot of effort is put by the whole treatment team – mostly composed of women, including the clinical director – into recreating '*un ambiente materno e familiare*' ('a maternal and family-like environment') in a setting that is purposefully rendered as similar to a 'home' as possible: professionals wear casual clothes and have a dedicated bedroom for the nightshift; after dinner, they spend time in the living room chatting, doing puzzles, watching movies or playing board games with the patients. The psychotherapist Carlotta explained that the treatment centre has 'a family-like functioning': 'After all, we are a group of adults who, like parents, organise the times and the rules of this shared life; and a group of patients who, like children, find themselves in the position of being looked after, no matter how old they are'.

Carlotta's explanation raises an interesting point on what is often called, in sociological studies of medicine, 'infantilisation' (for example, Marson and Powell 2014) – a 'behavioural pattern' in which a person of authority treats a grown-up person in a child-like manner. It would be easy to see 'infantilisation' here as a symptom of Goffmanian (1961) and Foucauldian (1991 [1975]) 'total institutions' and paternalistic care, but I want to take seriously the way professionals frame it: as a 'needed step' in the most severe phase of the illness, not only because of 'the extreme physical and psychological vulnerability' of patients at this stage, but also as part of a 'reparenting process' that is deemed fundamental to treatment. Most patients are deemed to have developed an eating disorder partly because, as the psychologist Flavia explained, 'they did not get to be children when they were children, and had to take adult responsibilities too soon':[7]

> They really need what they don't get from their parents, they look for parental figures. That is why the key to treatment, besides the work with food, is this *maternage* that we do with patients, the emotions it generates. The relatedness itself is good.

> The fact that they can experiment with healthy relationships. The fact that someone dedicates to them time without judging them or attacking them, but showing them affection.

The treatment team often used the French term '*maternage*' ('mothering') instead of the Italian term '*accudimento*' to refer to the attitude of maternal affection that they purposefully enact with patients. This was because the French term is the one commonly used in the language of psychotherapy to refer to therapeutic relationships that aim to tackle problems and traumas located in lack of parental care during infancy. And although the professionals connect the word to the fact that the treatment team is mostly composed of women, male professionals are equally and explicitly included in the *maternage* enterprise. The psychotherapist Mauro, for instance, is often referred to by colleagues as someone who is 'adopted as a parent' by the patients. We are seeing here how clinical detachment at Il Giardino is self-restrained but not unemotional in the way surgical practice would be, for example, in the operating room (cf. McDonald 2015: 51). The detachment that these professionals need and 'acquire' (ibid.: 52) is not the same lack of emotional display, but more a neutral stance in the perceived 'fight' between patients and their family carers, which keeps demanding affectionate engagement of a particular kind, as the psychotherapist Carlotta explains:

> It's a bit as if, during a football match, a player threw the ball to me – and I am the referee – asking me to start playing for his team. It's quite possible that I feel more sympathy for this player or for his team and its cause, because I am still a human being. But I know that, in my role, I can't. There is obviously the possibility that at this point the player will get nervous and angry ... and this happens here. But knowing that I have this role and that I cannot take the side of one person – be it the patient or a parent – allows me to bear that person's anger and the other negative emotions that might follow my refusal, much more than I could do in a personal situation. And this holds for virtually everything here, including the assistance with meals when a patient might ask you to let her leave the table without having finished the food on her plate. It's like telling her: 'Look, if it were for me, Carlotta, I could maybe agree with you, but as a professional I can't.

But staying 'neutral' or 'detached' is not an easy or 'natural' task for the professionals, especially because the very structure of treatment asks for parent-like practices. As Marta, an educator, explains:

> It's difficult. You see us as professionals, but we get attached too. When we do the night shift, for example, we see patients sleeping in their beds, brushing their teeth, straightening their hair ... it's an intimate thing. Il Giardino is a family for us too. But we must remain distant. As professionals, we have the duty to do it.

These invocations of clinical detachment are constant refrains. When it comes to work with the family, professionals have learnt to be affected in the way their profession demands, a way that they know will work for treatment. They know what a 'healthy attachment' is and they are supposed to be able to use that. Professionals strive to be caring in a way that mimics the family, but they are aware that they should not become 'too emotionally involved'. As Marta's words suggest, however, this is the ideal – what the treatment team strives for – not necessarily what always happens in practice, especially because of the residential structure of treatment, with its long shifts and prolonged contact with patients. Here, therefore, detachment is an aspiration (Anderson 2001), an uneasy and never complete ethical disposition that requires careful cultivation through practice and training (see McDonald 2015).

When we were discussing these matters, the psychotherapist Carlotta concluded that the treatment facility works as 'a relational laboratory' (*un laboratorio relazionale*), in which patients are given the opportunity to 'experiment with new ways of relating that can organise their subsequent experiences in a more functional way' compared to the 'relational styles' that they supposedly constructed with their own relatives while growing up:

> Sometimes there are relational styles that work in a maladaptive way – those who constantly avoid conflict for example. And we often see that both patients and their families deal with conflictual situations with us in the same way they deal with conflicts within their family. We are not interested in the result of the conflict per se, in who is right, who is guilty and the like – we are not policemen – but in how the conflict and the communication is managed, or mismanaged.

This is not the same kind of 'relational labor' that volunteers refer to in Andrea Muehlebach's (2011: 65) study of voluntarism in Italy, although most members of the treatment team, be it interns, volunteers, or professionals whose salaries barely reach 1,000 euros per month, also frame their work in similar terms. Nor is it exactly like the concept of 'moral laboratories' that Mattingly (2014a) uses to describe the experimental nature of people's struggle for a good life amidst deadly diagnoses for their children, although Carlotta's words also refer to the facility as a space that generates experiences of how life might be lived differently. Rather, this is closer to what Sarah Pinto (2011: 384) describes in her ethnography of psychiatric treatment in North India: in this treatment centre, relations are 'means, not just objects, of understanding', and – this is where the specificity of what goes on in Il Giardino lies – means of treatment too.

Among the most telling instances of how the treatment team works as a 'relational laboratory' by enacting what the professionals see as appropriate kinship care is the way they deal with patients' 'crises' during meals. I offer an example below.

Giada, a sixteen-year-old patient diagnosed with anorexia nervosa, is sitting at the table during 'nutritional therapy'. She has just finished her portion of plain rice and is waiting for the volunteer on shift to give her the 'second course'. When that is placed in front of her, her eyes widen in what seems to be panic. She starts shaking her head and frantically moving her right leg. The nutritionist Irma, who is monitoring the meal while standing next to me, notices Giada's reaction, and whispers to me that today the second course is canned tuna fish: 'It must be the oil', she says. She then walks to Giada, bends towards her while placing one arm on Giada's shoulder, and – still whispering – asks her what is happening. Giada, as Irma had imagined, says that she cannot eat the tuna as 'there is too much oil', and starts weeping silently. At this point, Irma asks Giada if she wants to exit the room with her for a moment, and Giada nods. They leave the dining room, while two other professionals walk around the other patients asking questions about their towns of origin and making jokes, in an effort, it seems, to draw their attention away from Giada's crisis. I can see that Irma is talking to Giada in the hall, trying to prevent her from shaking by keeping her own hands firmly but gently on Giada's shoulders, and looking straight into Giada's eyes. I cannot hear what she says, but she later tells me that she was telling Giada that most of the oil she saw was actually diluted in water, since that specific tuna has a very little amount of oil compared to what 'normal people eat'; that her body needed that little amount of oil to function, and that she had already eaten that kind of tuna may times, so she could do it – she just needed to breathe and eat it without thinking too much. After five minutes or so of conversation, Giada seems to calm down a bit. Irma smiles at Giada and gently strokes her arms while walking her back to her seat in the dining room. Giada sits down, looks at the tuna awaiting her, takes a deep breath and starts eating slowly. In the meantime, Irma keeps standing next to her, telling a story of something funny that has happened to her while coming to work that day and keeping one hand on Giada's shoulder while she eats. After ten minutes, Giada has finished the tuna.

This is one example of countless similar situations I witnessed, as crises like Giada's – some requiring much more work and time than this one – happened every day, at every meal. Although the kind and extent of these crises can vary widely, the ways in which professionals deal with them are always similar. When describing what they do, professionals say that they aim to be 'maternal and firm', but 'containing patients' irrational thoughts' and, most importantly, 'not taking their difficulties with food personally and overreacting, which is exactly what their parents tend to do'. When I asked about the frequent stroking, and in some cases hugging, that I observed both during mealtime crises and on other occasions in which patients were distressed, professionals explained that most patients 'need that physical affection' because most of them 'don't get it from their families'. They remarked that through this way of relating to patients, patients experiment with the fact that 'others can accept them even if they are angry, sad and needy'. This does not mean that professionals are never strict with patients. The key is seemingly to behave 'as one would behave with one's own kids: when they need scolding, scolding; when they need cuddles, cuddles' (nutritionist Irma). Here, kinship care is brought into the realm of the therapeutic and is understood to *become* therapeutic.

Even though treatment approaches in which the rehabilitation element leans on a family-like relational model are present in other community care settings, including for other psychiatric illnesses or addictions (see Myers 2015; Pinto 2011), the particularity of this case is that intervening in patients' kinship relationships, while at the same time 'reparenting' patients, is considered the only way to effectively act with lasting results on patients' eating-related behaviours, and, through that, to achieve a long lasting and 'healthy' transformation of their bodies. In Chapters 2 and 3 we have seen how the whole treatment path – from residential, to day-service, to outpatient treatment – ideally consists of a gradual shift from almost complete 'dependence' on the treatment team to more and more 'autonomy' through the different phases of treatment, and how professionals conceptualise their aim as that of 'becoming superfluous – so that patients will not need us anymore, eventually' (counsellor Carola). This path and aim are imagined as mimicking the steps that should emerge from a 'healthy parental relationship'. However, professionals are adamant that this can only happen if 'there has been healthy nurturing first' (ibid.).

Residential treatment is conceived to 'protect' patients from the triggers of the external world by keeping them in the facility in a phase in which they are deemed 'extremely vulnerable'. The idea is to gradually expose patients to the difficulties that they will encounter once discharged from treatment, teaching them how to cope with those difficulties and supporting them in the process – 'as any parent should do while their kids grow up' (counsellor Carola). We have seen in the previous chapter how this happens with food through the work with the nutritionists. But this also holds for matters of 'relatedness'. In their work with patients, psychotherapists, counsellors and educators dedicate a lot of time to discussing the difficulties of handling friendships, intimate relationships and relationships with family members. They encourage patients to 'experiment' with situations they find 'scary' and concretely support patients in matters such as finding hobbies they enjoy, finding a job that they like, obtaining a driving licence, learning to manage one's finances or moving out from one's family house.

This seems to suggest that, for the treatment team, 'health' and the 'autonomy' that should go with it do not equate to 'complete independence' from other human beings. The psychotherapist Mauro would often reiterate during group sessions that 'as humans, we are all born with a deficit and will always be deficient'. The paradox, he said, is that patients start restricting food because 'they want to be like God, completely self-sufficient'. And to pursue this, they end up in an illness that leads them 'to being completely dependent on others, which is the opposite of what they wanted' (ibid.). The treatment team, he insisted, tries to 'gradually bring them back to autonomy by being present, by nourishing them with familiar things. The aim is to make patients realise that, in order to be autonomous, one has to nourish oneself with healthy dependencies'. These, he explained, are those in which 'the human needs of warmth, of being listened to, of being seen, are met. In pathological dependence, instead, you can't live without that person or thing'. These statements suggest that 'autonomy' here derives not from complete independence, but from being 'attached well' (cf. Vogel 2018a: 520).

Conclusion

This chapter has traced how patients' parents shift from having to carry all the responsibility to make sure that their daughters survive – often beyond their capabilities and economic possibilities – to a situation in which they are suddenly asked and expected to 'step aside' and let professionals do what they had to do on their own until that moment: feeding their daughters, constantly monitoring their health and dealing with their crises. At the same time, parents 'have to be there' but 'in a different way': 'working on themselves' and learning how to deal with the needs of their daughters differently. We have seen that at Il Giardino kinship care is constructed as a substantial obstacle to treatment, but also as a potential solution to the problem if only it can be tinkered with and professionally channelled 'in the right way'. Kinship here has a toxic edge, since both 'too much' and 'too little' kinship care can get in the way of recovery.

The way the treatment team structures a specific form of detachment, by borrowing from kinship a kind of family care that is cleaned of its dysfunctionality, suggests how kinship care and its related 'emotions' can be turned into supportive tools towards recovery. This points to a form of detachment slightly different from that observed in other branches of medicine (cf. McDonald 2014, 2015). Professional detachment here is seen as what enables the affective *engagement* with patients that is seen as necessary for healing. Surgeons might cultivate detachment because the specific job that they need to do – opening up bodies – requires them to 'distance themselves' in the moment, to see those bodies as 'just bodies' and not as 'persons'. In that case, the process can be seen as one demanding an engagement that enables the cultivation of an attitude of 'detachment', which contains and holds at bay any emotional involvement or display (see McDonald 2015). In the world of Il Giardino, instead, what is framed as emotional involvement is needed as *part of* treatment, and it has to be both contained *and* displayed to patients. Detachment is again seen as a necessary precondition, 'within the self' of the professional, to enable involvement in practice. Detachment in this context has to be cultivated and maintained in a way that allows a 'healthy *maternage*' between professionals and patients – the contained affection and concern that patients seemingly need for recovery, because in their families they have experienced either complete enmeshment or complete abandonment. Detachment, in a way, is the background, the 'internal stance' that allows the reparenting process to occur without the risks that are seen to stem from relations between kin.

Finally, this chapter has suggested how medical practice engages in kin work not only by seeking to define the appropriate mechanics of kin care and by challenging the supposed boundaries between a 'domestic' or private sphere of kinship and a 'public' sphere of work (McKinnon and Cannell 2013; Yanagisako 2003), but also by making kinship one of its key therapeutic tools. We have seen how, in this residential facility, the 'domestic' of patients' family life is purposefully made public in the clinic, so that it can become an object of treatment and problems in kinship care can be addressed by professionals. At the same time, the clinic strives to construct a domestic space, 'but not too much': professionals borrow from kinship care in an effort to reparent patients, all the while making sure not to become 'too involved' in kinship care themselves. What goes on in Il Giardino is therefore a kind of relational healing: professionals frame patients as being constituted by and as constituting their family relationships. This suggests that acts of bodily transformation, in this 'Western' context too, are not confined to 'the biologically functional', but necessarily come with the reconfiguration of social relations. As Lambert and McDonald (2009: 5–10) put it, here 'bodies do not express, incorporate or embody the social ... Rather, bodies are social in their materiality'. What happens to patients' bodies is seen to be happening to the relations between patients and their kin – not only by analogy, but, as in the Melanesian context examined by Strathern (2009: 151–63), by the connections through which such relations are seen as constituting patients' bodies. Patients at Il Giardino are transformed through transforming the relations that constitute them.

Notes

1. In the relatively few cases in which patients are mothers, there are specific dynamics related to notions of responsibility for treatment and kinship care in addition to those I examine in this chapter. However, since those cases were a very small minority in the patient population that I encountered, I address them in a separate work.
2. For a history of 'parentectomy', which traces its origin to the treatment of children diagnosed with asthma in the United States, see Robinson 1972.
3. 'Enmeshment' is a concept from the psy sciences introduced by family therapist Salvador Minuchin to describe families where personal boundaries are not well-defined, and excessive concern for others leads to a loss of 'autonomous' development.
4. Although there were clear instances that pointed to expectations of 'traditional' family roles, in which mothers were seen as the main parents responsible for feeding, for example, fathers were equally problematised as 'absent' in the care of their children, especially 'emotionally', and as negatively impacting on their well-being.
5. The same holds for aspects of patients' sexuality or sexual identity, which, although surely important in some patients' experiences of their eating disorder and of treatment, did not emerge as central in my interlocutors' discussions, as they did not for Lester (2019: xxviii).

6. See Chapter 2.
7. The ways in which the professionals talk of treatment points to a world in which a distinct category of 'children' is important. International law, encoded in the United Nations Convention on the Rights of the Child, defines childhood as the period between the ages of 0 and 18, with childhood conceptualised as a separate space, protected from adulthood, in which children are entitled to special rights (Montgomery 2008). However, anthropologists, historians and social scientists have suggested that this notion of children as weak, dependent and vulnerable is both recent and culturally specific (e.g., Lancy 2014; Schwartzman 1978; Zelizer 1985). Most notably, the French historian Philippe Ariès claimed that our present-day ideas about the distinct nature of childhood have come to the scene relatively late in the history of Western Europe. He stated that, before the end of the fifteenth century, people had little conception of childhood as a phase in the life-course. In medieval society, for instance, the idea of childhood did not exist – not in the sense that people lacked affection for children, but in the sense that they lacked 'an awareness of the particular nature of childhood' (Ariès 1979 [1962]: 128). Ariès' thesis relied on analyses of medieval European art, in which, he claimed, children were depicted with the posture and muscles of adults but in smaller scale.

Chapter 5

Treating Patients 'Who Don't Speak'

The Challenge of Treating Children

These children are enigmatic. They have a mysterious world inside.

—Clinical director, weekly staff meeting, February 2019

'OK, I will be the housekeeper then'. The psychotherapist Michele nods from his crouching position on the floor of the group therapy room, seeming in this way to accept the role that he has just been assigned by Sofia. Sofia is eleven years old and has been living in the residential facility for the last five months. The other six patients present – all crouching in a disorderly circular shape together with Michele – giggle, apparently happy with this distribution of characters. They are all between ten and twelve years old, and have been admitted here in the past few months following a diagnosis of severe eating disorder. All of them exhibit what is deemed to be pathological behaviour towards food and a dangerously low weight for girls of their age. Sofia only eats first courses because she is convinced that second courses, sides and fruit make people fat.[1] Arianna barely eats solid food, and in extremely small quantities. Sara and Elena only eat food that is white. Susanna only eats food in liquid and semi-liquid form. Flavia and Alice refuse to eat anything but vegetables.

The other roles have been assigned: Sofia will be Arianna's mother, Susanna will be Arianna's father, and the others will be her paternal and maternal grandparents. Arianna will be Arianna, since the game is about her family. Next time, it will be about Sofia's family, and so on. The game works like this: after the chosen patient has drawn the scene of a 'family meal', patients and therapist have to enact it following the description of the patient, who works as a director and tells each character what they would do in that circumstance. This was the first group activity of this kind in the residential facility. 'I have never conducted a group session with preadolescents before', Michele had explained to me in a slightly nervous tone before the session started: 'You will see that, unlike in my group sessions with adolescents and adults, there will be no chairs in a circle. We will play on the floor'. The room had quickly filled with patients' voices and giggles after a few minutes of intimidated silence, during which Michele had explained the rules of the game: patients could do anything and say anything, as long as they did not hurt one another. During our discussion in the kitchen after the end of the session, Michele further explained to me what had just happened:

> As you saw, when you have patients so young – ten, eleven, twelve years old – you basically play with them. Because by choosing a specific game and specific ways to play that game, children tell stories about themselves, stories that you wouldn't get in a more direct conversation. Did you notice how Sofia, who never speaks to us, was actively participating and assigning roles?!

Michele continued that, although it looked like he was 'just playing' with the patients, in play 'there is a deeper level in which patients communicate their most intimate parts – their emotional experiences, and how they understand those'. This game, and the way Michele talked about it, is evocative of psychodrama. Initially developed in 1911 by the Romanian-American psychiatrist Jacob Levy Moreno through working with children at the *Stegreiftheater* (Theatre of Spontaneity) in Vienna, psychodrama involves group role play, theatrical representations and dramatic improvisations of a protagonist's experiences (Riva, Grassi and Belingheri 2020). The idea is that these practices work on the patient's 'internal experiences' through bodily action, allowing the 'truth of the soul' to be explored (von Ameln and Becker-Ebel 2020: 3). The use of 'surrogates' or 'agents' who 'represent' or 'embody' others' acts renders the game just described here a type of psychodrama. However, one can note that whereas the focus in psychodrama is on allowing the protagonists/patients to explore and understand their own 'internal experiences', the focus of this game is more on allowing *the therapist* to access the patient's internal world – otherwise perceived as inaccessible – by putting it on stage. Indeed, Michele pointed out that adolescents and especially adults are 'much more reflective and expressive of what goes on inside them', and that he had been trained and was used to dealing with *that* mode of communication. 'With preadolescents', he remarked, 'it is completely different, and therefore much more exhausting to get there'. Michele's words pointed to a model of the person in which patients are attributed internal worlds made of layers that the therapist needs to be able to traverse, with emotions ('there') appearing to be deep down, and harder to reach in children. This increased difficulty and the need to tackle it through play required Michele to 'participate more', hence his 'exhaustion'.

Michele was not the only one who had to learn new ways of dealing with patients during that time. Every professional, intern and volunteer had to, including the anthropologist. In fact, this was the first time in the history of Il Giardino that nearly half of the patients admitted (seven patients out of sixteen) were what professionals defined as '*preadolescenti*' ('preadolescents'), or more colloquially *'bambine'* ('children') – i.e., between ten and twelve years old. The clinical director would often point out that admitting such a high number of extremely young patients was unprecedented: 'We have had patients this young since we opened the centre in 2003, but we used to admit one once in a while, and it was always something exceptional; now we are admitting one every week! It is very disquieting'. This increase was a matter of concern not only because it found the treatment team unprepared, but also because it signalled a general trend whereby the average age of onset of eating disorders was seen to be becoming lower and lower. Professionals saw this as the effect of the damaging messages of mass media – to which children were increasingly exposed by having access to mobile phones, laptops and other internet devices at an 'inappropriately young age' – on an even more worrying 'deep distress and suffering'.

The whole treatment team agreed that the presence of so many children in the residential facility forced everyone to adapt to 'a very different kind of patient'. A second weekly planner of parallel daily activities – called *'Planner Piccole'* ('Little Ones Planner') – had to be put together by the coordinator. This was not an easy task, because it required one of the already few professionals on each shift to take time out of other pressing tasks to organise and lead the activities dedicated to children, with the complication that most professionals had rarely worked with children before. In the past, the one occasional patient who was considered too young to participate in some group activities would be entrusted to the care of a social worker and would play some board games during those hours. But with seven patients of the same age this was not manageable or acceptable, the clinical director insisted: if the treatment facility kept admitting children, it had to provide structured therapeutic activities that were tailored to their age. Interns and volunteers were all mobilised as precious resources to make this possible. As will become clear, however, this was far from being the greatest challenge that children posed to the treatment team.

We saw earlier how infantilisation techniques are deliberately used by professionals to impose treatment practices that patients would otherwise refuse, but also to give back to patients the 'proper childhood' they seemingly lacked when they were children (Chapters 2 and 4). Professionals argue that 'awareness' (*consapevolezza*), 'motivation' (*motivazione*) and 'autonomy' (*autonomia*) are supposed to gradually replace this period of infantilisation (Chapter 3). Against this conceptual background, we look here at what happens in treatment when patients *are* children (ten to twelve years old), and at how professionals find themselves having to adapt treatment practices to what are seen to be the specificities of preadolescent patients. I first situate how eating disorders in childhood are constructed by the clinical community as a worrying issue in treatment centres across Italy. I then zoom in on how those who work in the residential facility deal with this problem in practice. Focusing on the stories of two patients, I suggest that preadolescents with eating disorders are more difficult to treat than adolescents and adults because they fail to undergo the desired steps deemed essential for therapeutic transformation, putting into question the very paradigm of care of the treatment centre. In Chapter 4 I have shown how the family and family care are constructed by professionals as a potentially key resource in treatment; here I look at how the family is seen as the context and the very source of these children's conditions, while remaining the often-unchanged main network of relationships into which children will inevitably have to return after treatment discharge.

Eating Disorders in Children?

The child doesn't eat for herself, but for her mother: that the child eats is something that tests the caring abilities of the mother.

—Paediatrician, Annual National Conference on Eating Disorders, May 2019

Many cultural worlds have an intermediate state between what can be classified as 'childhood' and 'adulthood' – even if the ages of such stages can vary drastically – loosely demarcated by changes in responsibilities and by rites of passage that point to the potential dangerousness of such a liminal phase (Lancy 2014). However, a medicalised notion of 'adolescence' as a problematic life stage emerged as a peculiarly European and North American concept only in the twentieth century (e.g., Mead 1928) and subsequently became a 'worldwide phenomenon' through biomedical and broader 'globalisation' (Montgomery 2008: 15). Eating disorders have historically been mostly associated with adolescents and young adults – with what the psy disciplines in Italy call '*età dello sviluppo*' (literally 'age of development') and the profound changes and associated difficulties that this stage of life is seen to entail. Until a couple of decades ago, children or 'preadolescents' were not in the purview of professionals researching and treating eating disorders (Bryant-Waugh and Lask 1995). It was only in the 2000s that cases of patients as young as eight to twelve years old started being reported in Italy and elsewhere (Ammaniti et al. 2008; Rosen 2010). Still, until a few years ago, these cases were considered rare. In 2018–19, while I was conducting doctoral fieldwork, they were considered a hot topic for researchers and the clinical director was planning to publish a book about this 'emerging phenomenon'.

In May 2019 I flew to Sicily to attend the annual conference organised by a national scientific organisation that gathers researchers and clinicians who work on eating disorders from all over the country. The common framework of most presentations was the lack of resources invested by the Italian State to allow public facilities to treat eating disorders appropriately. One of the aspects felt to be particularly lacking was training for the appropriate treatment of 'eating disorders in childhood'. In fact, one afternoon was entirely dedicated to 'the increasing phenomenon of preadolescents diagnosed with anorexia nervosa', and to the specific difficulties they posed for treatment services. Specialists working in different treatment centres across the country reported an increasing number of patients under twelve years old in the last three years, and shared some key observations: i) that the 'psychological mechanisms' underlying eating disorders in preadolescents differ from those found in adolescents and adults; ii) that preadolescents – unlike older patients – have a 'physiological breakdown point' whereby from a state of malnutrition they can suddenly shift to an acute situation that requires emergency life-saving treatment; iii) that the most plausible cause of eating disorders in preadolescents is something gone awry in the process of 'building a healthy attachment' to the parents, especially the mother; iv) that, for this reason, 'specific mechanisms of transference and counter-transference' get activated between patients and professionals, which makes it more difficult to balance 'fully taking care' of the patient and the patient subsequently having to gradually 'detach' from the treatment milieu; and v) that notwithstanding these complications, if treated in a timely fashion the outcomes of treatment for the youngest patients are actually reassuring, indicating that patients can 'fully recover'. In the next section, we see how the professionals who work at Il Giardino deal with these aspects in practice, by tracing how these facts are 'done' (Mol 2002): we will see how working assumptions, reported as facts, effectively gain further factuality through their practice in the residential facility (cf. Latour 2005; Latour and Woolgar 1979).

The ways in which both the conference attendees and staff at Il Giardino talked of treatment for these younger patients point to a world in which a distinct category of 'children'[2] is important for clinicians: children are 'a different kind of patient' which requires 'specific training' and 'tailored therapeutic approaches'. The encounter between professionals and these younger patients also points to a series of interrelated assumptions about what characterises childhood and what a 'healthy childhood' should look like. In his work on the development of psychological techniques in Europe, Nikolas Rose (1990) also looks at how childhood became, starting in the 1950s, the most intensely governed of life periods. Rose claims that the introduction of children's rights was initiated both as a recognition of the child as a young citizen and as a means of making children an object of government through expertise. The site for this new government was primarily the family, within which the role of the mother was to make sure that the 'psychological well-being' of the child was achieved. This was seen to be possible by creating a fulfilling 'bonded relationship', along the lines espoused by the British paediatrician and psychoanalyst Donald Winnicott (1957, 1965) and the British psychologist and psychiatrist John Bowlby (1956, 1988). Rose argues that a link was thus established between the development of academic psychology and adult–child interactions in the home, with techniques of experts 'infiltrating' the domestic sphere: the family became both responsible and autonomous, and yet always open to state intervention if its 'products' were deviant. Rose's Foucauldian reading of this development will appear an obvious frame of reference for the material I present. However, I contend that a focus on governmentality and subjectification does not provide a full account of what is going on in this facility. Expanding on Rose's work, I will argue that, first, children (and their families, too) seem to be particularly impermeable to the experts' attempts at therapeutic 'infiltration'; and, second, that not only the techniques of experts infiltrate what seemingly belongs to the domestic sphere, but also the other way around, and with challenging consequences for the experts.

'How Do You Treat Patients Who Don't Speak?': Arianna and Sofia

Of the seven 'preadolescents' attending the group session in the opening of this chapter, Arianna had been the first one to be admitted to Il Giardino. On the day of her admission, she looked emaciated, and her gaze looked distant and scared. This was no wonder, professionals were quick to comment: she was hardly eating at the time and yet had kept going to school and doing things as usual until the week before, when she had been admitted to the children's ward of a nearby hospital because her weight had been declared dangerously low. Her BMI on admission was 11, a degree of 'underweight' that nutritionists reported as 'unclassifiable' on the growth curve that those working with children use as a reference point. The arrival of Arianna had therefore generated considerable anxiety in the treatment team, but also interest and affection towards what was perceived to be a particularly fragile and 'cute' patient.

Arianna's official diagnosis on admission was 'avoidant/restrictive food intake disorder' (ARFID),[3] but her nutritionist Monica reported 'smelling anorexic traits' from the beginning. It soon became clear that the treatment team would have a hard time working with Arianna. She was felt to take an 'excruciatingly long time' (nutritionist Monica) to finish the very little food she was given and often refused to finish it, with professionals having to make up for the 'lost calories'[4] by giving her nutritional supplements to drink. To complicate things, during both nutritional therapy and individual sessions with her nutritionist and her psychologist, Arianna barely spoke or answered questions – and, when she did, she used monosyllables or movement of her head to say 'yes' and 'no'.

For Fernanda, a young psychologist who had been working at Il Giardino for only one year, this was the first time she was assigned a patient this young. She would often report her worries about the fact that Arianna would not talk to her, wondering whether her inexperience was the issue. She wished she had received specific training to work with children, because she felt that it was 'totally different'. What Fernanda found most frustrating and difficult was Arianna's lack of '*introspezione*' ('introspection'): 'There is no awareness of what happens inside her ... so I struggle a lot. I have to come up with alternative ways. If I ask an adolescent to tell me how the past week went, she brings to me many things that we can discuss. If I ask the same to a ten-year-old, she answers: "I don't know." So what?' Fernanda eventually started reading stories, painting and drawing 'as a way to access Arianna's world': 'Now we are reading a book about emotions, with drawings that you can complete by using different colours, depending on what emotion you feel in that moment. Red for angry, purple for scared, yellow for happy ... we start from that and then I ask her why she feels that way. But it's difficult'.[5]

It is worth noting the assumption here of an internal world that the patient needs to 'be aware of' and 'work on' for recovery.[6] In Fernanda's experience, working with children is much more tiring and frustrating than working with older and 'more collaborative' patients. In fact, treatment with Arianna proceeded particularly slowly, the team felt. Her nutritionist Monica often found herself having to defend her slowed-down approach before other professionals, who thought that Arianna had to be pushed more and given more food because she was not gaining enough weight. Monica indeed said she had to increase the amount of food given to Arianna in an exceptionally slow way, by five grams every two weeks: 'I have never done this so slowly, but you have to consider that she started from eating ten grams of pasta!'

After six months in treatment, Arianna had gained five kilograms and two centimetres in height, reaching a BMI of 14. She had started going back to school in the morning and looked livelier and more playful. Arianna had also learned – Monica and Fernanda proudly reported during one staff meeting – to 'recognise that her stomach-ache, which she had always presented as the cause of being unable to eat, has to do with her emotions'. However, Arianna's weight was still considered well below a healthy weight, and yet she had become increasingly oppositional and refused any increase in her meal plan, displaying worries about 'growing up' and 'getting fat' but refusing to speak during therapy sessions. In the meantime, the treatment team were growing more and more concerned about her health and 'potentially irreparably stunted growth' (endocrinologist). During the days of negotiations about her meal plan, Arianna was caught walking on the ledge of the building between her bedroom's window and the window of the dining room. Since she could easily have slipped and fallen from a second-floor height, the treatment team decided to discharge her: Arianna had 'crossed the line' (clinical director), and the team did not want to risk being held responsible if something similar happened again, resulting in Arianna hurting herself or worse. Following that incident, Arianna continued her treatment path as an outpatient.

When Arianna left, the other six young patients were saddened by the decision, as they had become a close-knit group. One patient in particular – Sofia – seemed to feel deprived of her companion. Sofia, eleven years old, had been admitted a few weeks after Arianna. At that time, she was already being treated as an outpatient by Monica, who had initially thought that Sofia was a case of ARFID but quickly changed the diagnosis to that of anorexia nervosa. Sofia's parents had in fact reported that she had started reducing her portions of food and had stopped eating her snack at school altogether. Then, at a following outpatient session, Sofia brought a question to Monica, written on a piece of paper: 'How do thighs get fat?' This was when Monica had changed Sofia's suspected diagnosis into that of anorexia nervosa: 'It turned out that Sofia was convinced that second courses, fruit and vegetables make you fat, so she did all she could to avoid them'. At that point, Sofia was assigned to a psychotherapist who would see her on alternative weeks. But with her physical condition worsening and her parents becoming increasingly worried, she was soon admitted to the residential facility.

Like Arianna when she first arrived, Sofia looked emaciated and her gaze was defined 'empty' – probably a consequence of malnutrition, the team said. Sofia stubbornly refused food, especially meat, vegetables and fruit. Even more evidently than Arianna, who after a while had started being quite talkative, Sofia refused to speak to her therapists. Her ways of communicating amounted to a gentle shake of her head to say 'no', and an almost imperceptible shrug to say 'I don't know'. This did not change with time as it had changed in the case of Arianna. More precisely, it did not change with regards to the professionals: with other patients, Sofia would talk. In the rare occasions in which Sofia would speak during her individual sessions – her therapist Tessa reported – she would just talk about her fear of 'getting fat', which made Monica and Tessa feel increasingly 'helpless'. This situation of perceived impasse made the two professionals request Sofia's case[7] to be reviewed during the monthly supervision meeting that the treatment team routinely attended with an external, experienced psychotherapist. Things did not change much. In May, after almost five months of residential treatment and with Sofia having regained some weight, Monica and Tessa eventually decided to discharge her and keep treating her as an outpatient.

Challenging the Assumptions of Treatment

> *Preadolescent patients aren't aware of their illness, and they aren't motivated at all to recover. Telling them that if they don't eat we send them home doesn't work, because they can't wait to go home! They have been brought here by their parents totally against their will. The only thing that might work is telling them that, if they don't eat, they end up in hospital.*
>
> —Clinical director, weekly staff meeting, March 2019

Awareness of being ill and in need of help, a subsequent 'will to abandon the eating disorder' and responsibility for one's own treatment – demonstrated by active effort and 'collaboration' with the professionals – are all seen as essential to treatment, as we have seen in Chapter 3. But preadolescent patients seem to lack all this. With such young patients more than with others, treatment is something that professionals 'make them undergo' (clinical director). The fact that 'patients are still growing' makes it also more urgent for the treatment team to act when they keep losing weight or do not gain enough weight, 'because the damage done in this life stage in terms of bone density and loss of height can become permanent' (endocrinologist). On the other hand, Monica often insisted that, with the youngest patients, it was crucial to 'proceed very gradually and without insisting too much. Otherwise, the result might be that they start refusing everything'.

Here professionals representing different sciences – medical doctors on the one hand, and nutritionists and psychologists on the other – are vying for attention and seem to send conflicting messages. Such dynamics were particularly visible during weekly staff meetings: the endocrinologist would typically complain that patients were not gaining enough weight 'to be safe' and that their planned meals should be increased, whereas nutritionists and psychologists would make strong cases for proceeding slowly. Contrary to what one might expect given customary professional hierarchies in these sciences, it was the nutritionists and the psychologists who eventually decided if and how to increase a meal plan. They often remarked that medical doctors 'tend to only look at numbers' and are not the ones who spend time with patients, have sessions with them or have to make them eat every day: 'We are the ones who know how it works in practice, in the therapy room, and it's much more difficult than the doctors make it sound' (nutritionist Monica). As we have seen in Chapters 2 and 3, in this clinical world the numbers of calories, weight, BMI, growth curves, blood tests and so on are 'trusted' (Porter 1995), and construct realities that counteract patients' 'distorted ones' and redirect them towards recovery. However, here we see how some professionals can use these numbers contextually as a frame of distrust, precisely because of what they omit.

What is the aim of treatment with these young patients, one might then wonder, besides 'restoring a healthy weight'? Helping them become 'autonomous and responsible' – which, as noted in Chapter 3, seems to be the mantra for adolescent and adult patients – does not apply well to preadolescents. When I posed this question to the psychotherapist Carlotta, she told me that the aim was 'to reduce the strong sense of omnipotence that these children have developed in response to a situation in which their primary needs have not been listened to by their parents. As if: since none of my needs is satisfied, I take control of everything'. I asked how such an aim could be achieved. Carlotta explained that, ideally, treatment should proceed by working on the children's sense of frustration for their unmet needs. 'The aim – she continued – is to make that emotion tolerable, by giving them other instruments, different from the symptoms, to deal with it'. Carlotta's words seem to locate the source of the problem in children's families, in parents' inability to meet their children's needs. In the following section, we will return to the stories of

Arianna and Sofia and see how the particularly difficult traits of preadolescent patients tend to be ascribed to their growing up in 'dysfunctional families' – with the word 'dysfunctional' having both the literal meaning of 'families that do not function (properly)' and the more field-specific meaning of 'encouraging unhealthy thoughts and behaviours regarding food, eating and body shape' (clinical director).

Dysfunctional Families

These are all daughters of the wind.

—External psychotherapist, supervision meeting, March 2019

In her ethnography of a children's clinic for chronic pain in the United States, Buchbinder (2015) notes that it is important to distinguish between what are seen as the causes of chronic pain and the factors that interfere with recovery. She argues that regardless of whether a biological cause could be identified, the treatment team believed that many families did things, however unwittingly, that perpetuated or exacerbated their children's symptoms (ibid.: 135). Buchbinder suggests that whereas in 'onstage clinical spaces' professionals' explanatory model attributed pain to a flaw in the patient's 'neurobiological wiring' – laying the groundwork for a therapeutic approach that emphasised individual responsibility – in 'backstage clinical spaces', such as team meetings, another prevailing explanation circulated that targeted the family as a site of blame and intervention, and conceptualised children as 'vessels of their families' traumas' (ibid.: 111–12). Whereas the clinicians saw a flaw in neurobiological mechanisms as what Buchbinder calls the 'proximal cause' of chronic pain, problematic families were seen as the 'distal cause' (ibid.). This network of explanations challenges the notion of a singular, autonomous patient that has long been prevalent in North American and European biomedical settings, and illustrates how treatment is aimed not only at managing chronic pain but also at defining what constitutes 'good parenting' and a 'good family' (ibid.: 112). Buchbinder ultimately argues that paediatric pain treatment is a matter of 'making patients' but also of 'making parents', following specific cultural views of adolescent development, family roles and desirable parenting. Throughout this process, kin relationships and caregiving patterns become targets of clinical judgement and change (ibid.: 113). Similarly, in her ethnography of psychiatric care for women in India, Pinto (2014) has illustrated how clinical ethics are tied to kin ethics, with clinical rationality deployed to craft more ideal families.

As we have seen in Chapter 4, at Il Giardino parental behaviour becomes implicated in patients' treatment too, as part of a larger project of 'treating the family'. 'On stage' – during individual and group meetings for parents – families are never explicitly blamed but effectively constructed as a fundamental resource in treatment to secure their collaboration. 'Backstage', however – during weekly staff meetings, monthly supervision meetings and daily chats in the protected space of the kitchen – professionals explicitly put the blame for patients' conditions on their 'messed-up families'. Buchbinder (2015: 38) also reports that, at the pain clinic, the parents of younger children were depicted by clinicians as overprotective, whereas in the case of older adolescents parents' inattentiveness and precocious 'adultification' was more common. Instead, at Il Giardino, whereas one could find both situations in adolescent and adult patients (see Chapter 4), most younger children appeared to live in families in which lack of family care was described by the treatment team as the defining feature. If we return to Arianna and Sofia, we will see how their eating disorder and the character traits that make their treatment particularly difficult are put down to these children's families being 'dysfunctional' in several ways, and mostly to their parents failing to meet the expected parenting role.

Arianna's family was the object of many weekly staff meetings and discussions during mealtime breaks in the kitchen. Through regular sessions and phone conversations with her parents, Arianna's nutritionist Monica, her psychologist Fernanda and her assigned family counsellor Sara had put together a rather worrying picture of Arianna's home environment, completing Arianna's fragmentary descriptions. The first thing that had struck Arianna's therapists was that she never referred to 'my home' or 'our home', but always to 'grandma's home', 'mum's home' and so on. She had also drawn her house with wheels (see Figure 5.1), which was read as a clear sign of a perceived 'instability'.

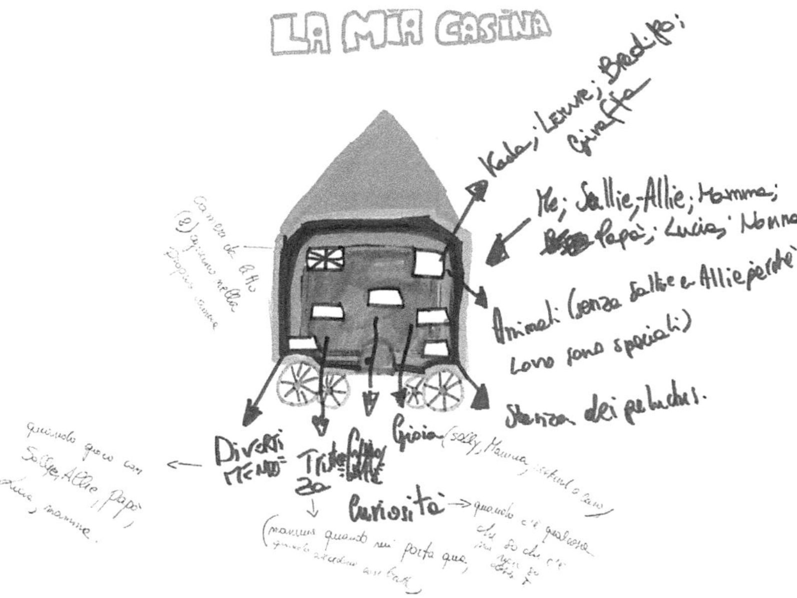

Figure 5.1. Arianna's drawing 'My little house'. Picture taken by author, 2019. © Giulia Sciolli.

When Arianna was asked to make a drawing of a typical family meal and describe it, it came out that she would usually eat 'some stuff' – not further specified – at her grandmother's house, either sitting alone at the kitchen table or in front of the TV. Her grandmother and occasionally her mother would eat in the house too, but often at different times and standing in the kitchen. Her father, instead, would mostly eat out in restaurants. Upon further investigation with Arianna's parents, her therapists reported that the whole family had 'dysfunctional behaviours' towards food and eating: Arianna's mother 'would never cook' and seemed not to know how to cook, so when she had to provide food for Arianna she would buy a takeaway in a trusted rotisserie in the neighbourhood; Arianna's father would never eat pasta, and would weigh himself every morning to make sure his weight was always in the same 300-g range. Even Arianna's grandfather seemed to be 'exceptionally worried' about food, to the point that he prevented himself and all his family members in his presence from eating any kind of ice cream other than ice lollies, which he considered healthier because they were just 'water and sugar'. All these 'weird behaviours towards food' – Arianna's therapists held – made it difficult for Arianna to have a clear idea of what 'normal eating' meant, since she lacked appropriate 'reference points'. They were also seen as dangerous predictors for the development of 'a full-blown anorexia' later, in her adolescence. Therapists felt that Arianna's current obsession with the quantity of her 'portions' was therefore also a way to ask for reference points that her own parents had failed to give her. Arianna's nutritionist and psychotherapist kept insisting with Arianna's parents that it was important for Arianna to have meals in their home during weekends, just the three of them sitting at a table and eating something that Arianna's mother would cook specifically for the occasion – suggesting quite strongly their normative reference point for an ideal 'functional' family.[8]

The lack of attention to Arianna's eating patterns on the part of her parents – and to her in general, professionals held – were so stark that nobody at home had noticed her substantial weight loss. It was Arianna's grandmother who eventually noticed and brought it to the attention of the parents. The treatment team found this 'astonishing', even more so because both Arianna's parents were medical professionals. Similarly, reconstructing Arianna's eating patterns since infancy had proved 'absurdly impossible'.

Another aspect of Arianna that worried her therapists was her 'relational difficulty', especially in establishing friendships with children of her own age: 'She hardly has any relationships with other children, other than a female cousin. Which is pretty much the same for her parents: they don't seem to have friends' (nutritionist Monica). The treatment team had soon recommended Arianna's parents to undergo psychotherapy themselves, but they proved very resistant, said Monica:

> They would really need that, because they are completely unable to draw boundaries for Arianna. Her mother reports that she never says 'no' to Arianna because Arianna doesn't listen to her, but it seems to me that it is more because she gets scared at Arianna's tantrums. Her father equally says that, if they fight, Arianna always wins. The result is that Arianna has no coordinates whatsoever: she doesn't know what is right, what is wrong, how much is too much, how much is too little ... she is so confused!

Monica kept explaining that she had to take Arianna around the town one afternoon to ask random people roughly how many grams of pasta they ate for their meals, because Arianna was convinced that eating 20 grams was 'normal': 'You should have seen her face when someone told her 150!' Professionals had concluded that the situation of Arianna's family was 'dysfunctional both in relational terms and as regards attitudes towards food', and that unless her parents realised that and did 'some work on themselves' to change, it would be difficult for Arianna to really get better. In this developmental context, healthy reference points are thus constructed, together with 'stability' (*stabilità*) and 'boundaries' (*confini*), as a vital ingredient of good parenting and as crucial to a child's orientation in the world.

Lack of boundary work, in particular, seemed to cause problems. As anticipated above, Sofia's family was not only at the centre of weekly staff meetings and informal discussions over lunch breaks in the kitchen, but also became a topic of the monthly supervision meeting. Each month, a 'particularly difficult case' was chosen among the admitted patients. An experienced psychotherapist who would otherwise work somewhere else would listen to the 'presentation of the case' by the treatment team and help them 'see what they could not see' due to their daily involvement with the patient in question. This suggests that the clinical detachment deemed to be essential in the clinic was not always easy to maintain. Sofia's case had been chosen because her therapists did not know 'what to do with her' and were growing increasingly frustrated at the fact that Sofia seemed to have nothing to tell them or, if she did, she would not tell them:

> I feel powerless ... because when you try to go in depth with her, it feels like you are standing in front of a black painting. She is completely empty and alone in her fears, she doesn't have an identity. She doesn't interact with anything. Even the other patients she seems to have bonded with, you realise she actually cares very little about them. (psychotherapist Tessa)

When the external psychotherapist asked about the history of the child and about what might have precipitated her anorexia, Sofia's nutritionist, Monica, reported what she had been told by Sofia's mother: Sofia – second child of four – had been breastfed 'for only twenty-four days' because her mother had to suddenly receive surgery for appendicitis. Sofia's weaning had proceeded 'normally', although she had always refused fruit and vegetables.[9] When she was very young, she had developed a severe allergic reaction after eating some hazelnuts, with her throat swelling and preventing her from breathing. She had also suffered from asthma and tonsillitis. These were all seen as potential risk factors. Starting from 2017, she had then become increasingly selective with food. In the same year her paternal uncle, to whom Sofia was very attached, had died of cancer. This sudden and early death was considered a highly possible 'precipitating factor'. Another likely precipitating factor was located by the treatment team in the beginning of marital problems between Sofia's parents, at around the same time that her uncle passed away. Moreover, during one of the meetings with the family counsellor, Sofia's mother had revealed she had never told anyone that she herself had 'suffered from anorexia' when she was sixteen, but that 'nobody had noticed' and the problem 'had gone away naturally' once she went to university – something that the treatment team struggled to believe. Even more interestingly for the professionals, Sofia's mother had reported that during the time she was ill she had also virtually stopped talking. The psychotherapist Tessa saw this as a striking similarity with Sofia's symptoms: 'It's as if Sofia's mother is unconsciously using her daughter to express the unsaid parts of herself'.

What the treatment team found particularly worrying in Sofia – besides her refusal to eat and talk to them – was her 'absolute incapacity to choose and to do anything on her own': 'She gets paralysed when she has to choose something. For example, the kitten she was gifted for Christmas, it still doesn't have a name because she can't choose one. And it's the same with her favourite colour, places she likes, where she wants to go … she always imitates others' (nutritionist Monica). The professionals related this trait to growing up with 'highly problematic and immature parents', notwithstanding the fact that they had both graduated from university and were economically well-off. Sofia's father was portrayed by the family counsellor as being 'very self-centred and not very present in the family', and as incapable of facing problems. At one point his worries and anxiety about Sofia's condition reportedly caused him to be admitted to hospital for heart issues. This, coupled with the fact that Sofia's mother had revealed only one year after Sofia had been in treatment that she had herself suffered from anorexia nervosa, made professionals suggest that Sofia's parents had issues with 'facing reality' and talking about it: 'We always end up knowing these important things late and through indirect ways. Which is the same dynamic that Sofia has with us' (psychotherapist Tessa). More than this, when Sofia was admitted, neither of her parents brought along the life-saving adrenaline doses that professionals soon found out (by reading her clinical record) that Sofia always needed to have ready in case she mistakenly ingested hazelnuts. Sofia's parents, who had been living in her mother's parents' house for a long time, were ultimately characterised by the external psychotherapist as 'unable to self-determine as parents'. 'They seem more like an older brother and sister, judging from how they behave with their children', she remarked. But patients' families were also seen by the professionals as examples of a more widespread fracturing of families in contemporary Italy, as the external psychotherapist pointed out:

> To me it seems like we are trying to draw the contemporary family here, and the figures don't add up. The eating disorder is the symptom of a fragile family. It feels like these are not daughters who have been desired and imagined; they are more like bio-objects – bodies that simply need to function. And the problem is not that their parents are distracted by other things and don't want to care for them; the problem is that these parents have fallen into a black hole themselves. It's not by chance that these little girls are trying to recreate a second family here. What you are doing here is quite heroic – the problem is where you send them back to.

Parents are therefore not simply seen as guilty: they are seen as victims as well, incapable of acting differently unless they themselves decide to undergo some psychotherapeutic work. The external psychotherapist was adamant that to really understand what was happening to the patients it was necessary to go back to their great-grandparents' generation and 'investigate the stories of the relationships between the generations'. Complicating taken-for-granted notions of mother–child attachment and bonding (cf. Scheper-Hughes 1987: 149), the psychotherapist seemed to be saying that parents cannot be nurturing if they have not been nurtured themselves: 'We are born since we are conceived in the head of those who want us. Our internal world is born from the internal world of our parents'. In the world of this treatment facility, people have 'internal worlds' that are inevitably interconnected with those of their kin and that are directly affected by those of their ancestors: Sofia did not know that her mother had suffered from an eating disorder and had stopped talking when she was sixteen, and yet, the external psychotherapist argued, 'her internal world knew because psychological life is passed on through generations'.

The professionals' discussion of Sofia's 'empty internal world' as the consequence of the absence of proper kinship ties is exemplary of Carsten's argument that kinship can be imagined as a way to engineer secure social landscapes and reliable histories (Carsten 2019a: 143). When kinship fails – the external psychotherapist seems to be saying – what should have been secure social landscapes and reliable histories fall apart. A 'substance' – in the wider sense of the term – that should ideally flow between parents and children, namely kinship care and the 'internal world' of the family that comes with it through generations, fails to be passed on, generating illness.

On a similar note, in her ethnography of child welfare institutions in Japan, Kathryn Goldfarb (2019) shows how children's bodies – their smaller body size, their inability to chew, improper chopstick use, left-handedness – are seen by social workers as carrying the signs of the absence of kinship care. She thus argues for a model of 'embodied relationality' that calls attention to the ways in which relatedness itself turns into biological materiality (ibid.: 155). The ways children in Japanese state care engage with their bodies – particularly at mealtimes – tell caregivers about a child's former caregivers. The staff view food practices as central to the institution's goal to produce a kin-like network for children, and to resocialise the children as 'normal' members of Japanese society (ibid.: 161). Here the child's body is very much an 'embedded body' – 'heavily impregnated by its own past and by the social and material environment within which it dwells' (Niewöhner 2011: 290). In the world of Il Giardino, such interpersonal histories are similarly seen to produce visible effects in patients' bodies, but through an additional intermediate step located in 'the mind': here there is a 'mind' distinct from and at the same time clearly entangled with 'the body'. If we take the 'embedded body' seriously as a language of analysis, then this mind-body is the body that patients have 'acquired' in their relational worlds (McDonald 2014, 2018).

In both Arianna's and Sofia's cases, their emaciated bodies – the corporeal aspect here of their ill minds – are seen as the result of the lack of proper family care, of what we might call relatedness. In summary, we can say that people acquire particular bodies in relational worlds, an important aspect of which here is acquiring particular forms of relatedness. It is worth noting how the body becomes privileged in this model of the person and family that professionals are working with. Here we have relational persons with bodies and minds: the mind is internal and is deep down, and finds expression through the corporeal body. It is also worth noting how a specific notion of the autonomous individual holds in this treatment centre, perhaps surprisingly to some since we are in Italy, which is commonly seen as the bearer of an exceptionally strong family ethos (Ghezzi 2012; Saraceno 2004, 2015; Vatta 2012). In this centre, instead, professionals can talk of relational issues and uphold an ideal of autonomous individual at the same time. As we have seen in the previous chapter, 'healthy' relatedness brings about autonomy, which is the ideal here. It is through relatedness that people acquire the capacity to take autonomous decisions. Moreover, it seems that there are different models of autonomy based on different kinds of patients, depending on age. Arianna's and Sofia's cases, as constructed by the professionals, seem to suggest that children need to develop a form of 'internal autonomy' before 'practical autonomy' can be achieved.

Complicating Clinical Detachment

It's boundaries that nurture the child.

—Psychotherapist Tessa, workshop for parents, May 2019

As we have seen for older patients in the previous chapter, professionals seem to agree that the children admitted for treatment need urgent 'reparenting', and that they themselves need to make up for the lacks and absences which patients experienced at home. Teaching them how to eat is central to this reparenting process. However, with these young patients there is more going on: reparenting patients does not seem to be simply a temporary phase of treatment in these cases, as it happens for older patients, because preadolescent patients will still be the children of their 'absent families' once discharged.[10]

In her work on Amazonian kinship, Aparecida Vilaça (2002: 361) argues that 'kinning' is a process whereby parents turn their babies 'into humans out of others' by 'individualising' them from an 'undifferentiated universe' of spiritual and especially animal subjectivities. This means that for babies to become kin to their human family they first need to be detached or 'de-kinned' from the relationships in which they find themselves enmeshed at birth, which happen to be those with spirits and animals. At Il Giardino, one could say, professionals try to 'de-kin' and then 're-kin' patients by similarly constructing the supposedly necessary 'boundaries' between these children and others. Interestingly, in this case the entities that children need to be de-kinned from through boundary work are not spirits or animals, but their own kin.

These children's perceived lack of boundaries seems to make it more difficult for the treatment team to maintain clinical detachment. The boundaries that the professionals have to create and maintain serve in part as a re-kinning process, with them acting as proxies for patients' family members. Most professionals – especially those who have individual sessions with children – report that they easily feel 'overinvolved' with these young patients, and that it is hard to stop thinking and worrying about them after their shifts. Preadolescents seem to generate an inevitable 'maternal instinct' here that makes it more painful and frustrating to treat them, especially when they keep refusing food and talk. The psychologist Mara was among those who spoke of 'the maternal function that kicks in' with preadolescent patients, which makes it more difficult to 'keep the boundaries'. This 'excessive' sense of protection is often related to the notion of being 'activated' by a patient, which the psychologist Fernanda explained as having to do with the notion of 'countertransference', i.e., with the parts of the professional's self that the patient touches. When professionals say that a patient 'activates' them – something that seems to happen more commonly with children – they refer to a state of hyperarousal, of 'physiological activation', that can be 'healthy because it makes you do things', but also 'dysfunctional because it doesn't help you see things from an external perspective' (psychologist Mara).

Here we see in a nutshell one key problem of the treatment apparatus as it stands: since one of the main causes contributing to the development of eating disorders is seen to lie in dysfunctional or absent kinship relationships, a therapeutic relationship between therapist and patient is seen as key to recovery. It is believed to be the tool through which patients can learn and experiment with what they could not learn in their family environments – i.e., how to deal with interpersonal relationships effectively. The problem is ascribed to the fact that this complicates the mantra of maintaining strict boundaries between patients and professionals (cf. Myers 2015). Certainly, this holds for therapeutic work with *any* patient in the treatment centre, as we will see in the next chapter. However, it specifically holds for preadolescents because with them the element of 'fiction' that professionals can resort to with adults and adolescents – i.e., that the reparenting dynamics of treatment are temporary and will gradually lead patients to find their own autonomy, as is expected for their age – is lacking.

Conclusion

We have seen in Chapter 3 how treatment practices in the residential and day-service facility are based on the assumption that the patient who is being treated has a psychological, internal world that she is aware of and capable of discovering and communicating about with her therapists. It is an internal world that has been relationally constructed and can be deconstructed through talk. It is also assumed that the aim of treatment – besides weight restoration – is to help patients regain some sort of 'autonomy'. This aim is based on the idea that part of the reason why patients developed an eating disorder in the first place has to do with their parents being 'overinvolved' or 'enmeshed', with their offspring thus lacking clear 'identity boundaries' (see Minuchin, Rosman and Baker 1978; Selvini Palazzoli 1978). Explicitly 'psychological' treatment mostly addresses these issues.

In this chapter I have shown that treating preadolescents with eating disorders puts into question the very paradigm of treatment and its underlying equation between health and autonomy, because children fail to undergo the desired steps deemed essential for therapeutic transformation. These young patients are found incapable of expressing their thoughts and feelings with the depth considered necessary for successful therapeutic work. The highly sought-after collaboration between health professionals and patients, which is thought to be at the heart of treatment, seems hard to reach when children are seen as lacking a supposedly coherent internal world to be disclosed to professionals during psychological therapy. It seems that these young patients are 'opaque' – in Joel Robbins' (2008) sense of the term – to themselves, and it is very hard for the clinicians to go behind that opacity and create a 'self-awareness' in them. Similarly, helping patients to regain their autonomy is difficult with children, who by virtue of their age cannot disentangle themselves from their families. This treatment logic, drawn primarily from the practice of clinical psychology, thus comes to an impasse with preadolescents, forcing professionals (and anthropologists) to question its basis and look for other ways to treat them.

'Dysfunctional' family dynamics, most notably characterised as lack of 'stability', 'reference points' and 'boundaries', come to be seen as the main roots of patients' illness. Well-entrenched family traits and relations are put under scrutiny, dissected and analysed as doctors might do with damaged body tissues in a patient with a physical ailment. This process has a further effect on the therapeutic relationship, as professionals find themselves having to reparent patients in a way that is not as clearly temporary as with older ones, who present as potentially autonomous in a near future. 'Maternal instinct' and 'activation' thus get in the way of the supposedly necessary clinical detachment. Whereas clinical detachment seems to be possible with older patients, with preadolescents professional boundaries are therefore harder to maintain, and the logic of psychological treatment must be ready to adapt in unexpected ways to produce new forms of therapeutic care. These children, professionals are aware, will eventually need to be sent back to the care of parents who seem to them unfit for the task.

Notes

* An earlier and shorter version of this chapter was originally published as: Sciolli, Giulia. 2025. 'Treating Patients "Who Don't Speak": The Challenge of Treating Children with Eating Disorders in a Residential Facility in Italy', in Mikkel Kenni Bruun and Rebecca Hutten (eds), *Towards an Anthropology of Psychology – Ethnographies of Mental Health and Psychotherapy*. Oxford: Berghahn Books.

1. In Italy, in 'nutritional' terms (see Chapter 3), first courses are typically composed of 'carbohydrates' such as pasta and rice; second courses include 'proteins' such as meat, fish, eggs or cheese; sides tend to be vegetables.
2. International law, encoded in the UN Convention on the Rights of the Child, defines childhood as the period between the ages of 0 and 18, with childhood conceptualised as a separate space entitled to special protection and rights (Montgomery 2008: 2, 6). However, historians, anthropologists and other social scientists have shown that this notion of children as dependent and vulnerable is both historically and culturally specific (see Ariès 1979 [1962]; Lancy 2014; Schwartzman 1978; Zelizer 1985).
3. Avoidant/restrictive food intake disorder (ARFID) is a condition defined in the *Diagnostic and Statistical Manual of Mental Disorders* (*DSM-5*) as 'avoidance' of certain foods or types of food and/or 'intake restriction' in terms of overall amount eaten. ARFID is typically associated with children and is distinguished from anorexia and bulimia nervosa in that 'beliefs' and 'worries' about weight and shape do not seem to contribute to the avoidance or restriction of food (American Psychiatric Association 2013).
4. For more on the measure of 'calorie', see Chapters 2 and 3.
5. The fact that therapists have to employ different tools to 'access children's internal worlds' – drawing, playing, telling stories – is not unique to the treatment of eating disorders, as the reader might guess, but also holds for other conditions seen to pertain to 'mental health'. However, in the case of eating disorders professionals have received no specific training to work with children and there is still very little clinical literature to which they can refer. Moreover, treatment for other children's conditions is usually at the outpatient level, except for 'acute' episodes briefly treated in hospital wards. At Il Giardino, instead, children may stay in the residential facility for months.
6. See Chapter 3.

7. In the world of the treatment centre, people and their stories become 'cases'. The upcoming discussion of Sofia's 'case' during the supervision meeting differed from the 'medical cases' described by Good (1993): in the distinct world of 'mental health', information and details about the patient's history, which may be disregarded as irrelevant by a physician treating what is seen as a bodily disease, become the very object of interest for the clinical gaze.
8. The reader might note that there seems to be much consensus within the treatment team on what a 'healthy family' should look like. This might partly have to do with the similar social background of the professionals working at Il Giardino. Most of them are from the same region in central Italy, whose inhabitants are renowned for their 'traditional views'.
9. Psychotherapists would often remark on the importance of looking at what happened during the weaning process of the child, and of exploring whether something had happened that might have affected the patient's current eating disordered behaviour.
10. It is important to note that the kind of 'lack of care' seen as negatively impacting these children's lives is rarely enough to take the children away from their families and put them in foster care. Professionals do sometimes conclude that the children would be better off if removed from their families, but they seldom have the 'right kind of evidence' needed for that. In most cases, the 'bad parenting' that is seen as causing the children's problems consists of aspects that are felt to be quite widespread in families and that are not prosecuted by law (e.g., 'unhealthy' attitudes towards food; family dynamics that only reward control and discipline, or inversely total lack of rules; marital problems; not enough time to spend with children because of work). The case of Arianna (whereby her parents did not notice her weight loss until it reached a critical stage) was quite extreme and unusual, and the fact that her parents were 'respectable medical professionals' in the region made it impossible for the treatment team to even think about removal action. The only instances in which professionals would contact social services to question the suitability of patients' parents and act so that patients could be removed from their families were cases in which there was suspected or proven physical and/or sexual abuse.

Chapter 6

When 'Things Don't Work'

Chronicity, Comorbidity and the Limits of Care

Here there's a tendency towards death, not life – through a whole set of self-destroying behaviours. You can feel the spectre of death always looming in the background.

—Psychotherapist Mauro, interview, June 2019

It is a Friday morning in January 2019. I am in a city one hour's drive away from Il Giardino, and I have just managed to reach the hospital wing where, on the sixth floor, I have been told I would find Maia's ward. She was admitted here a week ago. I am debating whether to take the stairs or the visibly old and shaky lift, when its metallic doors open to reveal Maia and another woman, her mother. 'Ohhh Giulietta, you found me!', Maia greets me with her characteristic enthusiasm, while her mother proceeds to introduce herself. Although I have known Maia for more than six months through my research and volunteer activities at the residential facility – where Maia had been staying until she was admitted to hospital – this was the first time I had seen her mother. Maia tells me that they are going 'to have the mid-morning snack' at the hospital café, and that I should join them. While we are sitting in the café chatting over a cappuccino, I cannot help but notice the dissonance between the liveliness of that moment and the fact that we are in a hospital because of Maia's continuous weight loss over the previous weeks, which had put her in a situation deemed to be at 'immediate risk for life'. The drip for intravenous nutrition that Maia's arm is attached to, connected to a plastic bag containing some white nutritious substance, is a visible reminder of that. What professionals at Il Giardino call 'the spectre of death', usually looming in the background, today is patently visible.

Patients diagnosed with anorexia or bulimia nervosa are reported to frequently experience severe health complications (Katzman 2005; Mehler, Crews and Weiner 2004). Longitudinal studies have suggested that, together with substance use addictions, these have the highest mortality rate of all mental illnesses[1]– seen as the result of the physical consequences of malnutrition and of suicide (Auger et al. 2021; Smink, van Hoeken and Hoek 2012). Anorexia nervosa in particular is associated with a fifty-fold increase in the relative risk of death from suicide (Franko and Keel 2006). One of the reasons behind these figures, the scientific literature suggests, is that rates of relapse after treatment are very high, and between 10% and 23% of cases develop into 'chronic conditions' (Fichter et al. 2017; Quadflieg and Fichter 2019).

Here it is important to pause on what 'chronic'[2] means when one talks of eating disorders. In their introduction to a special issue on 'new chronicities', Cinzia Greco and Nils Graber (2022: 3–10) have noted how, in the cases they consider, chronicity is mostly something that is hoped for and desired by patients and their families, as it amounts to a disease people now 'live with' rather than 'die of', as it used to be.[3] In her own contribution on metastatic breast cancer, Greco (2022: 110–12) reported that many patients and professionals contested the recent shift towards calling the disease a 'chronic condition', because of the misleading association with manageable, non-life-threatening diseases. Some of her interlocutors, instead, considered it a 'recurrent condition', as 'a series of acute episodes linked together by areas of more chronic stabilization' (ibid.: 114). As we will see, eating disorders could be considered recurrent conditions too, but here the association with 'chronicity', if present, is all but positive: since the premise is that eating disorders are curable with swift access to proper treatment, when a case is considered 'chronic' it means that something went wrong – that a person who could be freed from a very debilitating *and* life-threatening condition will, instead, probably have to not only 'live with it' for the rest of her life, but also, at some point, probably die prematurely *because of* it. Families tremble at the idea that their children might become 'chronic cases', and professionals experience futility when they find themselves dealing with them. Chronicity here is not a hope tied to access to biomedical innovations; it is an anxiety tied to lack of proper treatment.

Given this mortality risk, professionals who work with eating disorders inevitably lose some patients at some point during their careers. A multinational study of therapists' 'burnout' (Warren et al. 2013) suggests that high relapse rates and worry about patient survival are key factors that make these patients 'challenging' and 'emotionally exhausting' to treat. None of the patients I met died during my fieldwork, but I was informed of five patients who died a few years after their respective discharge – three as a consequence of more than twenty years of severe malnutrition, and two, much younger, as a consequence of a self-harming act.[4] In all instances the professionals I talked to were profoundly shaken, and I was too. But news about the death of other ex-patients and of prospective patients also reached the treatment team during my fieldwork. One case concerned a patient who had been in treatment at Il Giardino a few years before I arrived. The clinical director happened to receive an email from the patient's mother during one of the weekly staff meetings. The mother was replying to an invitation to a workshop for parents that would take place before Christmas. In the reply, she had written that her daughter had 'died of anorexia' the previous morning. A glacial silence had filled the room, with most staff visibly distressed and those who had known the girl almost in tears. On two more occasions, the clinical director told the treatment team that a patient who was on the waiting list to be admitted – and who had been 'kept on hold' because of bureaucratic problems with her authorisation – had 'died while waiting'. Commenting on what had happened, she said it was 'infuriating' that this was due to a system which keeps 'failing patients' because too often 'things don't work'.

We have seen in previous chapters how treatment aims at deconstructing 'the eating-disordered part of the patient's self', so that it can 'leave' the patient. Here I ask: when this does not happen and treatment is seen to fail, what are the reasons posited for failure?[5] One reason immediately obvious to any observer will be what can be framed as 'lack of resources'. As mentioned in Chapter 4, the State is seen as the main actor responsible for the numerous patients' deaths. Long waiting lists lead to residential treatment that, most of the time, is felt to be too short and disconnected from the wider network of day-service and outpatient care. The professionals who work at Il Giardino would often complain and worry about the 'ridiculously short time' (an average of twelve weeks) that they had to treat what were seen as extremely complex conditions, which should – 'in an ideal world', they said – be addressed with months and sometimes years of continuous treatment and support. These limited time frames are imposed by the authorisation that the patient's region of residence must grant for treatment in another region.[6] Since it is the patient's region of residence which pays for treatment, professionals routinely have to plead for the minimum of twelve weeks of admission, as well as for necessary extensions (cf. Lester 2009). When discharged from the residential or day-service facility, most patients go back to their regions, where outpatient services are often disorganised and lack staff that is specifically trained in eating disorders. Unless patients have the means to pay for private outpatient treatment, they may then start meeting a therapist once every two weeks. This discontinuity of care, professionals agree, 'blows up all the work done', often causing what is known in psychiatry as the phenomenon of the 'revolving door', whereby patients are readmitted in a cyclical pattern as a consequence of severe relapses. All these problems are in turn ascribed by the professionals to lack of enough public funding for what should be essential healthcare services accessible to everyone.

These systemic issues play an important role in constituting what the clinical director defined as 'treatment failure', and have recently been at the forefront of discussions in the national and international press.[7] Focusing on these factors would be in line with the anthropological scholarship[8] that depicts systems of care as so flawed that people are structurally unable to care in good ways for each other (Cook and Trundle 2020: 179). For eating disorders, we have seen that ethnographic works (Gremillion 2003; Lester 2019; Warin 2005) have examined how structural problems, coupled with the unintended iatrogenic effects of many treatment settings and with an ascription to patients of some inherent 'treatment resistance' by many professionals, all contribute to what the authors frame as treatment failure. These studies have importantly shown how looking beyond the patient–professional encounter is helpful to understand why 'things don't work'. In these accounts, what appears to be required is more resources that would enable the expansion of better-attuned care. As noted by anthropologists Joanna Cook and Catherine Trundle (2020: 179), however, this approach also risks limiting the possibility to think creatively about care. It implies that if people did have enough resources they would be able to solve everything, thus avoiding the question of tensions and uncertainties *within* the care practices. In this chapter I will show that something important can be missed when we lose focus on the patient–professional interaction, especially in the cases of patients who, like Maia, receive residential treatment in their region of residence, and therefore are not subject to the same time limits that the regionalised healthcare system imposes on others.[9] We will see here how care practices transform over time in unpredictable, complicated and conflicting ways – how care can both nurture and harm over time, unsettle and yet 'work to ensure the vitality of relational life' (ibid.: 181–82).

This chapter continues along the lines of Chapter 5, as it keeps questioning the treatment paradigm but by looking at treatment 'failure' in the form of chronicity. The chapter shows that it is not only preadolescent patients who challenge the key assumptions of treatment. Instead, the time of treatment and the time of illness intersect in important ways with the kind of care that is seen as key to patients' recovery. The temporal dimension of care here becomes salient – care emerges as an action in time which carries with it the hazards of relationality. We will see how, in 'chronic cases', the desired therapeutic transformation does not happen either, and the different constructions of the eating disorder – of patients on the one hand, and of professionals on the other – keep clashing. Once again, relationships of kinship care appear as crucial to treatment, but also as carrying the risk of producing disastrous effects. By focusing on two stories of so-called 'chronic' patients, I will explore the different ways in which the treatment team understands and deals with chronicity, and with 'the spectre of death' looming behind it. We will see how patients might never stop experiencing the professionals' caring work as going against their own self-care practices, and how the treatment team has to deal with the limits of their own care.

At Il Giardino, the explanations professionals give for 'failure' do not simply relate to wider structural impossibilities of doing good (as in Lester 2019). They also question two of the pillars that constitute the very logic of their treatment model: family-based care and framing the eating disorder as a part of the patient's self that can be dispensed with. I do not talk of 'failure' here as if accusing professionals of failure, but I focus instead on failure as they themselves experience and talk about it (see Carroll et al. 2017: 2). Although treatment failure mostly materialises in patients' bodies, which fail to gain weight or to maintain what is seen as a 'healthy' weight gain, we will see that it is mostly nonmaterial things that are seen to be failing when 'treatment fails': relationships, and especially relationships of kinship care. We will also see that failure here is not the direct opposite of 'success', as it works as a productive space for experimenting with novel forms of care.

Let us now return to Maia for a moment, and to the hospital visit in the opening of the chapter. Once back in her room on the ward, I asked Maia how she was doing. She told me that things were 'going well': she was regaining weight and was managing to avoid 'hyperactivity', the technical term used in the world of eating disorder treatment to refer to patients' tendency to constantly move with the aim of 'consuming calories' and therefore 'losing weight'.[10] The hardest part, Maia remarked, was 'staying away from Il Giardino' and from the treatment team. She could not wait for the moment she would be allowed to return. Yet, at the same time, she said she was worried that once returned she might go back to her 'dysfunctional habits'. This comment was striking in that it strongly resonated with the way most other patients I had met talked of their stay *in* the facility: the hardest part of residential treatment, many had been telling me, was being away from home and their families. They could not wait to return home, and yet were worried that once they found themselves in familiar spaces they might easily slip back into 'dysfunctional habits' – restricting food, purging, 'hyperactivity', using laxatives and so on. In Maia's words, instead, there was no desire to go 'home'. She wanted to go back to the residential facility and its treatment team. How could this make sense? By looking back at Maia's long history with her condition – now deemed 'chronic' by the professionals – it will become clear how the many years that she spent in treatment had turned Il Giardino into 'home' for her. But the very relationships with the professionals that made it home also put her life at risk.

When the Clinic Becomes Home: The Perils of Family-Based Care through Time

It isn't natural for anybody to stay in a treatment facility. One comes here when life outside is impossible. But keeping someone in a treatment facility for too long can cause dependence on the facility itself.

—Educator Flavia, interview, May 2019

'Oh, you met Maia then, our little scab', I was told by the psychotherapist Michele at the end of my first day of fieldwork at the residential facility. We were in the kitchen, and I was helping him to load the tray trolley for the patients' dinner. I had just come back from a 'guided tour' of the facility, arranged for me by the clinical director. I had soon realised that my guide was not a professional nor an intern, but a patient. Her blonde thin hair, puffed up in a way that made it the most voluminous part of her body, seemed to be leaving a trace of pale light behind while she walked, like a flame stubbornly burning on its candlestick when someone moves it around. 'Maia will tell you everything, she knows more of this place than we do!' the clinical director had commented when Maia was called to give me the tour. This comment, I would later learn, related to the fact that Maia had been an inpatient at Il Giardino for almost four successive years.

Several anthropologists (e.g., Biehl 2005; Myers 2015; Pinto 2014) have shown how inpatient facilities can contribute to the chronicisation of conditions that are biomedically classified as pertaining to 'mental health': people receiving care find themselves trapped in situations in which the criteria for being declared 'healthy' and capable of living a so-called 'normal life' seem impossible to obtain. This scholarship depicts inpatient treatment as riddled with ambiguous, if not outrightly harmful 'care'. This is also the case for the treatment of eating disorders, which are known to easily become chronic if not treated at the onset of symptoms. As I noted in Chapter 3, in her work on eating disorder treatment in Canada, the UK and Australia, Warin (2005) for instance shows how hospital inpatient programmes unwittingly reproduce the very configurations of space that support eating disordered practices, and calls for research on residential programmes that position themselves in contrast to hospital-based treatment. The treatment model of Il Giardino, we have seen, explicitly aims to distance itself from hospital-based approaches by reproducing a temporary 'second home' for patients. In this section I will explore how the residential facility can acquire a particular significance vis-à-vis a chronic patient's own home, in ways that are different from those of 'non-chronic' patients. I will suggest that Maia's specific needs, symptoms and disrupted kinship configurations and aspirations for a 'life outside' made the residential facility – and on occasion even a temporary stay in the hospital – a paradoxically 'vital' place in the midst of suffering and the looming spectre of death. But this very vitality, nurtured by the relationships with the professionals, also carried the risk of its end.

When we met Maia in Chapter 4, I suggested that the lack of her family's involvement in treatment was framed by the professionals as a major cause of her 'chronic state'. The reader will remember that Maia was a 33-year-old patient from a city nearby, who had been in and out of Il Giardino for the last ten years – the time 'out' spent mostly in hospital wards and other inpatient facilities. This is also why the treatment team referred to her as '*la nostra piccola crosta*' ('our little scab') – because she had been sticking to the facility for such a long time, 'like a mussel that keeps sticking to its rock' (psychotherapist Michele). From the beginning of my fieldwork, it became evident that Maia was a special patient. The first notable aspect was that Maia always had a personal assistant during meals. The staff explained that Maia had herself requested to have a professional sitting next to her for the entire duration of the meal, so that she could be watched 'second by second' and could not 'do the tricks that she knows she would otherwise do' (psychotherapist Michele). The second noticeable difference was her absence from shared spaces. Patients were supposed to spend as little time as possible alone in their rooms, and were often called if they failed to show up in the living room during the 'relaxation time' between meals and group activities. Maia, however, seemed to be exempt. Similarly, she seemed to be exempt from participating in the otherwise compulsory group activities that would not normally start until every single patient was in the therapy room. Why? Some (mostly the youngest professionals) told me this was just 'the way it is' – that it was impossible to keep running after her with all the other things to do, and pointless to do so because she would always find a way 'to sneak away'. Others (usually those who had been working in the facility for longer) would answer in a way that expressed anxiety and apprehension, and a sense of guilt: 'That is our biggest problem here, we don't know what to do with her anymore. We are failing her' (nutritionist Irma).

What did 'failure' mean here? Gradually, I came to realise that the failure professionals referred to was equated with giving up on the possibility that Maia would ever recover and have 'a life outside'. They felt they were now concerned with 'just keeping her alive'. A few months into my fieldwork, however, even 'keeping her alive' seemed to have become difficult. Maia, who had been 'stable' at a very low weight for a long time, started losing more and more weight. Professionals reported finding 'traces' of some of the ways in which she was perhaps managing to do that: notwithstanding the personal assistant during meals, Maia somehow managed to spread breadcrumbs on the floor and tomato sauce on the edge of her chair, unnoticed at the time. Some said they thought Maia was hiding food in her clothes and keeping some food in her mouth without swallowing it, so that she could spit it in the toilet after the meal. The treatment team therefore decided to make her undergo 'searches' right outside the dining room, before she could go anywhere else: one professional would first ask her to open her mouth to check that food had been swallowed, and then to empty the pockets in her clothes and pull up her T-shirt so that one could see if there was any food hidden between the clothes, including in her bra and underwear. Maia did not seem to oppose those invasive searches. Sometimes the professionals did find food, but they all agreed that this could not possibly be enough for her to lose so much weight, considering the high-calorie meal plan that she had. Instead, they located the greatest problem in Maia's 'hyperactivity' – in the fact that whenever she was not watched, she would 'constantly move to burn calories'. Volunteers reported seeing her walking up and down the stairs located in the bedroom area while the other patients were forced to stay in the living room or participate in group activities. Those on night shifts suspected that she spent most of the night walking in her bedroom. Frustratingly for those treating her, Maia did not deny any of this. She recognised that she was unable to control her 'urge to move', and even asked the treatment team to place a small gate at the entrance to the bedroom area to prevent her from sneaking out and spending hours moving up and down the stairs. Some suggested putting Maia in a wheelchair to reduce her movement, but others quickly reminded the team that they had already tried with a wheelchair in the past, and it had not worked: 'We would have to tie her to the wheelchair to prevent her from moving!'

Besides the supposedly obvious risks to Maia's physical health, her behaviours were a source of concern for the professionals because they seemed to be shrinking Maia's world, cutting her out of shared spaces and relationships. During a staff meeting, the coordinator of the facility pointed out how Maia's world was now 'reduced to those little stairs behind the bedrooms, where she walks up and down and keeps her nail polishes'. 'It's very sad, how do we shake her out of that?' she asked her colleagues. One psychotherapist pointed out that Maia needed someone with her all the time, all day, 'because she cheats everyone, with the excuse that she has to go to the toilet, or has to brush her teeth ... she is extremely manipulative. Everything has the aim of losing weight'. The clinical director therefore stipulated that, from that moment onwards, group activities would not start unless Maia was present. She reasoned that Maia would then feel a responsibility to participate, 'because if she doesn't, she prevents the others from receiving treatment'. A daily rota of shifts was also put together so that Maia would never be left alone: one intern or volunteer, with her all the time, would make sure she did not retreat into her 'hyperactivity world'.

The result, in practice, was mostly heated arguments between Maia and the intern or volunteer looking after her, and Maia falling asleep during group activities; a further proof – the professionals held – of the fact that she was so tired from constantly moving that as soon as someone forced her to stop she could not help but fall asleep. The new arrangements were then soon abandoned. Many professionals reported frustration at the fact that Maia kept asking for help, demanding that someone constantly control her, but would then become very aggressive with those same persons: 'Rationally, she knows she needs help, but then she can't stay with it. She wears you out' (psychotherapist Michele). The treatment team eventually came up with what was seen by some colleagues as 'a crazy idea': 'promoting Maia' to the role of staff assistant. The move was meant to 'shake her up', but many professionals were perplexed. This seemed a rather risky move to the anthropologist too, but an interesting reasoning behind it soon emerged.

What came to be known as 'the crazy proposal' was discussed during a supervision meeting with the external psychotherapist. Maia's case had been chosen because the whole treatment team felt 'stuck'. This was a common reason for a case to be selected for supervision, but this time something in the way the case was presented to the external psychotherapist seemed exceptional: the object of this supervision would not really be Maia, but *the relationship* that the treatment team had with her. This particular request came from a gradual realisation on the part of the team that they were 'unconsciously treating her differently from the other patients' (clinical director) and that it was important to understand how that was affecting her treatment. The clinical director was adamant that notwithstanding the role that Maia's family dynamics had played in the development and persistence of her condition, the impact of Maia's parents on her state was now 'virtually non-existent'. After all, the director insisted, she saw them 'barely thirty minutes per week':

> What we should reflect on, instead, is the dynamic that she has with *us*, and how we interact with her after all the time she has spent here. It's as if we have lost hope with her. The resignation that we see in her parents, she probably sees it in us. She can probably perceive that we are keeping her here just to keep her alive. It's hard to think something like this. She, but also *we* see this treatment as an end point, not as a transition towards something else. These behaviours lately with food are a challenge that she is throwing at us.

Maia's 'case' was presented to the external psychotherapist as one of 'pure anorexia',[11] 'extremely severe and incurable', with the patient having been 'really close to death' twice. The last time this had happened, Maia's BMI had reached 9, she had almost turned blind and was saved from a cardiac arrest. The main problem now, the treatment team felt, was that after almost four years in a row in the residential facility, Maia had recently started presenting again some 'old dysfunctional behaviours'. These behaviours – spreading breadcrumbs and tomato sauce around her seat, refusing to leave the bedroom area – were framed as possibly a way for her to tell the team that they were 'forgetting her'. Some professionals agreed that perhaps that was exactly what was happening: 'Rules don't exist for her anymore. We are so exasperated with her that we have stopped trying'.

Even more interestingly, some of the team read Maia's 'regressing behaviours' as symptomatic instead of a fear of being potentially discharged: 'She sees us as her family now, we are her only meaningful relationships. She doesn't have anything nor anyone waiting for her outside'. This was what prompted the 'crazy idea' of proposing an 'assistant role'. The plan was to ask her to assist the coordinator in carrying out administrative tasks for the centre, rather than participating in the patients' group activities. Maia would then feel reassured that she would not be 'abandoned' outside if her conditions improved, but would always have a place in the facility. Many, however, thought that it was absurd to even imagine Maia doing any kind of work, considering her physical state: 'We have tried to give her jobs in the past, when she was much better than now. She always tends to get worse physically once she starts working, and what do you do then? She literally burned whatever idea we came up with'. The endocrinologist noted how Maia, whose current BMI was 12, was already at a point of immediate risk to her life: 'A cold or a flu could be enough for her to die'. Eventually, the clinical director decided that although it was obvious to everyone that Maia was very ill, assigning those tasks to her amounted to 'a last, paradoxical intervention' to see if she finally turned towards 'the direction of health'. Arguing against this decision, Maia's nutritionist observed that Maia lacked 'the minimum motivation necessary for treatment', and that other patients with similar behaviours had been discharged because that kind of treatment was not seen as appropriate: 'Why haven't we discharged her? She is putting us at the limits of our capacities, and there is so much frustration among us. Is it possible that there is no alternative to keeping her here?' When the external psychotherapist asked why this case was different from the many other uncollaborative patients that the treatment team had had to deal with, the clinical director replied that it was because Maia was 'from here' (i.e., she was a resident in the region where Il Giardino is located): whereas other patients at some point had to be discharged and returned to their local outpatient services because their authorisation had an expiry date, with her this was not the case. It was also difficult to send her to a residential facility in a different region, because local health authorities tend to withhold authorisations for extra-regional treatment if the patient's region of residence has a comparable treatment facility. Moreover, that had already been done a few times in the past, without long-lasting improvements.

The 'crazy plan' was implemented for a few weeks, but Maia kept losing weight. As the reader knows from the opening of the chapter, she was eventually admitted to hospital for intravenous nutrition. However, that was not a solution to the problem that the treatment team had posed to the external supervisor. The hospital admission would last for a few weeks, after which Maia was supposed to return to a residential facility. Many team members at Il Giardino felt that Maia should be sent to a different facility upon discharge from the hospital, because they were 'too emotionally involved' and therefore 'unable to help her anymore' (coordinator). Others found the mere idea unthinkable for the same reason: 'We can't abandon her in such a difficult situation. We are the only meaningful relationships she has, her only family left' (educator Flavia). The clinical director herself – although she agreed that treatment in the facility was 'not working' – was very resistant to the idea of moving Maia somewhere else. At one point, she proposed to send Maia to a different residential facility that had opened a few years earlier as a 'spin-off' of Il Giardino in a region nearby. Other professionals saw that as a clear sign that the director wanted to do something for Maia but could not stand the idea of 'entrusting strangers with her care'. The team of the facility that she had in mind was in fact mostly composed of professionals who had previously worked or been trained at Il Giardino: 'But this is exactly why it wouldn't work. Most of them know Maia and have already been involved in her care here. There would be dysfunctional dynamics all the same', a team member pointed out. What Maia needed, most professionals held, was to be admitted to a residential facility 'where nobody knows her'. Only this way, it was felt, could she be treated 'as strictly as any other patient' and have some chance of getting better.

Just as Davis (2012: 221–23) pointed out in her analysis of psychiatric treatment in Greece, the dilemmas generated by patients breaking the rules of treatment can turn into 'tedious, repetitive, inconclusive debates' that amplify professionals' responsibilities towards patients, as they implicate both patients' survival and the professionals' capacity to help, often producing 'dependencies that are nearly impossible to dismantle'. In Maia's case, the difficulty of dismantling dependencies had to do with professional care being entangled with kinship care. In her account of psychiatric institutions in India, Pinto (2014) argues that the clinics are not so much a zone of social abandonment in which the normal is reasserted by keeping the unhuman confined there (as in Biehl 2005), but a place where people with very human difficulties inherently tied to kinship end up when kinship ties fall to pieces. In the eating disorder facility, and especially in the case of Maia's 'abandonment', perhaps what is defined and reasserted is the ideal nature of those kinship ties that are seen to have broken. When this reconfiguration fails, the patient is bound to stay in the clinic. But unlike Pinto's interlocutors, Maia does not want to get out – there is not 'an out' with other relationships for her anymore. In fact, she is scared of being discharged and of being abandoned once again, this time by her 'second family'.

After weeks of discussions, Maia was eventually sent to a different residential facility in northern Italy. The clinical director of Il Giardino knew the treatment team there, as the two facilities had been in a partnership for a while. But the other team – with a couple of exceptions – had not met Maia before, and that was seen to be enough. Here we see an interesting dynamic at work: the reparenting model of treatment, which is supposed to be a key ingredient for recovery, becomes problematic when the time a patient spends in the residential facility goes beyond the standard few months. In Maia's case this lasted for years, with the result that the treatment team literally substituted for Maia's family in her care. We have seen in Chapter 4 how Maia's exclusion from kinship care was understood, if not justified, by constructing her as incapable of recovering – as so many years of illness and treatment appeared to have shown. However, this was not enough for professionals to constitute her as unworthy of that care. In fact, the professionals made up for it while she was in treatment. In Maia's case, the boundaries between professional care and family care had thus become blurred, and professional care had suddenly found itself immersed in the same issues that are typically ascribed by the treatment team to family care: excessive 'emotional involvement', a subsequent inability to impose the rules necessary to tackle the symptoms of eating disorders, and exhaustion due to seeing that whatever one does to help, nothing seems to work. Once the treatment team realised this, they were eventually resigned to the idea that they had to do what patients' families have to do when their children are admitted to Il Giardino: delegate their care and entrust professional strangers with it.

One month after Maia was sent to the new facility, the director, the coordinator and four other members of the treatment team of Il Giardino drove for more than six hours each way to see her for the allowed one-hour visit. One of them, when telling me about the trip, noticed that although Maia was 'full of joy' and said she 'thought she was dreaming' when she saw them appearing in her room, the visit was probably something that had made *them* 'feel better'. The fact that Maia's family had not visited her yet added to the feeling that they were 'more of a family to Maia than her parents'.

The chronicity of eating disorders is certainly co-produced by lack of resources and of proper treatment, including stays in residential facilities that are felt to be too short. But the ethnographic material analysed here also suggests that one key working mechanism of treatment – i.e., family-based care – is strongly tied to the very fact that residential treatment *is* short term. One would need to see the extent to which the time patients spend in residential treatment could be helpfully extended before one starts observing the (unintentional) harmful dynamics that ended up characterising Maia's treatment path. Maia's case highlights that the temporal dimension of care can have unsettling effects on care practices. What should have been a 'transformational time' for Maia – admission to residential treatment – had gradually become 'everyday time' (see Baraitser 2017: 4), as the care she received did not generate any steady movement towards recovery. In Maia's story we see care taking the form of professionals waiting, delaying, enduring, returning, maintaining, preserving, remaining, to the point that time for Maia, and for the treatment team caring for her, looked akin to 'a circle with no rim'(ibid.). Although time is suspended, however, time is also passing, and with devastating effects. When the materiality of Maia's body starts deviating from the circle with no rim, but in the direction opposite to the one professionals are striving for, this care without ending is interrupted because it is recognised as leading to Maia's death. Long-term care in the same residential facility in this case complicates what otherwise allows clinical detachment: the treatment team ends up literally taking the place of the patient's family, with professional care and family care mixing 'too much' with one another. This was framed as the main cause of treatment failure for Maia. But an 'excessive' duration of residential treatment is not the only factor that puts into crisis the pillars of the centre's approach. In what follows, we will see that another kind of patient shakes the foundations of what it means, for professionals, to effect treatment.

When 'You Can't Take It All Away': Questioning the Dispensability of the Eating Disorder

> *Sometimes, the eating disorder protects the patient from another disorder that is underneath. In those cases, you can't take the eating disorder away. When there is only the eating disorder, one should thank God.*
>
> —President of the association Franca, interview, June 2019

One morning in May 2019, during the weekly staff meeting, the treatment team seemed to have become stuck while discussing the case of Giada, a sixteen-year-old girl from a nearby region who had been admitted to the residential facility one month earlier – for the second time, after a three-month admission the previous summer. Giada had been admitted with a 'double diagnosis' of severe anorexia nervosa and obsessive compulsive disorder (OCD).[12] Tessa, Giada's psychotherapist, was trying to convey to the rest of the team that they were at an impasse with her:

> It's becoming increasingly clear that Giada is at risk of psychosis, from which the eating disorder protects her. Her nutritionist and I have therefore agreed that it is best to leave the eating disorder there. We will provide Giada with just the necessary balance that would keep her away from the risk of death and allow her to have a decent quality of life when she goes home.

'Leaving the eating disorder there' sounded to the anthropologist like the opposite of what, until that moment, had appeared to be a key aim of treatment. But Tessa seemed to be saying that treating the eating disorder in this case would harm the patient, so the aim of treatment needed to be reframed. And yet even this reframed plan was proving increasingly difficult. Giada had been losing weight since she had been admitted, so her nutritionist had to slightly increase her meals – in practice, one more rusk for breakfast and one teaspoon of sugar in the tea for snack. This had generated 'a total crisis' in Giada, who had started scratching herself and crushing her head against a wall. Tessa kept explaining:

> She calmed down only after one hour of one-to-one discussion with the nutritionist. We feel completely stuck. I mean, you should have seen that crisis ... remember that she is that kind of patient who jumps from the stairs landing on her knees, and that she had jumped from a window when she was thirteen. We feel we can't add anything to her meal plan, but she keeps losing weight. We are basically facing an impossible choice: do we risk broken knees or extreme underweight? How can one decide?

Irma, the nutritionist who had been supervising dinner the previous day, agreed that Giada was 'at serious risk of a self-harming act'. She had had a very bad crisis during dinner because she had received tuna like the previous day,[13] and whatever alternative the nutritionist offered her, it seemed not to be OK: 'She seemed to be in a state of total despair, she kept biting her hands ... I would urge everyone not to insist with her during meals, for God's sake'. The team agreed that the only way to go forward with Giada was by doing 'extremely small and gradual changes' to her meal plan, but that one should not even try to 'take away' the eating disorder, because Giada was 'too fragile'. During subsequent team meetings, her therapists kept reporting that they were barely managing to keep Giada in a state of 'precarious psychological compensation' (psychotherapist Tessa).

Giada was not the first nor the only case of 'double diagnosis' at Il Giardino: several other patients were presented as displaying an eating disorder 'on top' of other (supposedly more severe) psychiatric conditions, ranging from OCD to borderline personality disorder, depression and dissociative disorders. In most of these cases of so-called 'comorbidity' – literally meaning 'with (another) illness' – the second, more severe and 'deeper' psychiatric condition was reported to be 'emerging' while the eating disorder symptoms (food restriction, food rituals, hyperactivity etc.) started subsiding. In these cases, the consensus among professionals was that the eating disorder could not be treated 'completely' – that 'some of it' had to be left there for the sake of the patient's well-being, because treating it completely would mean 'making the more severe disorder explode'.

In addition to the notion that the eating disorder is a psychopathology that assumes the form of a 'second self' which tries to take over the patient's 'very self' (see Chapter 2), we find here the view that in some cases the eating disorder is only the 'first layer' of psychopathology within a patient. These two conceptions of the self – external versus internal and an internal self made of 'layers' – exist side by side and are related. The eating disorder is externalised for the purpose of treatment: it is framed to patients and families as something 'external' to the self that became 'internal'. By virtue of this, the process can be reversed because the eating disorder is theoretically separable from the patient's self. We have seen, however, that some professionals also talk of the eating disorder as the embodiment of the 'untold parts of the patient', therefore as something that is *already within* a patient – that does not come 'from outside'. As the psychotherapist Mauro put it:

> When people say things like: 'It isn't you, it's the disorder that makes you do or think this ...' well ... it's like saying: 'Not only are you dissociated, but you are double, and when you are that other part, you don't even recognise it'. It's a part that acts without you noticing it, so there is a severe dissociation.

Mauro's critical view of the externalisation rhetoric seems to suggest that mental disorders should be framed, instead, as if emerging from the inside and going back inside during remission – as if they were all already there, inside the 'body-self'.

In patients with a 'comorbidity', the eating disorder thus becomes something that the patient's self has developed as a protection from a deeper, more severe psychopathology. These cases are therefore seen as 'particularly difficult', with the right balance between 'physical' and 'mental' health harder to establish. Sometimes, as in Giada's case, a second disorder – typically OCD – is framed as not only lying 'just underneath' the eating disorder, but also as itself covering a third, even deeper layer of what is usually characterised as 'psychosis'. In such cases, it is not infrequent to hear professionals (usually psychiatrists or psychotherapists) warn colleagues 'not to touch' (i.e., not even to attempt to treat) a patient's OCD, because by doing so they might run the risk of making patients 'turn towards a schizoid disorder'. Nevertheless, in many of these cases 'peeling off' the most debilitating symptoms of the eating disorder and 'leaving the second disorder there' seems to be possible at least. Giada's case was different in that the 'room for manoeuvre' on the eating disorder was much smaller. Her eating disorder seemed impossible to touch without consequences 'on the deeper layer': 'She is one of those who *need* the eating disorder' – the nutritionist explained – 'We can't take it away. For us nutritionists it's very difficult because we feel the urgency of the low weight, and yet we have to restrain ourselves'. The nutritionist felt she had to go against what her job would tell her to do after seeing the effects that increasing the meal plan had on Giada's 'mental stability'.

For these reasons, Giada's case was also brought to the monthly supervision with the external psychotherapist. Giada was presented as a patient with a 'very low tolerance to stress' and an 'absolute inability to modulate emotions: fear and anger are either not felt or felt uncontrollably'. As reconstructed by her psychotherapist and by her nutritionist, Giada's issues with food had started when she was twelve, when her weight had quickly dropped to 25 kg and she was admitted to the children's ward of the local hospital. From that moment, she alternated periods during which she was doing slightly better but would still mostly do home schooling and periods of severe 'relapses' followed by other admissions to hospital and feeding through a nasogastric tube. In July 2018, the day I started fieldwork, she had just been discharged from the children's hospital in her region and admitted to Il Giardino for the first time. 'Hyperactivity' was reported as her only compensatory behaviour alongside 'food restriction': she would walk outside, and at home, with a pedometer, and calculate the calories of everything she ate. She seemed to be a 'typical case of anorexia' (psychotherapist Tessa).

Things had started appearing 'suspicious' – her psychotherapist reported to the rest of team during the first staff meeting since Giada's second admission – when Giada seemed to be accepting all the food she was given after only ten days in the residential facility, without apparent crises. She had in fact gradually regained weight, and her only moments of crisis were related to anxiety for her return to school and fear of falling behind. She was discharged after three months, and during the following weeks as an outpatient her

BMI reached the 'normal threshold' of 18.5 for the first time. She had started going out with friends and had gone back to gymnastics. However, during the Christmas vacation, Giada reported that she had started having 'bad thoughts' about not being able to keep up with school, so she had stopped going to the gym and out with friends altogether. She had started restricting food again and walking a lot, and had gradually lost 7 kg. Eventually, Giada had to stop going to school, and at that point the local services contacted Il Giardino and urged them to admit her again.

During this second admission, it became clear to the psychotherapist Tessa that, although at that time Giada had only received a formal second diagnosis of OCD, she might be 'developing a psychotic disorder underneath', which would more clearly emerge with age but could explode 'at any moment':

> I have the feeling that she is really on the edge of developing a psychotic disorder, because from what she tells me she doesn't seem to have any internal containment. She seems to have a desert without any kind of boundaries. What I perceive is that she needs to control not only her body, but everything that happens inside her. She found in the eating disorder the way to control this chaotic void that she feels inside herself. She really needs a context that can keep her whole. I am trying to provide her with some boundaries, and the protective context here is working. But it's very difficult to make the family understand this.

Here we see once again how the patient's family is perceived and constructed by the treatment team as key to the patient's recovery. When the external psychotherapist asked Giada's therapists to describe her parents, everyone agreed that they *seemed* perfect: well dressed, always calm, never arguing nor getting angry, and with caring and supportive manners between one another and with Giada; but that 'underneath' they were 'angry with the world' for what had happened to their family through Giada's illness, and were constantly opposing and 'boycotting' the treatment team's suggestions regarding what Giada needed to recover. They were characterised as apparently incapable of understanding the severity of their daughter's condition and the risks that she was facing for her health.

Professionals were particularly startled by the way Giada's parents had reportedly reacted when Giada had jumped out of a window on the second floor of their house, when she was thirteen. She was at home on her own that afternoon, while her parents and sister were attending a family counselling session which was part of Giada's outpatient treatment path. After jumping and apparently landing without too much damage, Giada had gone back into the house and had called her parents to tell them what had happened. When they came back, after assessing that she only had 'a few scratches', nothing else followed: 'They didn't even bring her to a hospital, nothing! They said that because Giada is a gymnast, she knows how to land from high jumps without hurting herself' (psychotherapist Tessa). The same approach was reported by Giada's parents on another occasion when Giada acted in a way that was considered 'self-harming' by the professionals: she had repeatedly jumped from the top of a staircase and landed on her knees after a food-related argument during a meal at home, provoking severe bruises. When Tessa had asked them how they felt about those behaviours, Giada's parents had claimed that they were now 'used to it'. Moreover, they seemed to be very resistant to the professionals' suggestion that Giada would have benefited from changing school – moving from her current, competitive school to a private, less competitive school with special support. The reason behind this opposition was located by the treatment team in the fact that both Giada's parents had managed to reach a better economic situation and quality of life than the one they were born into thanks to studying in extremely competitive schools. In the reconstruction of the professionals, Giada's parents were worried that without a competitive school they would undermine Giada's future, and that Giada would later blame them for letting that happen. They also seemed really concerned that Giada risked failing to become 'autonomous enough' and capable of fending for herself, because in the future she would not have all the support she currently had. The school arrangements that Giada's parents wanted for her could be said to sit along a transgenerational continuum of kinship care: Giada's parents offered care in their own terms, even if the school they wanted for her was experienced by Giada, and seen by the professionals, as harmful (cf. Mody 2020: 196–98).

The treatment team reported frustration at the fact that, notwithstanding the understandable reasoning behind their position, Giada's parents could not see that Giada was 'really on the edge of exploding into a full-blown psychotic disorder', and there was no way this could be prevented without such a strong network of 'support and containment'. Giada's psychotherapist could not believe that her parents were still unmovable regarding the school matter, after she had explicitly told them that Giada, even with a heavy daily pharmacological treatment consisting of an antidepressant, an antipsychotic and lithium, risked a severe psychotic break: 'They are in complete denial, and I don't know what to do with them anymore. If they don't support our treatment plan, we can't do much'.

The external psychotherapist, after hearing further stories about Giada's family, concluded that Giada's condition was 'the result of the costs that her parents paid to reach the socio-economic position they reached, and of all the impulses that they had to suppress along the way, which ended up channelled into Giada – lives paid dearly at the level of the body'. Giada's parents, in the psychotherapist's reconstruction of their life, had to rigidly control reality by suppressing 'impulses' and 'excesses' to obtain a good social position. These 'suppressed impulses' were now 'inside Giada', who herself kept controlling them and suppressing them 'in her body', but sometimes exploded. Here again we see that patients' parents are not so much blamed for being the cause of their daughters' conditions. Rather, as we have seen in previous chapters, they are mostly constructed as victims themselves, as unwittingly contributing to the development of the patient's illness. What they are blamed for is the refusal to question themselves, and the lack of support to the treatment team.

Eventually, Giada was discharged in September 2019 and sent back to the local services in her region. The team felt it was impossible 'to keep working on Giada' without her parents backing up their strategies, as every individual session was now monopolised by anxiety about the return to school. Giada's psychotherapist agreed that, with the family constantly boycotting their ideas, nothing could be done. Here we see the treatment team unwillingly giving up. But the 'real failure' perceived by the treatment team was not so much located in the 'not doing' that Giada's comorbidity required with regards to her eating disorder. Although dealing with that was difficult for the professionals and made them question the aim of their work, the impossibility of really treating Giada's eating disorder had pushed the treatment team to look for novel forms of care – to focus their attention on Giada's family and school, while addressing her eating disorder symptoms as little as possible to keep her 'in balance'. We see here how 'not doing' and 'not intervening', rather than being always forms of clinical neglect and, therefore, of biomedical failure, can become a creative, deliberative, complementary and valuable aspect of treatment (see Borgstrom, Cohn and Driessen 2020). Moreover, doing 'nothing' is here reframed as 'something', because doing nothing is very hard to do for these professionals – it requires effort. Here 'not doing' is necessary to facilitate a 'good life with the illness' because life without the eating disorder would be even worse. 'Not doing' is therefore a specific act of treatment shaped by a specific patient configuration in which the object of 'doing' needs to be shifted from the eating disorder to 'what is around it': family, school and so on. However, these novel forms of care can themselves fail sometimes. What the professionals mostly perceived as 'failure' was the impossibility of enacting those alternative forms of care: Giada's family, and her parents' decision about Giada's school, ended up being 'untouchable' – unchangeable – like her eating disorder.

In her account of eating disorder treatment in the United States, Lester (2009: 284) argues that the 'double diagnosis' of borderline personality disorder allows clinicians to make sense of their impossibility to treat certain patients, and to feel OK discharging them. That, crucially, also has to do with the fact that in the context of managed care patients' lack of weight gain during treatment is – paradoxically – a key reason to withdraw insurance coverage. Clinicians in Lester's context, therefore, could never do what the treatment team of Il Giardino had decided to do with Giada. Nevertheless, what is interesting in Giada's case is that a focus on her double or triple diagnosis does not result in the professionals reconciling with the limits of their care. On the contrary, it makes them experience their limits in a way that is even more difficult to bear. The alternative forms of care they come up with do not point to any reconciliation with those limits.

Conclusion

The ethnographic material in this chapter suggests that 'failure' and 'success' are not simple binary opposites, nor are 'doing' and 'not doing' (Borgstrom, Cohn and Driessen 2020). The social function of failure emerges in that even if what is seen as failure is inherent to the system of care, it is made to appear as if it lies outside in order to bring a sense of coherence within (Carrol et al. 2017: 16): in Giada's case the failure to treat the eating disorder is framed as inevitable by professionals because of an additional, posited third 'agent' that is part of the patient's self (the more severe psychiatric disorder but also, on closer inspection, her uncollaborative family). In Maia's case the reason for failure becomes, in a sense, a category error (ibid.): family care becomes mixed with professional care, suggesting that when things go wrong the cause rests in the border-crossing, in practice and matter 'out of place' (à la Douglas 1966). In both instances, however, failure becomes, somehow, productive, because it motivates professionals to try different ways to care.

We have seen how 'failure' in these cases puts into question two of the pillars at the basis of treatment: Maia's story questions the model of family-based care for those 'chronic patients' who require more time in residential treatment than the standard few months. For those people, the kinship care enacted by the professionals might shift from being a partial and temporary therapeutic tool to assuming the total and permanent aspects of 'real' family care – including the 'dysfunctional ones' that are seen to prevent treatment from working by impairing the professionals' clinical detachment. Giada's case instead sheds light on the limits of the centre's construction of the eating disorder as a part of the patient's self that can be dispensed with. Here the removal of the eating disorder is seen as potentially harmful because it would let 'deeper and more serious disorders' come to the surface and 'completely dismantle the patient's self'. The eating disorder thus emerges as having a protective function. In a way, professionals here recognise the patient's eating disorder as a 'self-care practice': they do not agree with it, but they feel that the patient would be worse without it.[14]

Ethnographically, the treatment team acts with a desire to materialise a potentiality in the patients' bodies, but is thwarted in this. Two temporal scales and two kinds of bodies are at play here: on the one hand, there is the biomedical body and its temporalities of looming death; on the other hand, there is the body-self acquired through transgenerational family histories which can render it unresponsive to acts of care that would normally work. The disjuncture between the two creates a space of failure, but this failure is ultimately generative of further care work. In Maia's case, signs of failure prompted professionals to question their work with the patient and to realise that the relationship of care between her and the treatment team had changed over time, reaching a point that made it unhelpful. This, in turn, called for coming up with strategies 'out of the box' – the gate, the wheelchair, the 'crazy proposal' – that were not part of standard treatment, but a matter of continuously 'tinkering' with the resources that were available (Mol, Moser and Pols 2010). When it became clear that none of the tinkering within the facility would work, a new kind of care took shape in the delegation of Maia's treatment to a different team. This was not a case of careless abandonment driven by exhaustion, although the professionals *were* exhausted. It was a difficult and long-resisted decision that required effort and 'keeping emotions at bay' (clinical director). Similarly, Giada's relapse after the first admission generated more attentive care and experimenting with a different kind of work: limiting the physical damage of the eating disorder without 'taking it away' and shifting any intervening practice to what was *around* the disorder. In both cases, the generative work of failure highlights what is seen to really need more care. Problems with kinship care emerge as the reason for the need to delegate care to someone else. In Giada's case because her family care does not match and does not support professional care. In Maia's case because professional care becomes 'too much' like family care and unwittingly incorporates its 'dysfunctions' – its inability to stay clinically detached and impose the necessary rules for treatment.

Notes

* An earlier and shorter version of this chapter was originally published as: Sciolli, Giulia. 2023. 'When the Clinic Becomes Home: On the Limits of Kinship Care in an Eating Disorder Treatment Centre in Italy', *Anthropology & Medicine* 30(3): 262–77.

1. See Berkman, Lohr and Bulik 2007; Crisp 2006; Franko and Keel 2006; Herzog and Greenwood 2000.
2. 'Chronicity' indicates that something, such as pain or an illness, continues for a long time. In medicine, the 'long time' is often assumed to be the duration of the patient's life, which means that the condition in question is seen as 'incurable' and only 'manageable' to some degree (Smith-Morris 2010).
3. For example, see Feudtner (2015) on type 1 diabetes, and Kendal and Hill (2010) on AIDS.
4. More on these circumstances in the Conclusion.
5. In his account of treatment failure for a man's illness in Papua New Guinea, anthropologist Gilbert Lewis (2000) poses the question of what it means when we say that treatment has failed: what is it that fails, exactly? The answer, he suggests, depends on the different ways in which the aim of treatment is locally imagined. In his case, the complex healing ritual put together by the village can be said to have failed to save a man's life, but it did not fail to make the whole process of being ill and dying meaningful, and thus more bearable, to his kin. Lewis points out how the temporality of the illness profoundly shapes the way treatment is imagined, organised and enacted: an acute illness may require a sudden and unreflective response, which is not the same as a long-lasting condition. Anxiety about, hope for and belief in treatment test social ties in different ways. In an interesting parallel with eating disorder treatment, in Lewis' field site the man's illness is framed as an issue of possession

by a spirit that is seen as needing to leave the person for recovery to occur – and its persistence, eventually leading to death, is framed as the result of the spirit failing to depart.

6. This is because, as we have seen in Chapters 1 and 4, within the Italian national health service the central government defines the general framework and core benefits package, but each region manages its own regional health service.
7. See, for instance, in Italy Palazzo 2020a,b and Giancipoli 2024; in the UK Stevens 2020 and Marsh 2021.
8. For instance, Brodwin (2011, 2013), Han (2012) and Stevenson (2014) have criticised the employment of neoliberal ideologies of autonomy in care contexts; Biehl (2005) and Glenn (2010) have highlighted how care is often entangled with State violence; and Street (2014) and Ticktin (2011) how unequal practices of care are sometimes sustained through political and economic infrastructures.
9. Or in managed care contexts like the United States (see Lester 2019).
10. See Chapters 1 and 2.
11. We will see in the next section what this means, through comparison with its opposite.
12. Obsessive compulsive disorder (OCD) is defined in the *DSM-5* as being characterised by the presence of 'obsessions and/or compulsions'. Obsessions are described as 'recurrent and persistent thoughts, urges, or impulses that are experienced as intrusive and unwanted, and that in most individuals cause marked anxiety or distress'; compulsions are described as 'repetitive behaviors (e.g., hand washing, ordering, checking) or mental acts (e.g., praying, counting, repeating words silently) that the individual feels driven to perform in response to an obsession or according to rules that must be applied rigidly' (American Psychiatric Association 2013).
13. We have already encountered Giada dealing with tuna in Chapter 4, and on that occasion the nutritionist had managed to deal with her crisis and make Giada eat her food.
14. It is worth noting how the patient's eating disorder is 'legitimised' as a self-care practice when it is seen to protect the patient from another diagnosed mental disorder, but not when it is seen to do the same for experiences that cannot be categorised in medical terms, like dealing with painful family dynamics, for example.

Conclusion
The Social That Hurts

In 2013 a documentary filmed in an outpatient eating disorder service in Rome was released with the title *Ciò che Mi Nutre Mi Distrugge* (What Nourishes Me Destroys Me).[1] The 'what' stands for 'food' in this documentary, and the title points to the complicated relationship that people diagnosed with an eating disorder have with food in their daily lives. This book has shown, however, that when one talks about eating disorders the 'what' stands for a lot more than food. We have seen that it includes kinship care and a wider 'social' which infiltrates into treatment practices. And that it is not just that what 'nourishes' can 'destroy', but that the ambivalent factors seen to generate harm can be tinkered with through treatment practices so that their mortiferous effects can be avoided.

I first heard about 'refeeding syndrome' a few weeks into my fieldwork, during a weekly staff meeting. Roberta, aged seventeen, had just been admitted earlier in the morning, and the endocrinologist was briefing the rest of the team after her medical examination: 'This patient is extremely malnourished. She has been basically surviving on water, apple juice and fat-free yogurt for the last six months. We need to be really careful about refeeding syndrome with her, and keep watching out for any symptom'. Noticing the bewilderment in the eyes of the anthropologist and of the two newly arrived psychology interns, the endocrinologist paused to address our lost gazes: refeeding syndrome – she explained – is the medical term for a condition that can occur when nutrition is initiated in a severely malnourished patient. During prolonged fasting, she continued, the patient's body undergoes 'hormonal and metabolic changes' as a way to prevent muscle breakdown – a kind of 'automatic survival mechanism', she said. When the patient starts being 'refed' – whether through food by mouth, by 'enteral nutrition' (through a nasogastric tube), or by 'parenteral nutrition' (through an intravenous tube that brings the nutrients directly into the bloodstream) – the patient's newly adjusted 'metabolic balance' is disrupted, and the consequences can be severe. Using the language of biochemistry, the endocrinologist went on to say that the hallmark feature of refeeding syndrome consists of 'electrolyte imbalances', including 'hypophosphatemia' (low phosphorous in the blood), 'hypomagnesium' (low magnesium) and 'hypokalemia' (low potassium). The clinical features of refeeding syndrome are seen to occur as a result of the 'functional deficits' of these electrolytes and of the rapid change in metabolic rate that occurs because of sudden refeeding. Other warning signs are 'blood sugar fluctuations', 'vitamin deficiencies' and 'irregular heartbeat'. If these symptoms occur, the endocrinologist stressed, they need to be addressed immediately, as they can lead to neurological and respiratory issues as well as death from cardiac failure. It is therefore fundamental, she concluded, that refeeding occurs 'slowly and gradually', and with the support of phosphorous, magnesium and potassium supplements.

Here we see how 'nutrition' – the food that patients are given during treatment to keep them alive – can turn out to be potentially deadly if it is not given gradually and in small doses at the right time. Throughout the book we have seen that something similar holds for the specific form of kinship care that patients are thought to need, and which they have to be 'refed' by professionals. It is important to stress that for the treatment team this parallel is not just a metaphor: during that same staff meeting, the psychiatrist who had 'evaluated' Roberta pointed out how Roberta's eating disorder was not surprising given the context she had been living in. The girl, the psychiatrist explained, had grown up in a 'symbiotic relationship' with her mother, caused in turn by a situation of 'abandonment' due to her mother being a single parent with a job that kept her away from home all day:

> Her mother works as a cook and is away from early morning to late at night during the week, so Roberta has always been alone during mealtimes. In the weekend, when her mother is at home, she is so tired that she never cooks. Before the onset of the disorder they would spend the weekend by staying mostly in bed together, including while eating.

This has been a common theme running through the book: things that nurture – food and family – can also kill.

I started Chapter 2 of this book with the words of a young patient who had just been admitted to Il Giardino because a medical examination had declared her weight to be dangerously low and her life to be at risk without a professional intervention. The words that she used to describe her life before admission, however, pointed to a set of practices, of things that she would *do* every day to feel *better*. What professionals call 'eating disorder' was not a disorder in her framing: it was a way to cope with and move through life. The implications of this framing have carried through these pages a recurring conundrum: how do professionals care for people who frame their practices as self-care practices – and who therefore do not necessarily perceive themselves to be in need of professional care? In what follows I sum up what my ethnographic material suggests on this and on related questions. I then move on to take a focus on how this complexity plays out in patients' lives after discharge from Il Giardino, which, finally, helps us to rethink the relations between bodies and diseases and food and kinship.

Beyond the Body Multiple: The Multiplicity of Good Care

We have seen that patients and professionals at Il Giardino – and, within each category, different kinds of patients and professionals – each do 'the body' and 'the eating disorder' differently (see Mol 2002). For those who become patients, the eating disorder is a way to better cope with life by reshaping their body according to their will and control; but it is also a way to make themselves seen by their families and, through that, to receive care *from them* or paradoxically to care *for them*. For the professionals, the eating disorder is a pathology that has to be treated within the realm of medicine, a deviation from how 'normal', 'healthy' bodies and minds should 'function'. But within this second reality, there is more multiplicity: for endocrinologists and nutritionists the eating disorder is a pathology of the body whose symptoms are mostly caused by malnutrition – and which therefore can only be solved by refeeding, without which psychotherapy is pointless. For psychiatrists and psychologists it is a pathology of the mind, whereas malnutrition and its physical effects are the 'symptom of something else', the external form that 'inner mental distress' takes; it is a 'paradoxical act of self-care' chosen by patients to deal with problems that they feel they cannot manage. For philosophical counsellors it is a 'disorder of identity' whereby the eating disorder gives a person who does not know who she is an illusory answer, 'becoming an indivisible part of the patient's self'. In practice, therefore, the eating disorder and the body of the patient could be said to be more than one, but these different bodies and eating disorders are not fragmented. They are all intertwined and brought together in the practical meetings and discussions of treatment. Although the 'roots' of the eating disorder are framed as residing in the mind, the practicality of malnourishment in the body is seen in turn to play a key role in the worsening and 'crystallisation' of the disorder, as in a feedback loop. Even if there are tensions within these various bodies and disorders, they therefore depend on one another (cf. Mol 2002: 5).

Coordination is not always smooth, however. Mol (2002: 8) argues that in the case of atherosclerosis in the Netherlands the 'technicity of intervening' is more important than the 'consistency of facts', and that the work of treatment may go on as long as each of the 'variants' of the condition takes the other into account (ibid.: 116). She argues that 'a single patient tends to be supplied, if not with a single disease, then at least with a single treatment decision' (ibid.: 88). My book is an example that this is not always the case: at Il Giardino, the 'psy sciences' and the 'body sciences' do act on different fronts and take each other's 'eating disorder' into account, but sometimes their ontologies and the practices that follow end up clashing. In Chapter 6 we have seen how in some cases the treatment for 'malnutrition' – gradual increase in the meal plan – endangers the 'psychological integrity' of the patient. Here the condition that the endocrinologist and the nutritionist would treat does not match the condition that the psychotherapist and the psychiatrist would treat, resulting in an impasse. It is not only the singularity of the disease that is an accomplishment of the work of coordination, therefore, but also the singularity of treatment.

Different ontologies come with different ways of doing 'the good': when a patient is seen to be severely malnourished and at the same time on the verge of 'psychotic fragmentation', professionals find themselves stuck, facing an impossible choice: 'do we risk broken knees or extreme underweight? How can one decide?' In each case, the 'dis' of dis-ease is different – malnutrition, obsessive and intrusive thoughts, lack of kin care – and therefore the ideals that orientate treatment practices are different too, and can clash. Defining what is 'good', 'worse' and 'better' for each patient does not precede practice, but forms part of it – perhaps the most difficult part. Professionals can only try through 'small steps' to increase a patient's meal plan in a way that does not generate a psychotic crisis, but this requires getting as close to the limit as possible. It is a process that generates ambivalences, disagreements, insecurities and conflicts, even more so because the stakes are high. This means that 'good and bad' are never settled, and professionals have to continuously deal with new twists and complications (cf. Mol 2008: 75–76). Which brings us to the issue of what Mol (2002: 124) calls 'switching registers': professionals at Il Giardino are asked to turn their work from intervening in a malnourished body to intervening in a person's life and that of her family. Among these twists and complications, in fact, is that what happens in the treatment centre struggles to reach the world outside. This emerges in full force when patients are discharged.

Staying Afloat after Discharge

> *The body is not always at 100%. The body is not always strong and energetic. The body is not always free from pain or discomfort. Listening is essential to understand how to act in daily life. Resting and slowing down are part of this 'listening'. Unfortunately, we live in a society where slowing down, let alone stopping, is not allowed, even if we are physically or mentally unwell. Every day, the body sends us clear and distinct signals, and most of the time we are only capable of putting them on silent mode, suppressing the symptoms by taking a painkiller and diving headfirst back into our endless days, because we cannot afford to stop producing. But how functional is this? Thanks to the journey of growth and inner listening that I have been undertaking over the past few years ... I am learning that truly listening to those signals means nothing more than HEALING MYSELF. Because the body already knows everything.*

> *It knows how to recover and regain its energy and psychophysical health. You just need to listen to it. You just need to slow down, to stop. This involves: listening to what you feel like eating (and especially eating when you are hungry, without measuring portions); adjusting physical activity according to your energy levels and any pain or discomfort; and, above all, it involves letting go of what the others say, of what today's society wants us to believe is right to do ... because only by listening to ourselves can we find health and balance.*
>
> —Giada's Instagram post, December 2024, my translation

This is what Giada posted on her Instagram about five years after being discharged from Il Giardino,[2] under a photo depicting her in a yoga pose. Giada is now twenty-three years old; she lives at home with her parents and sister and has just finished university in her hometown in central Italy. She practises yoga, often going to retreats in the wilderness, walks a lot in nature, goes out with friends, travels, and does some volunteering work. In 2020, about one year after being discharged from Il Giardino, she published a book about her experience of illness, treatment and, as she calls it, 'rebirth'.[3] In the book she recounts how she has undergone numerous hospitalisations, and, because of her eating disorder, she was unable to experience her adolescence fully. Now, however, after her latest treatment at Il Giardino in 2019, she says she feels 'more aware and ready to face the real world again'. After years of struggles, Giada writes, she is proud of herself and of what she achieved, and says she wants to help all those who, like her, have fought 'to the bone' against their illness. In fact, another post on her Instagram proudly shows a picture of her talking to high school kids about her experience of suffering and recovering from anorexia, as part of an awareness campaign for schools in her region. Giada's Instagram is also filled with pictures of her walking in the countryside, of her studying, of the food she cooks and eats – all vegan, mostly locally sourced and homemade – and of some details of the furnishings at the local mental health centre where she keeps going for outpatient treatment and check-ups – sometimes a clock, sometimes a lamp, sometimes a sofa in the waiting room. Most of her pictures include a description which tells her followers how she felt in those moments, including in the moments, which she writes still occur, when she feels 'anxious' and 'not in control'. Her relationship with food, with anxiety, with control, is still complex and filled with difficulties at times, but these difficulties 'do not control her anymore', she says, and do not prevent her from living and enjoying life. Notwithstanding the worries of the treatment team of Il Giardino when they found themselves having to discharge her (see Chapter 6), it seems that the care Giada and her family received there not only allowed her to start recovering, but also gave her the tools that she still uses today to 'stay in balance', as she says.

The same can be said for Lisa, whom we met in Chapters 2 and 3. Lisa is now thirty-four and works as an editor. She lives with her partner and her cat, on the outskirts of a big city in northern Italy, which is her hometown.

Together they travel, go to concerts, do things with friends. She bought a used car and drives it when she needs to, even if she does not like it and it makes her anxious. She also started writing again. She had always been good at writing, her mother had told me during an interview in 2022, four years after Lisa was discharged from Il Giardino. I remembered Lisa's particularly evocative writing, together with her drawing skills, from the creative writing group sessions. In a word, like Giada, Lisa lives, she does not just survive her eating disorder. As the reader might guess now, this is not something that can be taken for granted, not even after months of apparently working treatment. For Lisa, in particular, this was not something that could be taken for granted at all. During the interview, her mother recalled the most distressing time of Lisa's stay at Il Giardino, when she was twenty-six and, at some point during her day-service treatment, had made an attempt to take her life.

I did remember that time too as the most difficult of my fieldwork. On Wednesdays I used to spend the whole day in the day-service facility: mornings were dedicated to the weekly 'weight monitoring' and to the 'meal planning group activity' – something that patients anxiously awaited and at the same time wanted to escape; the afternoons were dedicated to sessions of 'psychodynamic group therapy'. These sessions were always intense, and although patients enjoyed them and considered them extremely useful, they often left distressed. One cold, rainy Wednesday about five months into fieldwork, I had decided instead to go to the residential facility after lunch. I knew that two ten-year-old patients had just been admitted there, and I wanted to 'observe' how the professionals welcomed and approached the youngest patients they had ever had. The following morning, upon my arrival at the day-service facility, I saw Lisa in the relaxation room, sleeping all curled up in an armchair, with her psychotherapist Mauro, visibly tired and tormented, sitting in an armchair next to her as if constantly checking on her. I asked the nutritionist Isabella, who was in another room, if something had happened, and she told me that the previous evening, half an hour after the end of the group therapy session led by Mauro, Lisa had tried to jump from a window. Luckily, she was found while still standing on the window ledge by two other patients, who had promptly pulled her down. Lisa was my age, and I had 'followed' her treatment path since the moment she had been admitted to the residential facility. She was diagnosed with anorexia nervosa and reportedly showed 'depressive traits', the treatment team said, but she had never signalled that she could attempt anything like that. Knowing that she had tried to take her life was a shock for everyone. I had been with her until 2.30 pm the previous day, and she did look a bit distressed, but not more than any other Wednesday. We had been chatting right before I had left, and she had said goodbye with a smile. Four hours later, she was about to jump from a third-floor window.

This episode had deeply shaken both the group of patients and the treatment team, which felt that it was too risky for both Lisa and the 'stability' of the other patients to keep her in day-service treatment, especially given that, as many other patients, she spent the time outside the facility alone in a flat that her parents had rented for her in town (her hometown was miles away). The mother had then begged the treatment team not to discharge her, promising that she and her husband could take turns to be with her during the night and weekends. Lisa could then continue treatment for three more months and was discharged only in February, after 'visible progress', the team agreed. Everyone had noticed that after that extreme act Lisa had somehow got 'shaken' and had started 'taking treatment more seriously', actively collaborating and 'working on herself'. And yet, her mother recounted to me, the months after discharge from Il Giardino were full of difficulties, with Lisa struggling to stay in outpatient treatment because of discontinuities in her care: she had been given the contact of a psychiatrist in her region in northern Italy only after discharge, even if her mother had started asking for one in the very moment the treatment team had started talking about the idea of discharging Lisa. This meant that it took a whole month before she could see a psychiatrist for the first time after leaving Il Giardino. Moreover, the new psychiatrist seemed not to have been 'informed' about Lisa's case, in the sense that it did not seem the treatment team of Il Giardino had told him about Lisa's story; finally, Lisa reported that she did not feel at ease with him, nor with her new nutritionist. Things got so bad that by June 2020, her mother held, she was so underweight again that, in her view, she would have needed another admission to residential treatment. But Lisa refused any kind of help, to the point that she had a fight with the psychiatrist and stopped going to see him altogether. After this episode, however, her mother recalled, Lisa proactively chose to 'do some things that signalled she wanted to take care of herself': she booked a place for a holiday in the mountains, spending a few days there with her sister and then on her own; she bought a cat and started decorating her flat; she then bought a used car and started driving again (she had not driven since 2017). She also registered on an online dating app, and after a while she met a guy who then became her boyfriend and is now her partner. At that point, she decided to go to the local public mental health service, where she started seeing a psychiatrist and later a psychotherapist.

Barbara, a patient who had been admitted to Il Giardino a couple of months earlier than Lisa, and who had shared most of her treatment path with her, is also thirty-four now. She lives with her husband and three-year-old daughter in a small city in central Italy. In a public testimony at an awareness event for high school kids in her region, in October 2024, she said that she still has her 'demons' and 'monsters', but that today it is her who controls them, not the other way around: 'It's not them anymore who tell me if and what I can eat, if I deserve something or not'. This shift had come after many, many years of illness. She reported having had the first 'milder' issues with food when she was thirteen, because of trauma following an episode of sexual violence, until they 'erupted strongly' in 2011 when her father lost his job and her brother was diagnosed with a malignant lymphoma. It took Barbara four inpatient stays in hospital and other residential facilities, after which she always ended up losing weight again, to finally get herself admitted for what would be her last inpatient treatment – almost one year spent between the residential and day-service facilities of Il Giardino. In 2019, the same year in which she was discharged from her last admission, her brother passed away. But notwithstanding the extremely challenging time that followed, she managed to 'keep herself together' and 'not let the illness win again'.

Giordana is another patient who shared part of the treatment path at Il Giardino with Giada, Lisa and Barbara – but, like Giada, only the residential phase, since she was seventeen at the time and could not stay on her own in a town away from home for day-service treatment. She is now twenty-three and lives in a big city in central Italy, where she moved from her smaller hometown in 2021 to go to university. She is completing her graduate studies and lives in student accommodation, where she made close friends, fell in love, suffered from a breakup and fell in love again. She also went back to horse-riding, a passion she had to abandon when she got ill. Giordana had been discharged in 2019 after six months of residential treatment, where she had arrived directly from the hospital because her physical conditions had been deemed to cause an immediate risk for life. When she was discharged, she was 'another person', her mother said during the interview. Nevertheless, the months after discharge were difficult, because, as it was the case with Lisa, there was not enough support for outpatient treatment in her own region when she went back home. It was only thanks to private sessions and with active effort to maintain contact with the professionals of Il Giardino, including by travelling there frequently and recreating the network of care with a psychotherapist, a nutritionist and a family counsellor, that Giordana managed to stay afloat and later, the following year, to recover from a relapse that happened the first year she moved away from home, when she had decided to interrupt outpatient treatment. One of the last times I met her, in December 2024, she was giving a testimony of her illness and recovery to a group of people who were attending the presentation of a book written by the clinical director of Il Giardino. We bumped into one another while we were both searching for the room where the presentation would be held. She hugged me tight and later told me about her life at university and future projects.

I know of many other patients I had met during fieldwork having undergone similar paths, with ups and downs, better times and worse times, many of them still having a complicated relationship with food but also, day by day, choosing to stay in the world and enjoying staying in it, food included. They would all call these experiences 'recovery', even if treatment did not 'remove' the eating disorder completely from their life.

But others were less fortunate. Maia, whose story we have followed in Chapters 4 and 6, was thirty-four when she eventually passed away in November 2021 because of organ failure, a consequence of years and years of severe malnutrition. Asia was fifteen when, in the summer of 2021, she threw herself under a train that was passing through the station of her hometown in a small region in central Italy, about three hours away from Il Giardino. She had been treated there in residential treatment for six months in 2019, when she was thirteen. Her mother keeps carrying her testimony at awareness events and protests in the country, and keeps working actively to guarantee more support and public services in her region and in Italy. Ofelia, who had been treated for six months at the day-service facility of Il Giardino in 2019, was fifty-one when she died because of a coma induced by a hypoglycaemic crisis caused by fasting (she had type 1 diabetes), in 2022. Ofelia used to work as a cleaner at a bowling club doing mostly night shifts (something that did not help with managing her diabetes) and therefore sleeping during the day. This meant that she barely had friends and that her only source of support was her brother, since her parents had both passed away. But Ofelia was also a gifted painter. After discharge from day-service treatment, where she had managed to regain some weight, keep her diabetes under control, make some friends and start painting again, she had left her job as a cleaner and had started doing paintings and portraits on commission. But she had relapsed. Chiara, from a region in southern Italy, had been a patient in the day-service facility of Il Giardino for four months in 2019. She was thirty-eight and had two adolescent children when she passed away because of heart failure due to malnutrition in November 2024.

I learnt about these deaths either by a call or text from a member of the treatment team with whom I am still friends, or through Facebook posts of other patients who had asked for my 'friendship' when they were discharged. The differences in these patients' paths are stark, even if they had all been treated at Il Giardino during the same months or year, and therefore by the same healthcare professionals, with the same approach. Although for patients like Maia or Ofelia the treatment team had low expectations for their recovery, and somehow expected death to arrive at some point because of the countless years of malnutrition and the patients' fragile social networks, in other cases, like those of Asia or Chiara, death was not something that had crossed the professionals' minds. These different turns point to the fact, often repeated by the treatment team and by patients' parents during interviews – we have heard the external psychotherapist stressing it too in Chapter 5 – that even if what happens in treatment might be defined 'magic' or 'quite heroic', 'the problem is where you send them back to'. Although with this phrase the professionals referred mostly to patients' homes, here I want to show how even in cases where both the patients and the patients' parents have done 'work on themselves', sometimes that is not enough. Sometimes patients and their parents are left too alone in that work that is supposed to continue after discharge from residential or day-service treatment, including by other family members, friends, wider social networks, and also by treatment services and institutions.

What we might call 'the social' in some contexts hurts more than in others, and becomes like a black hole.

In the next section I illustrate some of the kinds of 'social' that hurts patients and families who are struggling to recover. I mostly draw from the interviews that I conducted with the parents of patients who had been discharged from the residential or day-service facility of Il Giardino,[4] including both families with very recent treatment experiences and those whose treatment experiences had happened several months or even years before the interview.

Returning to 'the Real World'

The problem is when they come back home.

—Maria's mother, interview, November 2022

As anticipated in Chapters 3 and 4, residential treatment aims to shield patients from external triggers during what is considered an extremely vulnerable phase, and to gradually prepare them for posttreatment challenges. In addition to a refamiliarisation with food, the treatment team helps patients navigate relationships, find fulfilling activities and manage practical life skills, and supports their transition to independence, according to their age. We have seen that day-service treatment keeps doing that, but that it also slowly and gradually allows for contact with the world *outside* treatment: patients spend every night and every weekend away from the facility – at home if they are from somewhere close to the town where Il Giardino is located, or, if they are from far away, in that very town with other patients and occasionally with their family members if they come for a visit. Once patients are discharged from these two treatment levels and switch to outpatient treatment, however, things change substantially in their daily life. Patients have to take 'full responsibility' for their own eating habits, since they are not anymore under the watchful and supporting eyes of the professionals. But they also have to navigate a world full of 'triggers' that might make them spiral towards eating disordered behaviour again (cf. Lester 2023). Such triggers not only include the countless 'dysfunctional' explicit and implicit messages regarding food, physical appearance, efficiency and productivity that can be found in mass media, school and work environments, or sport contexts, but also things that their closest relations – family members and friends – might do or say. In fact, although most parents, once their daughters and sons are discharged from Il Giardino, mostly know and have learned the best way to manage the patients' return home and support them in the process of readjusting to life outside the facility, the rest of the family and the circle of friends is often a very different matter.

Notwithstanding a few exceptions, in which parents reported that they had managed to 'train' their own parents and other family members who might come into contact with the discharged patient – mostly by reporting to them all of the things that they were learning during the group support meetings – the issue of lack of understanding and support from other family members recurred in almost every interview. This included other children (i.e., the patient's siblings), parents' own siblings, but especially their parents (i.e., the patient's grandparents). As one might expect, patients' parents understood that their other children had no responsibility for this, especially when they were young. Most parents actually felt guilty towards them, and were worried about the potential consequences of the lack of parental attention and care given to them as a consequence of focusing their efforts towards making sure the child with an eating disorder was treated and got better. In fact, in many cases, the patient's sibling or siblings also had or subsequently developed some kind of 'behavioural' or 'mental health issue', most frequently anxiety but often eating disordered behaviour – and in some cases even a 'full-blown' eating disorder. Parents lamented that although at Il Giardino there was plenty of support for families – through the weekly support meetings, the regular sessions and contact with the assigned family counsellor, and weekend workshops – all of these resources were very much tailored to parents, and rarely were they suitable for other family members, especially for the patient's siblings who were often young kids. I did occasionally see patient's siblings attending the weekly support meetings for families, but they rarely came a second time and often left the room before the meeting ended. The themes discussed and the language used were 'too intense' for kids, most parents and professionals agreed. As for other grown-up family members, I could occasionally see older siblings and partners, but very rarely aunts, uncles or grandparents, attending these group meetings or the individual ones with the assigned family counsellors. When I asked the parents why that was the case, many said that they experienced difficulties when trying to involve them, especially with their own parents – even if they often were the most important other family figures to involve because they were the ones who would take care of the children when the parents could not, including at mealtimes.[5]

In 'Mediterranean countries', including and especially Italy, the parents' generation, also due to the shortcomings of the welfare state combined with more precarious work conditions compared to those of the previous generation, heavily relies on grandparents ('*i nonni*') as providers of care and informal welfare (Grilli 2019: 69; Vatta 2012: 147–62). Even though grandparents mostly no longer live in the same house as their grandchildren, they often live close to them and visit frequently, especially when grandchildren are young (Grilli 2019: 67). Grandparents also make space for grandchildren within their homes to feed, care for, play with, and host them overnight weekly or for extended periods in the summer vacations. They accompany them on trips between home and school and vice versa, or on trips to and from gyms, language schools, or to entertainment venues (cinemas, shows, museums). They consistently provide time, availability, affection and financial resources, somehow prolonging their children's 'dependence' on them and their own 'infiltration' in choices regarding not only daily care practices (what, when and where grandchildren eat, what they wear etc.), but also decisions regarding which school their grandchildren may attend, which sport or after-school activity and so on. All of this even after their daughters or sons moved out from the parental home and created their own 'nuclear family' (ibid.: 69; D'Aloisio 2017).

The importance of the grandparent–grandchild relationship is inextricably linked to the significant demographic and social changes undergone by Italy: the lengthening of life; the marked improvement in the quality of life and health status of aging people; the processes of women's emancipation that have affected mothers; and the historical conjuncture that allowed today's grandparents to live in a period of growth, stability and abundance which enabled them to build homes, accumulate savings, acquire consumer goods and generous pensions, which they can now use for themselves and for their children and grandchildren, who are facing a completely different socio-economic horizon (Vatta 2012: 147–62). It is especially with grandmothers that children have the strongest relationship: grandmothers usually live longer, so they are present more or for a longer time, and they are predominantly the ones who are in charge of the nutrition, hygiene and care of the grandchildren (ibid.: 153). The support or 'substitution' of parental roles by grandparents is indispensable in most cases: increasingly, mothers seek to re-enter the workforce after childbirth but do not find or cannot afford adequate support from public or private services. Mothers are fully aware of this dependency, as well as of the need to ask for help and to feel grateful to their own mothers and mothers-in-law for stepping in.

This aspect of Italian kin care arrangements, however, proves particularly problematic when it comes to having to delegate the care of one's daughter with an eating disorder. Since grandparents belong to a generation who has experienced famine during or right after the Second World War – many parents explained to me – it is very difficult for them to understand and accept that their grandchildren would refuse and therefore 'waste' food and 'starve themselves'. This resistance and 'judgement' (*giudizio*) made it impossible for grandparents to understand the meaning and implications of an eating disorder, which often led the patient's parents to simply exclude them from the children's care. Grandparents were not only unable to provide support, but sometimes would even worsen the situation by criticising the children for not eating.

It was also generally difficult for grandparents, many parents said, to understand the notion of psy sciences, of mental health, and of the role of 'emotions' in parenting and in the development of the illness. Patients' grandparents were often characterised as 'rigid' and as having been very 'strict' parents to their kids (i.e., the patient's parents). Indeed, many mothers I interviewed talked of their own relationships with their parents as 'problematic' or 'dysfunctional', seemingly placing some of the responsibility for how they themselves behaved as parents, and in a way for how they were 'responsible' for their children's eating disorder, in the ways they themselves were parented. There was one mother of twins who had both developed anorexia nervosa in the space of the same year when they were twelve, to then be subsequently treated at the residential facility of Il Giardino two years before the interview took place. This mother stressed how, since then, she had been going to individual psychotherapy herself and had been working on her relationship with her own mother, whom she remembered as 'cold' and 'rational'. She could not remember a single occasion in which her mother had hugged her while she was a child, and said that the two completely lacked 'communication', something that she felt was passed down to her in the relationship with her daughters. As a grandmother, the girls' mother noted, she had been trying to be closer to her grandchildren, but always in what the mother described as 'an intellectual way': by sending pictures of landscapes, suggesting reading books together, but 'struggling to really give them physical affection'.

For similar reasons, the treatment team often noted that it was more difficult to do 'family work' with the parents of older patients, who might be in their seventies rather than in their forties or fifties: they were closer to the generation of grandparents and 'culturally' found it harder to understand eating disorders. These difficulties did not only have to do with age or generations, however. They also had to do with gender. Five mothers I interviewed[6] also reported that their husbands found it hard to understand eating disorders as something much more serious than a whim that their daughter was using to call for attention, and that they were sceptical towards the psy sciences and treatment in general, especially towards the strong focus that the treatment team placed on 'emotions'. In only one interview were the parts inverted, with the patient's father, divorced from his daughter's mother, being the one more involved in treatment. He depicted his ex-wife as sceptical and uncollaborative with the treatment team. In the other six interviews, mothers reported a slow but gradual understanding and increasing support from their husbands, even if they were often busy working and could not attend meetings and sessions as much as they would have wanted. More than this, mothers reported that thanks to this 'work on themselves' as parents, which they had undergone as a parallel path to their daughters' treatment path, they had also 'rediscovered themselves as couples', and in a few cases had even 'discovered themselves as real companions for the first time'.

Another recurring theme in the interviews with parents was having learned, during the patients' treatment path, the importance of letting both their children and themselves 'set boundaries' with their own family members – be these parents, siblings, grandparents – to maintain the 'balance' achieved with effort while in treatment. This often amounted to dismantling the (emotional) dependencies between patients' parents and grandparents, whose relationships were often characterised by the treatment team as 'too enmeshed'. In other cases, it was the relationship between the discharged patient and a sibling that was deemed to be 'too enmeshed' and in need of boundaries, especially in the case of twins or children very close in age. In others, again, it was the relationship between the patient and the parents themselves that needed 'more boundaries'. These were understandably the most difficult boundaries for the parents to set and respect, especially because often they were also, at the same time, the only carers that could help and support the patient just discharged. Here it would seem that not only are contemporary Italians, after all, 'dividual persons' à la Strathern, but also that they are somehow 'too dividual', and being too dividual leads to illness, hence the need to 'set boundaries'.

'The Older the Patient, the More Difficult It Is': Life as an Adult after Treatment

Further difficulties were reported by the parents of adult patients, both because in those cases the eating disorder had often become somehow 'chronic' and was harder to treat, as we have seen in previous chapters, and also because of the very ways in which services were structured and institutions could offer support. And, not ultimately, because of the extent to which they as parents could 'intervene' in their daughters' lives. For example, the simple fact that adult children, when discharged, might not return home to their parents but go and live on their own or with housemates meant that it was easier for them to slip back into disordered eating habits, since nobody was there to check on them or support them in difficult times. Giordana's mother, for instance, reported that her daughter's recovery had proceeded steadily for the first couple of years after discharge, when she had returned home with her parents. Even if the lockdown caused by Covid-19 made outpatient treatment difficult and often having to happen remotely, the family could take the time to stay together, and this had 'helped a lot'. But when Giordana later moved to a bigger city to start her undergraduate studies and decided to interrupt outpatient treatment because she felt she could now 'manage things on her own', a relapse happened. She was far away from home, had to adjust to a new place, new life and new people, had started working in an organic grocery store, and did not have any therapeutic support. Although she is now fine after having started outpatient treatment again and having changed her side job to babysitting, her mother stresses that knowing she is far away and could technically decide to stop outpatient treatment whenever she wants is often a concern: 'You know, once they are eighteen they just do what they want to do, you can't force them'.

Maria's and Lisa's parents reported similar experiences: upon discharge from Il Giardino, both returned to their hometown but decided not to move back with their parents – they were almost thirty years old and had already lived on their own for many years before inpatient treatment. Although this was something that the treatment team had supported, because it was in line with the aim of disentangling them from difficult family dynamics and making them 'autonomous', it also meant that they were left on their own when it came to eating. These parents lamented that the current system keeps parents 'too excluded' from information about their daughters' treatment and possibility of intervention: 'Just because they are not minors, it doesn't mean they are capable of doing everything on their own and taking the best decisions'. Lisa's mother was particularly frustrated at the fact that she was not 'kept informed enough' about Lisa's treatment path, especially during the day-service phase, when, she argued, that would have been more important because Lisa spent more time on her own. She recalled with anger that when Lisa had tried to jump from the window of the facility the treatment team had called her only the following day, and had told her to come as early as she could because Lisa was 'undergoing a difficult time', without telling her what had really happened (it was Lisa who, the night her mother arrived, told her what she had done):

> In the previous weeks it was clear to me from phone calls with Lisa that the situation was getting worse, that things weren't going well, that Lisa was unwell. And not being able to interact with her psychotherapist and speak freely unless Lisa was present ... this issue of the inability for a psychiatrist to speak with the family if the patient is an adult ... I ask myself: if someone has a stroke and is unable to make decisions about their own life, the spouse, the husband, the father, the mother, can interact with the doctors. The doctors report, the doctors talk, and there can be a discussion. But if someone is unable to communicate, for instance someone who attempts to commit suicide during a treatment path like the one Lisa was going through, it is evident that this person was capable of understanding and making decisions only up to a certain point, right? So, in a process like this, why can't the family interact with her therapist? The same holds for follow-ups: the family should be involved in a process where follow-up checks are tightly scheduled, and where the family is equally responsible and aware. When my daughter told me, 'Look, starting from June, there are no more follow-ups', I thought wow, just two follow-ups, but I could only believe her. And if this weren't true? Things might have gone differently after discharge. I mean, there were times in which we would look at the times Lisa checked WhatsApp just to know if she was still alive or not.

Maria's parents faced similar problems and anxieties. They expressed frustration at the fact that they were not involved enough in their daughter's treatment just because she was an adult, even if she was 'clearly not capable of choosing the best for herself' (Maria's father). This brings back the question of (in)competence that we addressed in Chapters 2 and 3. Here, however, we have parents questioning the very notion of 'focal incompetence', i.e., the idea that those who suffer from an eating disorder are only incompetent regarding choices that have to do with food and eating but are competent for all the rest. Moreover, here the questioning of competence is also a matter for those who provide kin care: they experience a loss of *their* own sense of competence when those for whom they feel responsible are taken elsewhere, to be 'cared for properly' (Jenkins 1999: 226). When I interviewed Maria's parents, in November 2022, they were preparing for the moment Maria would be discharged from day-service treatment. They feared that things would soon go back to square one, as had happened in countless ways following her previous hospitalisation in other facilities, when Maria would live on her own, find a job that would give her 'excuses' to skip meals, meet a boyfriend, break up and stop eating altogether. From those experiences, they had learnt that this time Maria would have to stay at home with them at least for a while, so that they could make sure she would keep following her meal plan. But they knew she was not happy about this. They were also particularly worried because they had recently received a text from Maria saying: 'I have no friends, I won't be able to have children, I won't be able to do anything ... so what's the point of living?' and a few days after that they had found a bunch of pills that she had not taken when she was supposed to, perhaps to use them later all together in an attempt to take her life (as she had already done once, after a previous discharge from hospitalisation). Maria's father had been trying to find a job or a volunteering activity that could keep Maria busy while making her feel she had a purpose without tiring her too much, and which would allow her to eat at regular times. But it was proving difficult. Moreover, he and his wife were terrified at the idea that once discharged and back in her own region Maria would not keep going to outpatient treatment because the professionals working at the public services available had already proved they 'did not know what to do with her'. Shortly before she was admitted to Il Giardino, these professionals had told her that she was 'a lost case, without hope'. Maria's family did not have the money to pay for private treatment, and her father felt that their situation was much more complex than those of the majority of families attending the weekly support meetings:

> You see, these support groups are helpful, but most of the experiences that parents share here regard patients who are much younger and have just fallen ill. We have already gone through all of those experiences and phases, multiple times. It would be more helpful for parents who are in our situation to talk to other parents with a long history of illness. Otherwise, we can only give to others, we cannot take much that we can use.

A nurse I interviewed at Il Giardino during the same period also seemed to agree that it was much harder to think of and support a 'postdischarge' plan for adult patients, compared to preadolescents or adolescents:

> The life context and life stage of a 35-year-old is obviously very different from that of a fifteen-year-old or a twelve-year-old in terms of lifestyle, expectations, social life, school or work environments. There are many more factors that influence the treatment and recovery itself. The greater the patient's age, the more complex the situation becomes, as more variables need to be integrated into the treatment process. The postdischarge plan itself becomes increasingly complex and perhaps more limited as the person gets older. Conversely, the younger the patient, the more

> opportunities we have and the more resources we can use, such as in education, sports and other activities, because everything is just beginning. For older patients, leaving here often means returning home alone or with one parent, because they might have abandoned their studies, they might have lost their job … and then what do we rely on? People in these situations, without a supportive context around them, what kind of help can we provide outside?

I want to start from the nurse's question and suggest that since it is the social outside the treatment facility which often hurts again after treatment and turns into disordered eating – which can eventually turn into a full relapse or even death – treatment centres would need to be able to act on the social outside, going beyond patients' immediate carers. This is because the social, it should now be clear, often fails patients once they are discharged from a treatment path in which they worked hard and suffered to get even a tiny bit better. The social, as will become even clearer in the next section, makes persons not just as social entities, but as material entities too, through an effect on their eating (or not eating) practices.

Food as a Substance of Relatedness, Relatedness as a Substance of Feeding

We have seen that an 'eating disorder' is many different things at the same time, which requires coordinating not only different 'bodies' and 'diseases', but also different 'goods' and 'bads' in treatment. This complex coordination, I have suggested in this book, requires tinkering with food and family: it requires temporarily eradicating food from the social – cleansing it from the messiness of commensality by scientising it and turning it into 'nutrition'. In the meantime, the family needs to be cleansed of its harmful aspects too, so that after discharge from the facility, when commensality will be put back into food, it will not harm the patient. Doing that requires not only turning the patient's family into a patient itself – into an object of treatment. It also requires professionals to practise kinship care with patients: to 'reparent patients' in a 'healthier way', so that that they can unlearn 'dysfunctional' dynamics of relatedness and learn more 'functional' ones.

In concluding this book, I want to focus on the implications of this observation: that in the world of this treatment centre, patients' relational histories are seen to produce visible effects on their bodies, through an additional intermediate step which is located in 'the mind'. The relationality that professionals privilege in their understanding of the patients' conditions and in their treatment is relations of kinship, especially of the close kin that are the family. This ethnographic finding calls for rethinking Anne Becker's (1995, 2004b) argument that eating disorders do not emerge in social contexts in which people's bodies are understood as the result of how their relational community cares for them because they would not make sense. As I traced in the Introduction to this book, in her ethnography of bodily aesthetics in Fiji she has convincingly pointed out that the interest in reflexively cultivating one's body (which, taken to the extreme, includes eating disordered practices) depends on the cultural validation of personal agency with respect to the body, which is in turn linked to the experience of self vis-à-vis the community; it presupposes that the body represents a personal resource for expression. In Fiji, instead, the cultivation of bodily space is a collective rather than a personal enterprise: bodies and the crafting of their form are the responsibility of the community that cares for them (Becker 1995: 5). Therefore, what bodily form communicates is how one has been nurtured or neglected in his or her social universe, not the attitude of one's personal self. Although it is certainly the generally European and North American identification of the self with an individuated body, seen as a reflexively and personally manageable resource, that makes the antagonistic relationship between any body and its governing self possible (ibid.: 134), the ethnographic material I examined here also strongly suggests that the dichotomy Becker draws between 'Western' notions of bodies as projects of bounded selves, and 'others' whose bodily transformations are the result of the care of their micro-communities, might be too simplistic.

There are recent ethnographic examples in the literature that seem to fit this sharp dichotomy: as shown by Rupert Stasch (2009) in his work in West Papua, among the Korowai, children are understood as signs of past relational histories: they are seen as signs of their parents' actions of 'making good', as parenting is described as a matter of giving food and children are defined by what they lack, and therefore by the care they need (ibid.: 170). Similarly, as already mentioned in Chapter 5, in child welfare institutions in Japan children's bodies are seen by social workers as carrying the signs of the absence of kinship care, suggesting how relatedness itself turns into biological materiality (Goldfarb 2019). In both these cases, like in Fiji, children's bodies are very much 'embedded bodies' – bodies constituted by their own past and by the social and material environment they inhabit (Niewöhner 2011: 290). But patients' emaciated bodies at Il Giardino – the corporeal aspect here of their ill minds – are also similarly seen by the treatment team as the result of the lack of proper family care. In the world of this treatment centre, eating disorders are the result of the embedded bodies that patients acquired through kinship, and which can be treated through kinship.

What are the implications of this argument for our understanding of the relationship between food and kinship? My ethnography has shown that not only is food a 'substance of relatedness' that generates kinship (Carsten 1995, 1997), but that the reverse is also true: food can function as a substance to make and unmake kinship (by refusing it), and, in turn, kinship itself becomes a sort of 'substance' – a medium – that shapes whether and how food is incorporated into persons. It is not only that food makes people into kin; kinship also makes and unmakes people through food – with consequences that, for some people, can make the difference between life and death. The fact that food is a substance of relatedness, but also the other way around, is precisely what allows the professionals to tinker with food and family in the treatment centre – by turning food into 'nutrition' first and then, later, by putting relatedness back into food but in a modified form.

Whereas previous analyses of eating disorders have framed (the refusal of) food as a way to rebel against kinship care, to negate kinship care, or to ask for more kinship care – with food always framed as a medium whose 'end' is kinship – here we see that an ethnographic lens can illuminate how medium and end are not static. What has been framed as an end can become a medium itself and, in turn, what has been framed as a medium can become an end. In this treatment centre, not only is food a substance of relatedness, relatedness is also a substance of feeding – although a recalcitrant one.

Where to Go Now?

I conclude with this question, so that further research may add to what I have offered in these pages. I hope that by challenging the dichotomy of 'failure' versus 'success' in studying eating disorder treatment I have done some justice to the immensely complex and difficult work of both living with an eating disorder and treating eating disorders – as much as it is possible for a temporary visitor to do so. Arjun Appadurai (2016: xxi) has highlighted that failure is a 'volatile and variable' concept, not really a fact but a human judgement, shaped by local assumptions which change over time and through encounters with other ideas about failure. This is evident in the stories of Giada, Lisa, Barbara and Giordana. Some might think that treatment for them somehow 'failed' because they still have some issues with food and are more or less vulnerable to relapses; although, if you look at their lives, they are not 'less functional' than many others who do not have issues with food, and, if you ask them, they will tell you that they feel they have recovered. But what about the other stories? Failures in the care of Maia, Asia, Ofelia, Chiara have surely produced other forms of care that neither the professionals nor their family carers might have imagined otherwise. But is this enough? In the face of their stories it is hard not to ask who failed at what, and who failed whom. As noted by Catherine Alexander (2023: 11–12) in her introduction to a recent special issue entitled 'After Failure', perhaps in certain contexts ethnographers should choose not to relativise failure but to see that people *have been failed*, and have been failed systematically, especially when failures have to do with care and with the neglect of moral and legal obligations by authorities to citizens. Keeping this stance and trying, at the same time, to see the generative aspects of failure are not mutually exclusive.

Moreover, Alexander (2023: 11) helpfully reminds us, whether failure is taken as given, ethnographically or analytically, or as judgement paused, there are always 'temporal ethics' at play which should challenge the notion of failure as a singular post hoc judgement. This is particularly evident in Giada's story: healthcare professionals at Il Giardino felt that their care had 'failed' Giada, even after they had adjusted it to different forms of care to accommodate what had seemingly prevented their first approach from working (i.e., Giada's comorbidity), because her problematic family care had proved as untouchable as her eating disorder. And yet, contrary to their expectations and to the fact that previous hospitalisations had already 'failed', Giada is now living a healthy and full life. On the other hand, Asia, who when arrived at Il Giardino had just developed an eating disorder and whose mother seemed much more collaborative with the treatment team, once discharged was hurt so much by the social outside the clinic that she took her own life when she was only fifteen.

One thing that can surely be said of the 'failure' of eating disorder treatment in Italy is that it is not, as Lester (2019) showed is the case for the United States, (wrongly) ascribed to the patients. Lester's ethnography is all too perfect an example of the neoliberal 'reallocation' of systemic failure through a moralised reorientation to individual (in)capacity and lack of will, in which, rather than provide care, the state tells citizens to be self-reliant (Alexander 2023: 189). Even when people are most vulnerable and least able to care for themselves, like the patients described by Lester, failure to care for oneself is immediately translated into 'self-inflicted illness', which legitimises withdrawal of support. In Italy, instead, it is broadly held that when someone dies of an eating disorder it is not that person who has 'failed', nor, in most cases, is it the healthcare professionals who have 'failed' her. The narrative, coming from patients, their families, healthcare professionals and even the media, is quite blunt: there are not enough state-funded services and resources, which means that many people cannot access appropriate care soon enough, nor receive enough care during and after intensive treatment. In this situation, what is left for the ethnographer to do?

One thing I have tried to do in this book is to show that the kinds of failures I have described are not only due to an already acknowledged lack of care on the part of the state, although this is certainly the biggest problem to be addressed, and with urgency too. This 'macro-level' of failure is also entangled with accumulations of other failures at the 'meso' and 'micro' level. That Maia, Asia, Ofelia, Chiara and all the others who did not 'win the battle' against their eating disorder have been failed is not something that can be argued. But even in their case the 'diagnosis' or narrative of failure is not neat. Rather, the chain of failures is long and convoluted, with many things and people entangled at different levels. What ethnographers can do in these contexts is to highlight the precise cracks where the resources that should be mobilised to address an already recognised systemic failure should be directed. In particular, this book suggests that in addition to more public funding systematically dedicated to public treatment services and specialised training for healthcare professionals, for all the levels of care (outpatient, day service, residential and hospital ward), the following measures need to be urgently implemented: i) weekly support groups not only for the patients' parents but also for other relatives, distinguished by age and role in the family. It is especially important to have support groups tailored to grandparents and to young siblings, which seem to be two 'forgotten categories' in research about eating disorder treatment; moreover, even if they are less numerous, it is important that partners/spouses and daughters/sons of adult patients have tailored support meetings too; ii) specialised support groups for relatives of people with a long history of illness and treatment, who inevitably face different complexities and have different needs; iii) a greater involvement of patients' parents or closest family carers even when the patients are adults, with consent of the patient and on the basis of the patient's therapist's assessment of every specific situation; iv) a systematic plan for helping adult patients on their way to be discharged from residential or day-service treatment to find jobs in organisations and services whose managers take into account their difficulties and allow them to have regular meals; v) a systematic 'flow' of information from the treatment team of residential or day-service treatment to the treatment team of outpatient service if this is going to be different, arranged in a way that guarantees that patients who are discharged have already scheduled their first outpatient visit; this is so that they are not left alone in the very vulnerable phase that is the weeks immediately after discharge; and finally vi) awareness campaigns not only in schools but also in universities, organisations and workplaces regarding eating disorders and more generally the damaging effects of toxic work culture.

Surely there is even more that can be done. This book only opened some lines of inquiry that I hope will bring themes dear both to anthropologists and to those treating these conditions – the relationships between bodies, illness, kinship, food, detachment and boundaries – under further scrutiny, and, perhaps, generate more collaborative endeavours. More than anything else, I hope that this book will generate questions that will serve as a springboard for unravelling what remains to be unravelled about caring for people living with eating disorders. I see two particularly important avenues for further ethnographic research, which regard the youngest patients on the one hand and the 'oldest' patients on the other: the first avenue would entail exploring how eating disorder treatment is being adapted, in Italy and elsewhere, to the increasing number of preadolescent patients, and what this could reveal about taken-for-granted notions of 'dependence' and 'autonomy'; the second avenue would give attention to the forms that care could take, within and outside clinics, for the many 'chronic' patients who end up living with an eating disorder for the rest of their lives, and for whom clinics sometimes become homes but who in other cases are left to themselves. These two ends of the spectrum often fall through the cracks of research and treatment both because of their marginality and because of the enormous rethinking and restructuring that addressing them seriously would entail. Addressing them is therefore a matter of research ethics and clinical ethics. Even more so because their perhaps still 'marginal' numbers are inevitably destined to increase, and because the two issues seem to be intertwined: not intervening promptly and appropriately in children easily makes the eating disorder chronic, which might in turn mean that future mothers and fathers will raise children who themselves have a much higher risk of developing an eating disorder compared to their peers.[7]

In these challenging endeavours, I hope that the tenacity of both people living with an eating disorder and of those who care for them will inspire tenacity in those who set out to disentangle the complexity that is care. Living with an eating disorder, caring for someone who suffers from an eating disorder, writing about eating disorders, and demanding changes for better care, all call for tenacity.

Notes

1. See Brunetti and De Laurentis 2013.
2. I am still in contact with Giada, as with the other patients I mention here. They all gave me consent to use this material in the book.
3. The exact title of the book is not provided because it would lead to the identification of Giada's real name.
4. See Chapter 1.
5. Arianna's story in Chapter 5 is one example of this.
6. As detailed in Chapter 1, out of twelve interviews most of them were with patients' mothers, three with both parents present, and only one with a patient's father.
7. See Bould et al. 2015; Watson, O'Brien and Sadeh-Sharvit 2018.

References

Accornero, Ferdinando. 1941. 'L'Anoressia Mentale, una Priorità Italiana e l'Osservazione di 4 Casi', *Rivista sperimentale di Freniatria* 67: 447.
Addley, Esther. 2023. 'Friday Briefing: Eating Disorders Are Soaring in the UK – and So Are Wait Times for Vital Support', *The Guardian*, 4 August.
Alexander, Catherine. 2023. 'Writing Failure: Knowledge Production, Temporalities, Ethics, and Traces', *Journal of the Royal Anthropological Institute* (N.S.): 8–30.
American Psychiatric Association. 1952. *Diagnostic and Statistical Manual of Mental Disorders: DSM-I.* Washington: American Psychiatric Publishing.
American Psychiatric Association. 1968. *Diagnostic and Statistical Manual of Mental Disorders: DSM-II. Second Edition.* Washington: American Psychiatric Publishing.
American Psychiatric Association. 1980. *Diagnostic and Statistical Manual of Mental Disorders: DSM-III. Third Edition.* Washington: American Psychiatric Publishing.
American Psychiatric Association. 1994. *Diagnostic and Statistical Manual of Mental Disorders: DSM-IV. Fourth Edition.* Washington: American Psychiatric Publishing.
American Psychiatric Association. 2000. *Diagnostic and Statistical Manual of Mental Disorders: DSM-IV-TR. Fourth Edition, Text Revision.* Washington: American Psychiatric Publishing.
American Psychiatric Association. 2013. *Diagnostic and Statistical Manual of Mental Disorders: DSM-5. Fifth Edition.* Washington: American Psychiatric Publishing.
Ammaniti, Massimo, et al. 2008. 'Psicopatologia dello Sviluppo e Anoressia Infantile: Continuità Omotipica ed Eterotipica', *Noos* 3: 197–216.
Anderson, Amanda. 2001. *The Power of Distance: Cosmopolitanism and the Cultivation of Detachment.* Princeton: Princeton University Press.
Appadurai, Arjun. 2016. 'Introduction', in Failure. Special Issue (ed.) Argjun Appadurai. *Social Research: An International Quarterly*, 83(3): xxi–xxvii.
Arcelus, Jon, et al. 2011. 'Mortality Rates in Patients with Anorexia Nervosa and Other Eating Disorders. A Meta-analysis of 36 Studies', *Archives of General Psychiatry* 68(7): 724–31.
Ardener, Edwin. 1989. *The Voice of Prophecy and Other Essays*, ed. M. Chapman. Oxford: Blackwell.
Ariès, Philippe. 1962. *Centuries of Childhood.* New York: Vintage Books.
Arteaga, Ignacia M. 2018. 'Life Must Go On: Everyday Experiences of Colorectal Cancer Treatments in London'. Ph.D. Thesis. London: University College London.
Auger, Nathalie, et al. 2021. 'Anorexia Nervosa and the Long-Term Risk of Mortality in Women', *World Psychiatry* 20(3): 448–49.

Banks, Caroline G. 1992. '"Culture" in Culture-Bound Syndromes: The Case of Anorexia Nervosa', *Social Science & Medicine* 34(8): 867–84.
Baraitser, Lisa. 2017. *Enduring Time*. London: Bloomsbury.
Barbagli, Marzio, and David Kertzer. 1990. 'An Introduction to the History of Italian Family Life', *Journal of Family History* 15(4): 369–83.
Barbero, Joan, and Aitor Gabilondo. 2020. 'Madres: Amor y Vida'. Produced by IMDBPro.
Barret, Robert J. 1996. *The Psychiatric Team and the Social Definition of Schizophrenia: An Anthropological Study of Person and Illness*. Cambridge: Cambridge University Press.
Basaglia, Franco. 1959. 'L'Anoressia Mentale è una Nevrosi o una Psicopatia?', *Medicina Psicosomatica* 4: 263.
BBC. 2006. 'I Am a Child Anorexic'. Produced by the BBC.
Beccari, Jacopo B. 1745. *De Bononiensi Scientiarum et Artium Instituto atque Academia Commentarii. Tomi Secundi, Pars Prima: Commentarii de Longa Cibi Potusque Omnis Abstinentia*. Bologna: ex Typographia Laelii a Vulpe.
Becker, Anne E. 1995. *Body, Self, and Society: The View from Fiji*. Philadelphia: University of Pennsylvania Press.
Becker, Anne E. (ed.). 2004a. 'New Global Perspectives on Eating Disorders' [Special Issue], *Culture, Medicine and Psychiatry* 28(4).
Becker, Anne E. 2004b. 'Television, Disordered Eating, and Young Women in Fiji: Negotiating Body Image and Identity during Rapid Social Change', *Culture, Medicine and Psychiatry* 28(4): 533–59.
Bell, Kirsten. 2019. 'The "Problem" of Undesigned Relationality: Ethnographic Fieldwork, Dual Roles and Research Ethics', *Ethnography* 20(1): 8–26.
Bell, Rudolph M. 1979. *Fate and Honor, Family and Village: Demographic and Cultural Change in Rural Italy since 1800*. Chicago: University of Chicago Press.
Bell, Rudolph M. 1985. *Holy Anorexia*. Chicago: University of Chicago Press.
Belmonte, Thomas. 1979. *The Broken Fountain*. New York: Columbia University Press.
Benedetti, Alessandro. 1533. *Collectionum Medicinalium Libellum, Liber XI, cap. X*. Venezia: La Giunta.
Benson, Susan. 1997. 'The Body, Health and Eating Disorders', in Kathryn Woodward (ed.), *Identity and Difference*. London: Sage, pp. 121–66.
Berkman, Nancy D., Kathleen N. Lohr and Cynthia M. Bulik. 2007. 'Outcomes of Eating Disorders: A Systematic Review of the Literature', *International Journal of Eating Disorders* 40: 293–309.
Berliner, David, et al. 2016. 'Anthropology and the Study of Contradictions', *Hau: Journal of Ethnographic Theory* 6(1): 1–27.
Bernini, Stefania. 2004. 'Natural Mothers: Teaching Morals and Parent-Craft in Italy, 1945–60', *Modern Italy* 9: 21–33.
Biehl, João. 2005. *Vita: Life in a Zone of Social Abandonment*. Berkeley: University of California Press.
Bonaccorso, Monica M. E. 2009. *Conceiving Kinship: Assisted Conception, Procreation and Family in Southern Europe*. Oxford: Berghahn Books.
Bordo, Susan. 1993. *Unbearable Weight: Feminism, Western Culture, and the Body*. Berkeley: University of California Press.
Borgstrom, Erica, Simon Cohn and Annelieke Driessen. 2020. 'We Come in as "the Nothing": Researching Non-intervention in Palliative Care', *Medicine Anthropology Theory* 7(2): 202–13.
Bould, Helen, et al. 2015. 'Do Eating Disorders in Parents Predict Eating Disorders in Children? Evidence from a Swedish Cohort', *Acta Psychiatrica Scandinavica* 132(1): 51–59.

Bowlby, John. 1956. 'The Growth of Independence in the Young Child', *Royal Society of Health Journal* 76: 587–91.
Bowlby, John. 1988. *A Secure Base: Parent-Child Attachment and Healthy Human Development*. New York: Basic Books.
Bozzola, Elena. 2024. 'A 8 Anni i Primi Segnali di Anoressia, l'Allarme dei Pediatri' [First Signals of Anorexia at 8 Years Old, the Alarm of Paediatricians], *La Repubblica*, 24 September.
Bradley, Bridget, and Stefan Ecks. 2018. 'Disentangling Family Life and Hair Pulling: Trichotillomania and Relatedness', *Medical Anthropology* 37(7): 568–81.
Brodwin, Paul. 2011. 'Futility in the Practice of Community Psychiatry', *Medical Anthropology Quarterly* 25(2): 189–208.
Brodwin, Paul. 2013. *Everyday Ethics: Voices from the Frontline of Community Psychiatry*. Berkeley: University of California Press.
Bruch, Hilde. 1962. 'Perceptual and Conceptual Disturbances in Anorexia Nervosa', *Psychosomatic Medicine* 24(2): 187–94.
Bruch, Hilde. 1978. *The Golden Cage: The Enigma of Anorexia Nervosa*. Cambridge, MA: Harvard University Press.
Brugnoli, Giovanni. 1875. 'Sull'Anoressia', *Memoria dell'Accademia delle Scienze dell'istituto di Bologna* 3: 351.
Brumberg, Joan J. 1988. *Fasting Girls: The Emergence of Anorexia Nervosa as a Modern Disease*. Cambridge, MA: Harvard University Press.
Brunetti, Raffaele, and Ilaria De Laurentis. 2013. 'Ciò che mi Nutre mi Distrugge'. Produced by B&BFILM, co-produced with RAI3. Retrieved from https://www.cinemaitaliano.info/ciocheminutremidistrugge.
Bryant-Waugh, Rachel, and Bryan Lask. 1995. 'Annotation: Eating Disorders in Children', *Journal of Child Psychology and Psychiatry* 36(2): 191–202.
Buchbinder, Mara. 2015. *All in Your Head: Making Sense of Pediatric Pain*. Berkeley: University of California Press.
Burns, Maree. 2004. 'Eating Like an Ox: Femininity and Dualist Constructions of Bulimia and Anorexia', *Feminism and Psychology* 14(2): 269–95.
Button, Eric. 1986. 'Body-Size Perception and Response to Outpatient Treatment in Anorexia Nervosa', *International Journal of Eating Disorders* 5: 617–29.
Bynum, Caroline W. 1987. *Holy Feast and Holy Fast: The Religious Significance of Food to Medieval Women*. Berkeley: University of California Press.
Candea, Matei. 2007. 'Arbitrary Locations: In Defence of the Bounded Field-Site', *The Journal of the Royal Anthropological Institute* 13(1): 167–84.
Candea, Matei, et al. 2015. 'Introduction: Reconsidering Detachment', in Thomas Yarrow et al. (eds), *Detachment: Essays on the Limits of Relational Thinking*. Manchester: Manchester University Press, pp. 1–31.
Caplan, Pat. 2003. 'Introduction: Anthropology and Ethics', in Pat Caplan (ed.), *The Ethics of Anthropology: Debates and Dilemmas*. New York: Routledge, pp. 1–33.
Carroll, Timothy, David Jeevendrampillai and Aaron Parkhurst. 2017. 'Introduction: Towards a General Theory of Failure', in Aaron Parkhurst et al. (eds), *The Material Culture of Failure: When Things Do Wrong*. London: Bloomsbury Academic, pp. 1–20.
Carsten, Janet. 1995. 'The Substance of Kinship and the Heat of the Hearth: Feeding, Personhood, and Relatedness among Malays in Pulau Langkawi', *American Ethnologist* 22(2): 223–41.
Carsten, Janet. 1997. *The Heat of the Hearth: The Process of Kinship in a Malay Fishing Community*. Oxford: Oxford University Press.

Carsten, Janet. 2019a. 'The Stuff of Kinship', in S. Bamford (ed.), *The Cambridge Handbook of Kinship*. Cambridge: Cambridge University Press, pp. 133–50.

Carsten, Janet. 2019b. *Bloodwork: Life and Laboratories in Penang*. Durham, NC: Duke University Press.

Casadio, Andrea. 2020. 'Fame d'Amore'. Produced by RAI 1.

Castel, Robert. 1981. *La Gestion des Risques: De l'Anti-psychiatrie à l'Après-psychanalyse*. Paris: Èditions de Minuit.

Cavanna, Donatella, and Renata Nacinovich. 2024. 'Nodi Clinci per l'Identificazione e il Trattamento dei Disturbi Alimentari in Età Evolutiva. Un Invito alla Discussione', *Psicologia clinica dello sviluppo. Rivista quadrimestrale* I: 111–26.

Charcot, Jean-Martin. 1889. *Clinical Lectures on Diseases of the Nervous System*. London: New Sydenham Society.

Cheney, Ann M. 2012. 'Emotional Distress and Disordered Eating Practices among Southern Italian Women', *Qualitative Health Research* 22(9): 1247–59.

Cheney, Ann M. 2013. 'Altering the Social: An Ethnography of Disordered Eating among Southern Italian Women', *Food and Foodways* 21(2): 87–107.

Cheney, Ann M., Steve Sullivan and Kathleen Grubbs. 2018. 'The Morality of Disordered Eating and Recovery in Southern Italy', *Medical Anthropology Quarterly* 32(3): 443–57.

Chesney Edward, G. M. Goodwin and S. Fazel. 2014. 'Risks of All-Cause and Suicide Mortality in Mental Disorders: A Meta-review', *World Psychiatry* 13(2): 153–60.

Chua, Jocelyn L. 2011. 'Making Time for the Children: Self-temporalisation and the Cultivation of the Anti-suicidal Subject in South India', *Cultural Anthropology* 26(1): 112–37.

Cirino, Ilaria. 2005. 'Briciole'. Produced by IMDbPro.

Clemente, Ignasi. 2015. *Uncertain Futures: Communication and Culture in Pediatric Cancer Treatment*. Chichester: Wiley Blackwell.

Collier, David A., and Janet L. Treasure. 2004. 'The Aetiology of Eating Disorders', *The British Journal of Psychiatry* 185: 363–65.

Cook, Joanna, and Catherine Trundle. 2020. 'Unsettled Care: Temporality, Subjectivity, and the Uneasy Ethics of Care', *Anthropology and Humanism* 45(2): 178–83.

Cooper, Peter J., et al. 1986. 'The Development and Validation of the Body Shape Questionnaire', *International Journal of Eating Disorders* 6: 485–86.

Corica, Alessandra. 2022. 'Disturbi Alimentari, in Lombardia Casi Aumentati del 30% in Due Anni: in Ritardo la Rete di Aiuti' [Eating Disorders, in Lombardy 30% More Cases in Two Years: the Network of Care is Falling Behind], *La Repubblica*, 16 March.

Counihan, Carole. 1988. 'Female Identity, Food, and Power in Contemporary Florence', *Anthropological Quarterly* 61(2): 51–62.

Counihan, Carole. 2004. *Around the Tuscan Round Table: Food, Family and Gender in Twentieth-Century Florence*. New York: Routledge.

Crisp, Arthur H. 1980. *Anorexia Nervosa: Let Me Be*. London: Academic Press.

Crisp, Arthur H., et al. 2006. 'Death, Survival and Recovery in Anorexia Nervosa: A Thirty-Five-Year Study', *European Eating Disorders Review* 14: 168–75.

Crow, Scott J., et al. 2009. 'Increased Mortality in Bulimia Nervosa and Other Eating Disorders', *The American Journal of Psychiatry* 166(12): 1342–46.

Cubelli, Roberto, and Paolo Nichelli. 1990. 'Giovanni Brugnoli and the Origin of Neuropsychology in Italy', *The Italian Journal of Neurological Sciences* 11: 501–5.

Cuj, Miguel, Lisa Grabinsky and Emily Yates-Doerr. 2021. 'Cultures of Nutrition: Classification, Food Policy, and Health', *Medical Anthropology* 40(1): 79–97.

Cullather, Nick. 2007. 'The Foreign Policy of the Calorie', *The American Historical Review* 112(2): 337–64.
Cuzzolaro, Massimo, et al. 2000. 'Body Uneasiness Test, BUT', in Luciano Conti (ed.), *Repertorio delle Scale di Valutazione in Psichiatria*. Firenze: SEE, pp. 1759–61.
D'Abano, Pietro (*Petri de Abano*). 1958. *Conciliator Controversiarium quae inter Philosophos et Medicos Versantur*. Venezia: Giunta.
D'Aloisio, Fulvia. 2017. 'Un Approccio Etnografico ai Legami Generazionali e al Supporto della Parentela. Necessità e Contraddizioni a Confronto tra Napoli e Bologna', in Alessio Fornasin and Claudio Lorenzin (eds), *Per una Storia della Popolazione Italiana nel Novecento*. Udine: Forum, pp. 360–77.
Dalla Ragione, Laura, and Lucia Giombini. 2014. *Solitudini Imperfette: Le Buone Pratiche di Cura nei Disturbi del Comportamento Alimentare* [Imperfect Solitudes: Good Treatment Practices for Eating Disorders]. Italy: Ministero della Salute.
Dalla Ragione, Laura. 2023. 'Ritratto di Laura Dalla Ragione: Pensare Fuori dagli Steccati', *Recenti Progressi in Medicina* 114(11): 694–96.
Dalle Grave, Riccardo, et al. 1991. 'Approccio Multidisciplinare e Flessible nella Terapia dell'Anoressia Nervosa', *Rivista Sperimentale di Freniatria e Medicina Legale delle Alienazioni Mentali* 2: 283–301.
Dalle Grave, Riccardo, et al. 1993. 'Inpatient Treatment for Anorexia Nervosa: A Lenient Approach', *European Eating Disorders Review* 1(3): 166–76.
Dalle Grave, Riccardo. 1996. *Anoressia Nervosa: I Fatti*. Verona: Positive Press.
Das, Veena. 1995. 'National Honour and Practical Kinship: Unwanted Women and Children', in Faye D. Ginsburg and Rayna Rapp (eds), *Conceiving the New World Order: The Global Politics of Reproduction*. Berkeley: University of California Press, pp. 212–33.
Davis, Elizabeth A. 2012. *Bad Souls: Madness and Responsibility in Modern Greece*. Durham, NC: Duke University Press.
Davis, John. 1973. *Land and Family in Pisticci*. London: Athlone Press.
De Bac, Margherita. 2024. 'Anoressia, l'Allarme dei Familiari: "Pochi ambulatori e attese infinite" [Anorexia, the Alarm of Family Carers: 'Few Outpatient Services and Neverending Wait Times'], *Il Corriere della Sera*, 15 March.
Deiana, Federica. 2012. 'Seeing with New Eyes: Field Research and Self-analysis in a Clinic for Treatment of Eating Disorders', *Medische Anthropologie* 24(1): 57–71.
Delinsky, Sherrie S., and G. Terence Wilson. 2005. 'Mirror Exposure for the Treatment of Body Image Disturbance', *International Journal of Eating Disorders* 39(2): 108–16.
Devoe, J. Daniel, et al. 2023. 'The Impact of the COVID-19 Pandemic on Eating Disorders: A Systematic Review', *International Journal of Eating Disorders* 56(1): 5–25.
Di Angelantonio Emanuele, et al. 2016. 'Body-Mass Index and All-Cause Mortality: Individual-Participant-Data Meta-analysis of 239 Prospective Studies in Four Continents', *Lancet* 388(10046): 776–86.
Di Nicola, Vincenzo F. 1990. 'Anorexia Multiforme: Self-starvation in Historical and Cultural Context; Part II, Anorexia Nervosa as a Culture-Reactive Syndrome', *Transcultural Psychiatric Research Review* 27(4): 245–86.
Di Silvio, Rossana. 2012. 'Learning to "Parenting": Peer-to-Peer Educational Actions in the Italian Associations of Adoptive Families', *Mediterranean Journal of Social Sciences* 30(10): 21.

Dogliotti, Giulio C. 1936. 'Sulla Magrezza Ipofisaria Giovanile', *Rivista Critica di Clinica Medica* 37: 303.
Dotti, Federico. 1950. 'Il Problema Diagnostico e Terapeutico dell'Anoressia Nervosa e della Malattia di Simmonds', *Giornale di clinica medica* 31: 1431.
Douglas, Mary. 1966. *Purity and Danger: An Analysis of Concepts of Pollution and Taboo*. London: Routledge.
Dragojlovic, Ana, and Alex Broom 2018. *Bodies and Suffering: Emotions and Relations of Care*. New York: Routledge.
Eknoyan, Garabed. 2008. 'Adolphe Quetelet (1796–1874) – the Average Man and Indices of Obesity', *Nephrology, Dialysis, Transplantation* 23(1): 47–51.
Eli, Karin. 2012. '"4st 7lbs": Eating Disorders, between Horror and Survival'. *UBVO Opinion Paper Series* 3.
Eli, Karin. 2014. 'Between Difference and Belonging: Configuring Self and Others in Inpatient Treatment for Eating Disorders', *PLoS ONE* 9(9): 105452.
Eli, Karin. 2016. '"The Body Remembers": Narrating Embodied Reconciliations of Eating Disorder and Recovery', *Anthropology & Medicine* 23(1): 71–85.
Eli, Karin. 2018. 'Striving for Liminality: Eating Disorders and Social Suffering', *Transcultural Psychiatry* 55(4): 475–94.
Eli, Karin, and Megan Warin (eds). 2018. 'Anthropological Perspectives on Eating Disorders: Deciphering Cultural Logics' [Special Issue], *Transcultural Psychiatry* 55(4).
Eli, Karin, and Anna Lavis. 2022. 'Material Environments and the Shaping of Anorexic Embodiment: Towards a Materialist Account of Eating Disorders', *Culture, Medicine & Psychiatry* 46(2): 344–63.
Eli, Karin, and Stanely Ulijaszek. 2023. 'Anorexia Nervosa', *Oxford Bibliographies*, 23 March. Retrieved 14 January 2025 from http://www.oxfordbibliographies.com/view/document/obo-9780199766567/obo-9780199766567-0116.xml.
Esposito, Nicholas J. 1989. *Italian Family Structure*. New York: Peter Lang.
Fainzang, Sylvie. 2002. 'Lying, Secrecy and Power within the Doctor–Patient Relationship', *Anthropology & Medicine* 9(2): 117–33.
Fairburn, Christopher G. 1981. 'A Cognitive Behavioural Approach to the Treatment of Bulimia', *Psychological Medicine* 11(4): 707–11.
Fairburn, Christopher G., Zafra Cooper and Roz Shafran. 2003. 'Cognitive Behaviour Therapy for Eating Disorders: A "Transdiagnostic" Theory and Treatment', *Behaviour Research and Therapy* 41(5): 509–28.
Fassino, Secondo, et al. 2009. 'Factors Associated with Dropout from Treatment for Eating Disorders: A Comprehensive Literature Review', *BMC Psychiatry* 9: 67.
Fausto, Carlos, and Luiz Costa. 2013. 'Feeding (and Eating): Reflections on Strathern's "Eating (and Feeding)"', *The Cambridge Journal of Anthropology* 31(1): 156–62.
Feudtner, Chris. 2015. *Bittersweet: Diabetes, Insulin, and the Transformation of Illness*. Chapel Hill: University of North Carolina Press.
Fichter, Manfred Maximilian, et al. 2017. 'Long-Term Outcome of Anorexia Nervosa: Results from a Large Clinical Longitudinal Study', *International Journal of Eating Disorders* 50(9): 1018–30.
Foot, John. 2015. *The Man Who Closed the Asylums: Franco Basaglia and the Revolution in Mental Health Care*. London: Verso.
Foucault, Michel. 1986 [1984]. *The Use of Pleasure: The History of Sexuality, Volume 2*. London: Viking.
Foucault, Michel. 1991 [1975]. *Discipline and Punish: The Birth of the Prison*. London: Penguin Books.

Franko, Debra L., and Pamela K. Keel. 2006. 'Suicidality in Eating Disorders: Occurrence, Correlates, and Clinical Implications', *Clinical Psychology Review* 26: 769–82.
Freud, Sigmund. 1918. *From the History of an Infantile Neurosis*. London: Vintage.
Freud, Sigmund, and Joseph Breuer. 2004 [1895]. *Studies in Hysteria*. Translated by Nicola Luckhurst. London: Penguin Books.
Funk, Leberecht. 2021. 'Feeding as an Attachment System among the Tao (Taiwan)'. *European Network for Psychological Anthropology (ENPA) Conference, Helsinki, 2 June 2021*. University of Helsinki. Retrieved 15 January 2025 from ENPA2021_Conference_Programme_Abstracts.pdf.
Galdi, Francesco, et al. 1936. *Adiposità e Magrezze Patologiche: Relazione al Quarantaduesimo Congresso della Società Italiana di Medicina Interna*. Roma: Pozzi.
Galt, Anthony H. 1991. *Far from the Church Bells: Settlement and Society in an Apulian Town*. Cambridge: Cambridge University Press.
Gard, Maisie C. E., and Chris P. Freeman. 1996. 'The Dismantling of a Myth: A Review of Eating Disorders and Socioeconomic Status', *International Journal of Eating Disorders* 20(1): 1–12.
Garfinkel, Paul E., and David M. Garner. 1984. 'Perceptions of the Body in Anorexia Nervosa', in Karl M. Pirke and Detlev Ploog (eds), *The Psychobiology of Anorexia Nervosa*. Berlin: SpringerVerlag.
Garghentini, Piero G., et al. 2003. 'Historical Perspective', in Giovanni M. Ruggiero (ed.), *Eating Disorders in the Mediterranean Area: An Exploration in Transcultural Psychology*. New York: Nova Science Publishers, pp. 165–75.
Garner, David M., and Kelly M. Bemis. 1982. 'A Cognitive-Behavioural Approach to Anorexia Nervosa', *Cognitive Therapy and Research* 6(2): 123–50.
Geschiere, Peter L. 2003. 'Witchcraft as the Dark Side of Kinship: Dilemmas of Social Security in New Contexts', *Etnofoor* 16(1): 43–61.
Ghezzi, Simone. 2012. 'Parenthood and the Structuring of Time among Urban Households in Northern Italy', *Ethnologie française* 42(1): 37–44.
Giancipoli, Danila. 2024. 'La Cura dei Disturbi Alimentari Non Può Essere un Privilegio', *Il Sole 24 Ore*, 29 January.
Gibson, Dennis, Cassandra Workman and Philip S. Mehler. 2019. 'Medical Complications of Anorexia Nervosa and Bulimia Nervosa', *Psychiatric Clinics of North America* 4: 263–74.
Giordano, Cristiana. 2011. 'Translating Fanon in the Italian Context: Rethinking the Ethics of Treatment in Psychiatry', *Transcultural Psychiatry* 48(3): 228–56.
Giordano, Cristiana. 2018. 'Political Therapeutics: Dialogues and Frictions around Care and Cure', *Medical Anthropology* 37(1): 32–44.
Giordano, Simona. 2005. *Understanding Eating Disorders: Conceptual and Ethical Issues in the Treatment of Anorexia and Bulimia Nervosa*. Oxford: Clarendon Press.
Glashouwer, Klaske A., et al. 2019. 'The Role of Body Image Disturbance in the Onset, Maintenance, and Relapse of Anorexia Nervosa: A Systematic Review', *Clinical Psychology Review* 74: 101771.
Glenn, Evelyn N. 2010. *Forced to Care: Coercion and Caregiving in America*. Cambridge, MA: Harvard University Press.
Goddard, Victoria A. 1996. *Gender, Family and Work in Naples*. Oxford: Berg.
Goffman, Erving. 1961. *Asylums: Essays on the Condition of the Social Situation of Mental Patients and Other Inmates*. Garden City, NY: Anchor Books.

Goldfarb, Kathryn E. 2019. 'Embodied Relationality beyond "Nature" vs "Nurture": Materializing Absent Kinships in Japanese Child Welfare', in S. Bamford (ed.), *The Cambridge Handbook of Kinship*. Cambridge: Cambridge University Press, pp. 153–78.
Good, Byron J. 1993. *Medicine, Rationality and Experience: An Anthropological Perspective*. Cambridge: Cambridge University Press.
Gooldin, Sigal. 2008. 'Being Anorexic: Hunger, Subjectivity, and Embodied Morality', *Medical Anthropology Quarterly, New Series* 22(3): 274–96.
Gordon, Richard A. 2000. *Eating Disorders: Anatomy of a Social Epidemic*. Oxford: Blackwell Publishing.
Greco, Cinzia. 2022. 'The Nebula of Chronicity: Dealing with Metastatic Breast Cancer in the UK', *Anthropology & Medicine* 29(1): 107–21.
Greco, Cinzia, and Nils Graber. 2022. 'Anthropology of New Chronicities: Illness Experiences under the Promise of Medical Innovation as Long-Term Treatment', *Anthropology & Medicine* 29(1): 1–13.
Green, Katie. 2013. *Lighter Than My Shadow*. London: Jonathan Cape.
Gremillion, Helen. 1992. 'Psychiatry as Social Ordering: Anorexia Nervosa, a Paradigm', *Social Science & Medicine* 35(1): 57–7.
Gremillion, Helen. 2003. *Feeding Anorexia: Gender and Power at a Treatment Center*. Durham, NC: Duke University Press.
Grilli, Simonetta. 2018. 'È Tutto l'Altra Madre. Costruzioni Procreative e Pratiche della Genitorialità nella Maternità Lesbica', in Martina Giuffrè (ed.), *Essere Madri Oggi tra Biologia e Cultura*. Pisa: Pacini, pp. 39–70.
Grilli, Simonetta. 2019. *Antropologia delle famiglie contemporanee*. Roma: Carocci Editore.
Guerzoni, Corinna S. 2020. *Sistemi Procreativi. Etnografia dell'Omogenitorialità in Italia*. Milano: Franco Angeli.
Guerzoni, Corinna S. 2023. 'Same-Sex Parents: A Case Study from Italy', in Clare Huntington, Courtney G. Joslin and Christiane Von Bary (eds), *Social Parenthood in Comparative Perspective*. New York: NYU Press, pp. 33–49.
Guerzoni, Corinna S. 2024. 'Moral and Ethical Dilemmas of Italian Embryo Recipients', *L'Uomo* 14(1): 89–112.
Guisinger, Shan. 2003. 'Adapted to Flee Famine: Adding an Evolutionary Perspective on Anorexia Nervosa', *Psychological Review* 110(4): 745–76.
Gull, William Withey. 1997 [1874]. 'Anorexia Nervosa (Apepsia Hysterica, Anorexia Hysterica)', *Transactions of the Clinical Society of London* 7: 22–8, republished in *Obesity Research* 5(5): 498–502.
Hacking, Ian. 2006. 'Making Up People', *London Review of Books* 28(16): 1–9.
Halbeisen Georg, Gerrit Brandt and Georgios Paslakis. 2022. 'A Plea for Diversity in Eating Disorders Research', *Frontiers in Psychiatry* 13: 820043.
Han, Clara. 2012. *Life in Debt: Times of Care and Violence in Neoliberal Chile*. Berkeley: University of California Press.
Harari, Daniel, et al. 2001. 'A Computer-based Method for the Assessment of Body-Image Distortions in Anorexia Nervosa Patients', *Information Technology in Biomedicine* 5(4): 311–19.
Hargrove, James L. 2007. 'Does the History of Food Energy Units Suggest a Solution to "Calorie Confusion"?', *Nutritional Journal* 6: 44.
Harris, John. 2024. 'Your Illness Worsens – So Care Is Cut Off. This Is the Scandal Playing Out in Eating Disorder Treatment', *The Guardian*, 25 February.
Hastrup, Kirsten. 1993. 'Hunger and the Hardness of Facts', *Man, New Series* 28(4): 727–39.

Hendricks, Jennifer. 2003. *Slim to None: A Journey through the Wasteland of Anorexia Treatment.* Columbus, OH: McGraw-Ill.

Herzfeld, Michael. 2024. 'Afterword. Beyond Rhetorical Binaries: The Anthropology of Italy and the Politics of Critique', in Paolo Heywood (ed.), *New Anthropologies of Italy: Politics, History and Culture.* Oxford: Berghahn Books, pp. 376–93.

Herzog, David B., and Dara N. Greenwood. 2000. 'Mortality in Eating Disorders: A Descriptive Study', *International Journal of Eating Disorders* 28: 20–26.

Heywood, Paolo. 2018. *After Difference: Queer Activism in Italy and Anthropological Theory.* Oxford: Berghahn Books.

Heywood, Paolo. (ed.). 2024. *New Anthropologies of Italy: Politics, History and Culture.* Oxford: Berghahn Books.

Hochschild, Arlie R. 2003 [1983]. *The Managed Heart.* Berkeley: University of California Press.

Hornbacher, Marya. 1998. *Wasted: A Memoir of Anorexia and Bulimia.* New York: Harper Collins.

Ingold, Tim. 2000. *The Perception of the Environment: Essays on Livelihood, Dwelling and Skill.* London: Routledge.

Istituto Superiore di Sanità (ISS). 2012. 'Conferenza di Consenso sui Disturbi del Comportamento Alimentare (DCA) negli Adolescenti e nei Giovani adulti', *Rapporti ISTISAN* 13/6.

Janet, Pierre. 1907. *The Major Symptoms of Hysteria.* London: Macmillan.

Janowski, Monica, and Fiona Kerlogue. 2007. *Kinship and Food in South East Asia.* NIAS Press.

Jenkins Richard. 1999. 'Towards a Social Model of (In)Competence', in Richard Jenkins (ed.), *Questions of Competence: Culture, Classification and Intellectual Disability.* Cambridge: Cambridge University Press, pp. 222–29.

Katzman, Debra K. 2005. 'Medical Complications in Adolescents with Anorexia Nervosa: A Review of the Literature', *International Journal of Eating Disorders* 37(6): 52–59.

Keel, Pamela K., and Tiffany A. Brown. 2010. 'Update on Course and Outcome in Eating Disorders', *International Journal of Eating Disorders* 43(3): 195–204.

Keel, Pamela K., et al. 2005. 'Postremission Predictors of Relapse in Women with Eating Disorders', *American Journal of Psychiatry* 162(12): 2263–68.

Kendall, Carl, and Zelee Hill. 2010. 'Chronicity and AIDS in Three South African Communities', in Lenore Manderson and Carolyn Smith-Morris (eds), *Chronic Conditions, Fluid States: Chronicity and the Anthropology of Illness.* New Brunswick: Rutgers University Press, pp. 175–94.

Kendall, Sacha. 2011. 'Ethics and Involuntary Treatment for Anorexia Nervosa in Context: A Social Work Approach'. Ph.D. Thesis. Sydney: UNSW.

Key, Adrienne, et al. 2002. 'Body Image Treatment within an Inpatient Program for Anorexia Nervosa: The Role of Mirror Exposure in the Desensitization Process', *International Journal of Eating Disorders* 31(2):185–90.

Keys, Ancel, et al. 1950. *The Biology of Human Starvation (2 Vols).* Minneapolis: University of Minnesota Press.

Keys, Ancel, et al. 1972. 'Indices of Relative Weight and Obesity', *Journal of Chronic Diseases* 25: 329–43.

Khalsa, Sahib S., et al. 2017. 'What Happens after Treatment? A Systematic Review of Relapse, Remission, and Recovery in Anorexia Nervosa', *Journal of Eating Disorders* 14(5): 20.

Kleinman, Arthur, and Byron Good. (eds). 1985. *Culture and Depression: Anthropology and Cross-Cultural Psychiatry of Affect and Disorder*. Berkeley: University of California Press.

Kleinman, Arthur. 1988. 'Neurasthenia: Weakness and Exhaustion in the United States and China', in *The Illness Narratives: Suffering, Healing, and the Human Condition*. New York: Basic Books.

Kleinman, Arthur. 2010. 'Caregiving: The Divided Meaning of Being Human and the Divided Self of the Caregiver', in J. Michelle Molina and Donald K. Swearer (eds), *Rethinking the Human*. Cambridge, MA: Harvard University Press, pp. 17–29.

Koopman, Colin. 2019. *How We Became Our Data: A Genealogy of the Informational Person*. Chicago: The University of Chicago Press.

Krause, Elizabeth L. 2001. '"Empty Cradles" and the Quiet Revolution: Demographic Discourse and the Cultural Struggles of Gender, Race, and Class in Italy', *Cultural Anthropology* 16: 576–611.

Krause, Elizabeth L. 2005. *A Crisis of Births: Population Politics and Family-Making in Italy*. Belmont, CA: Wadsworth.

Laidlaw, James. 2013. *The Subject of Virtue: An Anthropology of Ethics and Freedom*. Cambridge: Cambridge University Press.

LaMarre, Andrea, and Carla Rice. 2021. 'Recovering Uncertainty: Exploring Eating Disorder Recovery in Context', *Culture, Medicine and Psychiatry* 45(4): 706–26.

Lambek, Michael. 2010. 'Introduction', in M. Lambek (ed.), *Ordinary Ethics: Anthropology, Language, and Action*. New York: Fordham University Press, pp. 1–36.

Lambek, Michael. 2011. 'Kinship as Gift and Theft: Acts of Succession in Mayotte and Israel', *American Ethnologist* 38(1): 2–16.

Lambert, Helen, and Maryon McDonald. 2009. 'Introduction', in Helen Lambert and Maryon McDonald (eds), *Social Bodies*. Oxford: Berghahn Books, pp. 1–15.

Lancy, David F. 2014. *The Anthropology of Childhood: Cherubs, Chattel, Changelings*, 2nd edn. Cambridge: Cambridge University Press.

Landecker, Hannah. 2011. 'Food as Exposure: Nutritional Epigenetics and the New Metabolism', *BioSocieties* 6(2): 167–94.

Landecker, Hannah. 2013. 'Postindustrial Metabolism: Fat Knowledge', *Public Culture* 25(3 71): 495–522.

Landecker, Hannah. 2017. 'Metabolism, Autonomy, and Individuality', in Scott Lidgard and Lynn K. Nyhart (eds), *Biological Individuality: Integrating Scientific, Philosophical, and Historical Perspectives*. Chicago: The University of Chicago Press, pp. 225–48.

Lasègue, Charles. 1997 [1873]. 'On Hysterical Anorexia', *Medical Times and Gazette*, Sept. 6, 265–6; Sept. 27: 367–9, republished in *Obesity Research* 5(5): 492–7.

Latour, Bruno, and Steve Woolgar. 1979. *Laboratory Life: The Social Construction of Scientific Facts*. London: Sage Publications.

Latour, Bruno. 2004. 'How to Talk about the Body? The Normative Dimension of Science Studies', *Body & Society* 10(2–3): 205–29.

Latour, Bruno. 2005. *Reassembling the Social: An Introduction to Actor-Network-Theory*. Oxford: Oxford University Press.

Lavis, Anna, Emma-Jayne Abbots and Luci Attala. 2015. 'Introduction: Reflecting on the Embodied Intersections of Eating and Caring', in Emma-Jayne Abbots, Anna Lavis and Luci Attala (eds), *Careful Eating: Bodies, Food and Care*. London: Routledge, pp. 1–22.

Lavis, Anna. 2015. 'Careful Starving: Exploring (not) Eating, Care and Anorexia', in Emma-Jayne Abbots, Anna Lavis and Luci Attala (eds), *Careful Eating: Bodies, Food and Care*. London: Routledge, pp. 91–108.

Lavis, Anna. 2016. 'A Desire for Anorexia: Living through Distress', *Medicine Anthropology Theory* 3(1): 68–76.

Lavis, Anna. 2018. 'Not Eating or Tasting Other Ways to Live: A Qualitative Analysis of "Living through" and Desiring to Maintain Anorexia', *Transcultural Psychiatry* 55(4): 454–74.

Lederman Rena. 2013. 'Ethics: Practices, Principles, and Comparative Perspectives', in James G. Carrier and Deborah B. Gewertz (eds), *The Handbook of Sociocultural Anthropology*. London: Bloomsbury, pp. 588–611.

Lee, Seung-Hyun, T. P. Ho and L. K. George Hsu. 1993. 'Fat Phobic and Non-fat Phobic Anorexia Nervosa: A Comparative Study of 70 Chinese Patients in Hong Kong', *Psychological Medicine* 23(4): 999–1017.

Lee, Sing. 1996. 'Reconsidering the Status of Anorexia Nervosa as a Western Culture-Bound Syndrome', *Social Science & Medicine* 42(1): 21–34.

Leira, Arnlaug, and Chiara Saraceno. 2006. 'Care: Actors, Relationships, Contexts', *Sosiologi i Dag* 36(3): 7–34.

Lester, Rebecca J. 1997. 'The (Dis)embodied Self in Anorexia Nervosa', *Social Science & Medicine* 44(4): 479–89.

Lester, Rebecca J. 2007. 'Critical Therapeutics: Cultural Politics and Clinical Reality in Two Eating Disorder Treatment Centers', *Medical Anthropology Quarterly* 21(4): 369–87.

Lester, Rebecca J. 2009. 'Brokering Authenticity: Borderline Personality Disorder and the Ethics of Care in an American Eating Disorder Clinic', *Current Anthropology* 50(3): 281–302.

Lester, Rebecca J. 2014. 'Health as Moral Failing: Medication Restriction among Women with Eating Disorders', *Anthropology & Medicine* 21(2): 241–50.

Lester, Rebecca J. 2017. 'Self-governance, Psychotherapy, and the Subject of Managed Care: Internal Family Systems Therapy and the Multiple Self in a US Eating Disorders Treatment Center', *American Ethnologist* 44(1): 23–35.

Lester, Rebecca J. 2018. 'Ground Zero: Ontology, Recognition, and the Elusiveness of Care in American Eating Disorders Treatment', *Transcultural Psychiatry* 55(4): 516–33.

Lester, Rebecca J. 2019. *Famished: Eating Disorders and Failed Care in America*. Berkeley: University of California Press.

Lester, Rebecca J. 2023. 'Trigger Warnings: Danger, Desire and Declensions of the Will in Eating Disorders Treatment', in Patrick McKearney and Nicholas H. A. Evans (eds), *Against Better Judgment: Akrasia in Anthropological Perspectives*. Oxford: Berghahn Books, pp. 34–49.

Lewis, Gilbert. 2000. *A Failure of Treatment*. Oxford: Oxford University Press.

Linardon, Jake, et al. 2022. 'A Systematic Scoping Review of Research on COVID-19 Impacts on Eating Disorders: A Critical Appraisal of the Evidence and Recommendations for the Field', *International Journal of Eating Disorders* 55(1): 3–38.

Littlewood, Roland. 1995. 'Psychopathology and Personal Agency: Modernity, Culture Change and Eating Disorders in South Asian Societies', *British Journal of Medical Psychology* 68(1): 45–63.

Lock, Margaret. 1993. 'Cultivating the Body: Anthropology and Epistemologies of Bodily Practice and Knowledge', *Annual Review of Anthropology* 22: 133–55.

Lock, Margaret, and Vinh-Kim Nguyen. 2010. *An Anthropology of Biomedicine*. Oxford: Wiley.

Lupton, Deborah. 2016. *The Quantified Self: A Sociology of Self-Tracking*. Cambridge: Polity.

MacSween, Morag. 1993. *Anorexic Bodies: A Feminist and Sociological Perspective on Anorexia Nervosa*. London: Routledge.

Mahmood, Saba. 2005. *Politics of Piety: The Islamic Revival and the Feminist Subject*. Princeton: Princeton University Press.

Malson, Helen, et al. 2004. 'Constructing 'The Eating Disordered Patient': A Discourse Analysis of Accounts of Treatment Experiences', *Journal of Community & Applied Social Psychology* 14: 473–89.

Malson, Helen. 2008. 'Deconstructing Un/healthy Body-Weight and Weight Management', in Sarah Riley et al. (eds), *Critical Bodies: Representations, Identities and Practices of Weight and Body Management*. London: Palgrave Macmillan, pp. 27–42.

Marks, Andrea. 2019. 'The Evolution of Our Understanding and Treatment of Eating Disorders over the Past 50 Years', *Journal of Clinical Psychology* 75(8): 1380–91.

Marsh, Sarah. 2021. 'Eating Disorders: Families Tube-Feeding Patients at Home amid NHS Bed Shortage', *The Guardian*, 22 April.

Marson, Stephen M., and Rasby M. Powell. 2014. 'Goffman and the Infantilization of Elderly Persons: A Theory in Development', *The Journal of Sociology & Social Welfare* 41(4): 143–58.

Martin, Emily. 2007. *Bipolar Expeditions: Mania and Depression in American Culture*. Princeton: Princeton University Press.

Martinotti, Giovanni. 1953. 'Un Metodo di Cura dell'Anoressia psichica', *Lavoro Neuropsichiatrico* 13: 121.

Marzano, Michela. 2011. *Volevo Essere una Farfalla. Come l'Anoressia mi ha Insegnato a Vivere*. Milano: Mondadori.

Mattingly, Cheryl. 2010. *The Paradox of Hope: Journeys through a Clinical Borderland*. Berkeley: University of California Press.

Mattingly, Cheryl. 2014a. *Moral Laboratories: Family Peril and the Struggle for a Good Life*. Oakland: University of California Press.

McDonald, Maryon. 2014. 'Bodies and Cadavers', in Penny Harvey et al. (eds), *The Routledge Companion to Objects and Materials*. Abingdon and New York: Routledge, pp. 128–43.

McDonald, Maryon. 2015. 'Some Merits and Difficulties of Detachment', in Thomas Yarrow et al. (eds), *Detachment. Essays on the Limits of Relational Thinking*. Manchester: Manchester University Press, pp. 35–57.

McDonald, Maryon. 2017. 'The Ontological Turn Meets the Certainty of Death', *Anthropology and Medicine* 24(2): 205–20.

McDonald, Maryon. 2018. 'From "the Body" to "Embodiment", with Help from Phenomenology', in Matei Candea (ed.), *Schools and Styles of Anthropological Theory*. Oxford: Routledge, pp. 185–94.

McKearney, Patrick. 2017. 'L'Arche, Learning Disability, and Domestic Citizenship: Dependent Political Belonging in a Contemporary British City', *City & Society* 29(2): 260–80.

McKearney, Patrick. 2018. 'The Weight of Living: Autonomy, Care, and Responsibility for the Self', *Journal of Disability & Religion* 22(3): 266–82.

McKearney, Patrick. 2021. 'What Escapes Persuasion: Why Intellectual Disability Troubles "Dependence" in Liberal Societies', *Medical Anthropology* 40(2): 155–68.

McKinnon, Susan, and Fenella Cannell. (eds). 2013. *Vital Relations: Modernity and the Persistent Life of Kinship*. Santa Fe, NM: SAR Press.
Mead, Margaret. 2001 [1928]. *Coming of Age in Samoa*. New York: Harper Collins.
Mehler, Philip S., Cyntia K. Crews and Katherine Weiner. 2004. 'Bulimia: Medical Complications', *Journal of Women's Health* 13: 668–75.
Mezzenzana, Francesca. 2020. 'Between Will and Thought: Individualism and Social Responsiveness in Amazonian Child Rearing', *American Anthropologist* 122(3): 540–53.
Mezzenzana, Francesca. 2021. 'Feeding and Being Fed: Child Care and Food Consumption among the Runa of the Ecuadorian Amazon', *European Network for Psychological Anthropology (ENPA) Conference, Helsinki, 2 June 2021*. University of Helsinki. Retrieved 15 January 2025 from ENPA2021_Conference_Programme_Abstracts.pdf.
Milano, Walter, and Anna Capasso. 2019. 'Psychopharmacological Options in the Multidisciplinary and Multidimensional Treatment of Eating Disorders', *The Open Neurology Journal* 13: 22–31.
Minelli, Massimiliano, and Veronica Redini. 2015. 'Il "Caso", la Vita e le Sue Condizioni. Per una Antropologia Politica del Welfare State in Italia', *Anuac* 4(1): 145–69.
Ministero della Sanità. 1998. 'Commissione di Studio per l'Assistenza ai Pazienti Affetti da Anoressia e Bulimia Nervosa', *Annali della Sanità Pubblica*, pp. 9–20. Rome.
Ministero della Salute. 2017. 'Linee di indirizzo nazionali per la riabilitazione nutrizionale nei disturbi dell'alimentazione', *Quaderni del Ministero della Salute* 29, September 2017.
Minuchin, Salvador, Bernice L. Rosman and Lester Baker. 1978. *Psychosomatic Families: Anorexia Nervosa in Context*. Cambridge, MA: Harvard University Press.
Miskovic-Wheatley, Jane, et al. 2023. 'Eating Disorder Outcomes: Findings from a Rapid Review of over a Decade of Research', *Journal of Eating Disorders* 11: 85.
Mitchison, Deborah, et al. 2014. 'The Changing Demographic Profile of Eating Disorder Behaviors in the Community', *BMC Public Health* 14: 943.
Mody, Perveez. 2020. 'Kinship Care', in Loraine Gelsthorpe, Perveez Mody and Brian Sloan (eds), *Spaces of Care*. Oxford: Hart, pp. 183–200.
Mol, Annemarie. 2002. *The Body Multiple: Ontology in Medical Practice*. Durham, NC: Duke University Press.
Mol, Annemarie. 2008. *The Logic of Care: Health and the Problem of Patient Choice*. New York: Routledge.
Mol, Annemarie, Ingunn Moser and Jeannette Pols. (eds). 2010. *Care in Practice: On Tinkering in Clinics, Homes and Farms*. New York: Columbia University Press.
Molé, Noelle J. 2008. 'Living It on the Skin: Italian States, Working Illnesses', *American Ethnologist* 35: 189–210.
Molé, Noelle J. 2012. *Labor Disorders in Neoliberal Italy: Mobbing, Well-Being, and the Workplace*. Bloomington: Indiana University Press.
Montgomery, Heather. 2008. *An Introduction to Childhood: Anthropological Perspectives on Children's Lives*. UK: Wiley Blackwell.
Mosley, Philip E. 2009. 'Bigorexia: Bodybuilding and Muscle Dysmorphia', *European Eating Disorders Review* 17(3): 191–98.
Moss, Leonard W., and Walter H. Thompson. 1959. 'The South Italian Family: Literature and Observation', *Human Organization* 18: 35–41.

Moulding, Nicole. 2003. 'Constructing the Self in Mental Health Practice: Identity, Individualism and the Feminization of Deficiency', *Feminist Review* 75: 57–74.

Muehlebach, Andrea. 2011. 'On Affective Labor in Post-Fordist Italy', *Cultural Anthropology* 26(1): 59–82.

Muehlebach, Andrea. 2012. *The Moral Neoliberal: Welfare and Citizenship in Italy*. Chicago: The University of Chicago Press.

Muehlebach, Andrea. 2013. 'The Catholicization of Neoliberalism: On Love and Welfare in Lombardy, Italy', *American Anthropologist* 115(3): 452–65.

Munro, Calum, Louise Randell and Stephen M. Lawrie. 2017. 'An Integrative Bio-Psycho-Social Theory of Anorexia Nervosa', *Clinical Psychology & Psychotherapy* 24(1): 1–21.

Murray, Stuart B., and Leslie K. Anderson. 2015. 'An Introduction to the Special Issue on Innovations in Family Therapy for Eating Disorders', *Eating Disorders* 23(4): 279–80.

Murray, Stuart B., et al. 2017. 'The Enigma of Male Eating Disorders: A Critical Review and Synthesis', *Clinical Psychology Review* 57: 1–11.

Musolino, Connie, et al. 2015. '"Healthy Anorexia": The Complexity of Care in Disordered Eating', *Social Science & Medicine* 139: 18–25.

Musolino, Connie, et al. 2016. 'Developing Shared Understandings of Recovery and Care: A Qualitative Study of Women with Eating Disorders Who Resist Therapeutic Care', *Journal of Eating Disorders* 4: 36.

Musolino, Connie, Megan Warin and Peter Gilchrist. 2018. 'Positioning Relapse and Recovery through a Cultural lens of Desire: A South Australian Case Study of Disordered Eating', *Transcultural Psychiatry* 55(4): 534–50.

Myers, Neely L. 2015. *Recovery's Edge: An Ethnography of Mental Healthcare and Moral Agency*. Nashville, TN: Vanderbilt University Press.

Niewöhner, Jörg. 2011. 'Epigenetics: Embedded Bodies and the Molecularisation of Biography and Milieu', *BioSocieties* 6: 279–98.

Niola, Marino. 2015. *Homo Dieteticus: Viaggio nelle Tribù Alimentari*. Bologna: Il Mulino.

Noxon, Marti. 2017. 'To the Bone'. Produced by Netflix.

O'Connor, Richard A., and Penny Van Esterik. 2008. 'De-medicalizing Anorexia: A New Cultural Brokering', *Anthropology Today* 24(5): 6–9.

Oeye, Christine, Anne K. Bjelland and Aina Skorpen. 2007. 'Doing Participant Observation in a Psychiatric Hospital: Research Ethics Resumed', *Social Science & Medicine* 65(11): 2296–306.

Orbach, Susie. 1986. *Hunger Strike: The Anorectic's Struggle as a Metaphor for Our Age*. London: Faber.

Orsini, Gisella. 2017. '"Hunger Hurts, but Starving Works". The Moral Conversion to Eating Disorders', *Culture, Medicine, and Psychiatry* 41(1): 111–41.

Orsini, Gisella. 2021. 'Compliance and Resistance to Treatment in an Italian Residential Centre for Eating Disorders', *Anthropology and Medicine* 29(2): 193–207.

Orsini, Gisella. 2023. 'Beautiful, Moral, Functional: Bodily Self-alteration in an Italian Center for Eating Disorders', in Jean-Paul Baldacchino and Christopher Houston (eds), *Self-alteration: How People Change Themselves across Cultures*. New Jersey: Rutgers University Press, pp. 111–27.

Ottonello, Paolo. 1937. 'Contributo alla Delimitazione Clinica dell' Anoressia Mentale', *Rivista di Patologia Nervosa* 50: 353.

Palazzo, Cristina. 2020a. 'I Sogni del Nostro Lorenzo, ucciso a Vent'anni dall'Anoressia e dalla Legge', *La Repubblica*, 16 February.
Palazzo, Cristina. 2020b. 'Famiglie Sole Davanti all'Anoressia? Sì, in Piemonte Mancano le Strutture', *La Repubblica*, 18 February.
Parker, Ripley. 2023. 'Everything Now'. Produced by Netflix.
Pearce, John M. S. 2004. 'Richard Morton: Origins of Anorexia Nervosa', *European Neurology* 52(4): 191–92.
Piasere Leonardo. 1998. 'Le Culture della Parentela. Un Approccio Cognitivo Fuzzy', in Leonardo Piasere and Pier Giorgio Solinas (eds), *Le Culture della Parentela e l'Esogamia Perfetta*. Roma: CISU, pp. 1–202.
Pinto, Sarah. 2011. 'Rational Love, Relational Medicine: Psychiatry and the Accumulation of Precarious Kinship', *Culture, Medicine and Psychiatry* 35: 376–95.
Pinto, Sarah. 2014. *Daughters of Parvati: Women and Madness in Contemporary India*. Philadelphia: University of Pennsylvania Press.
Pitkin, Donald S. 1985. *The House That Giacomo Built: History of an Italian Family*. Cambridge: Cambridge University Press.
Plesset, Sonja. 2006. *Sheltering Women: Negotiating Gender and Violence in Northern Italy*. Stanford, CA: Stanford University Press.
Pols, Jeannette. 2015. 'Towards an Empirical Ethics in Care: Relations with Technologies in Health Care', *Medicine, Health Care and Philosophy* 18(1): 81–90.
Porta, Simone. (Simonis Portiis) 1951 [1551]. *De Puella Germanica, que Fere Biennium Vixerat sine Cibo, Portuque (Disputatio)*. Firenze: L. Torrentini.
Porter, Theodore M. 1995. *Trust in Numbers: The Pursuit of Objectivity in Science and Public Life*. Princeton, NJ: Princeton University Press.
Pozzi, Marco. 2010. 'Maledimiele'. Produced by 3Per s.r.l.
Preston, John D., John H. O'Neal and Mary C. Talaga. 2013. *Handbook of Clinical Psychopharmacology for Therapists*, 7th edn. Oakland, CA: New Harbinger Publications.
Prince, Raymond. 1985. 'The Concept of Culture-Bound Syndromes: Anorexia Nervosa and Brain-Fag', *Social Science & Medicine* 21(2): 197–203.
Probst, Michel, et al. 1995. 'Body Size Estimation in Eating Disorder Patients: Testing the Video Distortion Method on a Life-Size Screen', *Behavioural Research and Therapy* 33: 985–90.
Probst, Michel, et al. 1998. 'The Significance of Body Size Estimation in Eating Disorders: Its Relationship with Clinical and Psychological Variables', *Eating Disorders* 24: 167–74.
Quadflieg, Norbert, and Manfred Maximilian Fichter. 2019. 'Long-Term Outcome of Inpatients with Bulimia Nervosa: Results from the Christina Barz Study', *International Journal of Eating Disorders* 52(7): 834–45.
Rabinbach, Anson. 1992. *The Human Motor: Energy, Fatigue, and the Origins of Modernity*. Berkeley: University of California Press.
Raevuori, Anu, Anna Keski-Rahkonen and Hans W. Hoek. 2014. 'A Review of Eating Disorders in Males', *Current Opinion in Psychiatry* 27(6): 426–30.
Reher, David S. 2004. 'Family Ties in Western Europe: Persistent Contrasts', in Gianpiero Dalla Zuanna and Giuseppe A. Micheli (eds), *Strong Family and Low Fertility: A Paradox?* European Studies of Population, vol. 14. Dordrecht: Springer, pp. 45–76.
Rilke, Rainer M. 1962 [1934]. *Letters to a Young Poet*. New York: Norton & Company.
Ritenbaugh, Cheryl, et al. 1996. 'A Cross-cultural Review of Eating Disorders in Regard to DSM-IV', in Juan E. Mezzich, Arthur Kleinman, Horacio Fabrega and Delores L. Perron (eds), *Culture and Psychiatric Diagnosis: A DSM-IV Perspective*. Washington, D.C.: APA Press, pp. 171–86.

Riva, Michele, Luca Grassi and Michael Belingheri. 2020. 'Jacob L. Moreno and Psychodrama – Psychiatry in History', *The British Journal of Psychiatry* 217(1): 369.
Robbins, Joel. 2008. 'On Not Knowing Other Minds: Confession, Intention, and Linguistic Exchange in a Papua New Guinea Community', *Anthropological Quarterly* 81(2): 421–29.
Robinson, George. 1972. 'The Story of Parentectomy', *Journal of Asthma Research* 9(4): 199–205.
Rose, Nikolas. 1990. *Governing the Soul: The Shaping of the Private Self.* London: Routledge.
Rose, Nikolas. 1996. *Inventing Ourselves: Psychology, Power and Personhood.* Cambridge: Cambridge University Press.
Rosen, David S. 2010. 'Identification and Management of Eating Disorders in Children and Adolescents', *Pediatrics* 126(6): 1240–53.
Rossini, Romolo. 1959. 'Brevi Considerazioni in Tema di Patogenesi e di Inquadramento Nosografico dell'Anoressia Mentale', *Rivista Sperimentale di Freniatria* 83: 36.
Ruggiero, Giovanni M., Marcello Prandin and Mario Mantero. 2001. 'Eating Disorders in Italy: A Historical Review', *European Eating Disorders Review* 9(5): 292–300.
Ruggiu, Valentina. 2016. 'Eccellenze Rare, Altrove si Finisce in Psichiatria', in 'Disturbi Alimentari: Curarsi è un'Odissea', special issue of *La Repubblica*, 12 August.
Rusconi, Alessandra. 2004. 'Different Pathways out of the Parental Home: A Comparison of West Germany and Italy', *Journal of Comparative Family Studies* 35(4): 627–48.
Russell, Gerald, F. M. 1979. 'Bulimia Nervosa: An Ominous Variant of Anorexia Nervosa', *Psychological Medicine* 9(3): 429–48.
Russell, Gerald F. M., et al. 1987. 'An Evaluation of Family Therapy in Anorexia Nervosa and Bulimia Nervosa', *Archives of General Psychiatry* 44(12): 1047–56.
Rynkiewich, Michael A., and James P. Spradley. 1976. *Ethics and Anthropology: Dilemmas in Field Work.* New York: Wiley.
Sachdev, Perminder, et al. 2008. 'Brains of Anorexia Nervosa Patients Process Self-images Differently from Non-self Images: An MRI study', *Neuropsychologia* 46: 2161–68.
Salvatori, Clarida. 2024. 'Anoressia e Bulimia, Meno fondi nel Lazio: Appena 70 Posti Letto nelle Strutture Residenziali', *Il Corriere della Sera*, 21 October.
Saraceno, Chiara. 2004. 'The Italian Family from the 1960s to the Present', *Modern Italy* 9(1): 47–57.
Saraceno, Chiara. 2011. 'Beyond Care. The Persistent Invisibility of Unpaid Family Work', *Sociologica – Italian Journal of Sociology* 1: 1–15.
Saraceno, Chiara. 2015. 'Trends and Tensions within the Italian Family', in E. Jones and G. Pasquino (eds), *The Oxford Handbook of Italian Politics*. Oxford University Press, pp. 465–79.
Scheper-Hughes, Nancy. 1987. '"Basic Strangeness": Maternal Estrangement and Infant Death – A Critique of Bonding Theory', in Carolyn M. Super (ed.), *The Role of Culture in Developmental Disorder*. New York: Academic Press.
Schilder, Paul. 1935. *The Image and Appearance of the Human Body.* London: Kegan Paul.
Schmidt, Ulrike, et al. 2016. 'Eating Disorders: The Big Issue'. *The Lancet Psychiatry* 3(4): 313–15.
Schneider, Jekaterina, et al. 2023. 'A Mixed-Studies Systematic Review of the Experiences of Body Image, Disordered Eating, and Eating Disorders during the COVID-19 Pandemic', *International Journal of Eating Disorders* 56(1): 26–67.

Schwartzman, Helen B. 1978. 'The Invention of Childhood', in Helen B. Schwartzman, *Transformations: The Anthropology of Children's Play*. New York: Plenum Press.

Selvini-Palazzoli, Mara. 1963. *L'Anoressia Mentale*. Milano: Feltrinelli.

Selvini-Palazzoli, Mara. 1965. 'Interpretation of Mental Anorexia', in J. E. Meyer and H. Feldmann (eds), *Anorexia Nervosa*. Stuttgart: Thieme.

Selvini-Palazzoli, Mara. 1978. *Self-starvation: From the Intrapsychic to the Transpersonal Approach to Anorexia Nervosa*. London: Chaucer.

Silverman, Sydel. 1975. *Three Bells of Civilization: The Life of an Italian Hill Town*. New York: Columbia University Press.

Slade, Peter D., and Gerald F. M. Russell. 1973. 'Awareness of Body Dimensions in Anorexia Nervosa: Cross Sectional and Longitudinal Studies', *Psychological Medicine* 3: 188–99.

Smink, Frédérique R. E., Daphne van Hoeken and Hans W. Hoek. 2012. 'Epidemiology of Eating Disorders: Incidence, Prevalence and Mortality Rates', *Current Psychiatry Reports* 4(4): 406–14.

Smith-Morris, Carolyn. 2010. 'The Chronicity of Life, the Acuteness of Diagnosis', in Lenore Manderson Carolyn Smith-Morris (eds), *Chronic Conditions, Fluid States: Chronicity and the Anthropology of Illness*. New Brunswick: Rutgers University Press, pp. 21–37.

Sontag, Susan. 1978. *Illness as Metaphor*. New York: Farrar Straus and Giroux.

Squire, Sarah. 2003. 'Anorexia and Bulimia: Purity and Danger', *Australian Feminist Studies* 18(40): 17–26.

Stasch, Rupert. 2009. *Society of Others: Kinship and Mourning in a West Papuan Place*. Berkeley: University of California Press.

Stevens, Jenny. 2020. '"I Was at War with My Body": My Year as a Day Patient on an Eating Disorders Ward', *The Guardian*, 28 November.

Stevenson, Lisa. 2014. *Life besides Itself: Imagining Care in the Canadian Arctic*. Berkeley: University of California Press.

Strathern, Marilyn. 1988. *The Gender of the Gift: Problems with Women and Problems with Society in Melanesia*. Berkeley: University of California Press.

Strathern, Marilyn. 2009. 'Using Bodies to Communicate', in Helen Lambert and Maryon McDonald (eds), *Social Bodies*. Oxford: Berghahn Books, 148–69.

Strathern, Marilyn. 2018. 'Persons and Partible Persons', in Matei Candea (ed.), *Schools and Styles of Anthropological Theory*. London and New York: Routledge, pp. 236–46.

Street, Alice. 2014. *Biomedicine in an Unstable Place: Infrastructures and Personhood in a Papua New Guinean Hospital*. Durham, NC: Duke University Press.

Strober Michael, and Craig Johnson. 2012. 'The Need for Complex Ideas in Anorexia Nervosa: Why Biology, Environment, and Psyche All Matter, Why Therapists Make Mistakes, and Why Clinical Benchmarks Are Needed for Managing Weight Correction', *International Journal of Eating Disorders* 45(2): 155–78.

Sturm, Bonnie A. 2004. 'Ethics and Care: An Ethnographic Study of Psychiatric Community Health Nursing Practice', *Archives of Psychiatric Nursing* XVIII(3): 106–15.

Swartz, Leslie. 1985. 'Anorexia Nervosa as a Culture-Bound Syndrome', *Social Science & Medicine* 20(7): 725–30.

Tait, Gordon. 1993. '"Anorexia Nervosa": Asceticism, Differentiation, Government', *Journal of Sociology* 29(2): 194–208.

Tanassi, Lucia M. 2004. 'Compliance as Strategy: The Importance of Personalised Relations in Obstetric Practice', *Social Science & Medicine* 59(10): 2053–69.

The Lancet Diabetes & Endocrinology. 2023. 'Eating Disorders: Care Not Keeping Up with Demand', *The Lancet Diabetes & Endocrinology* 11(9): 625.
Ticktin, Miriam. 2011. *Causalities of Care: Immigration and the Politics of Humanitarianism in France.* Berkeley: University of California Press.
Touyz, Stephen, and Phillipa Hay. 2015. 'Severe and Enduring Anorexia Nervosa (SE-AN): In Search of a New Paradigm', *Journal of Eating Disorders* 3: 26.
Trace, Sara E., et al. 2013. 'The Genetics of Eating Disorders', *Annual Review of Clinical Psychology* 9: 589–620.
Treasure, Janet. 2010. 'Introduction', in Janet Treasure, Ulrike Schmidt and Pam Macdonald (eds), *The Clinician's Guide to Collaborative Caring in Eating Disorders.* Hove: Routledge.
Treasure, Janet, Daniel Stein and Sarah Maguire. 2015. 'Has the Time Come for a Staging Model to Map the Course of Eating Disorders from High Risk to Severe Enduring Illness? An Examination of the Evidence', *Early Intervention in Psychiatry* 9(3): 173–84.
van der Geest, Sjaak, and Kaja Finkler. 2004. 'Hospital Ethnography: Introduction', *Social Science & Medicine* 59(10): 1995–2001.
van der Geest, Sjaak. 2007. 'Is It Possible to Understand Illness and Suffering?', *Medische Antropologie* 19(1): 9–21.
van Dongen, Els. 2002. 'Theatres of the Lie: Crazy Deception and Lying as Drama', *Anthropology & Medicine* 9(2): 135–51.
van Ginkel, Rob. 1998. 'The Repatriation of Anthropology: Some Observations on Endo-ethnography', *Anthropology & Medicine* 5(3): 251–67.
Vandereycken, Walter, and Ron van Deth. 1994. *From Fasting Saints to Anorexic Girls: The History of Self-starvation.* London: Athlone.
Vandereycken, Walter, Leopold Depreitere and Michel Probst. 1987. 'Body-oriented Therapy for Anorexia Nervosa Patients', *American Journal of Psychotherapy* 41(2): 252–59.
Vatta, Barbara. 2012. 'La Dipendenza fa la Famiglia: Forme e Culture Familiari nel Friuli Venezia Giulia Contemporaneo'. Ph.D. Thesis. Italy: Università degli Studi di Udine.
Vermeulen, Eric. 2004. 'Dealing with Doubt: Making Decisions in a Neonatal Ward in the Netherlands', *Social Science & Medicine* 59(10): 2071–85.
Vilaça, Aparecida. 2002. 'Making Kin out of Others in Amazonia', *The Journal of the Royal Anthropological Institute* 8(2): 347–65.
Vogel, Else. 2018a. 'Operating (on) the Self: Transforming Agency through Obesity Surgery and Treatment', *Sociology of Health & Illness* 40(3): 508–22.
Vogel, Else. 2018b. 'Metabolism and Movement: Calculating Food and Exercise or Activating Bodies in Dutch Weight Management', *BioSocieties* 13(2): 389–407.
von Ameln, Falko, and Jochen Becker-Ebel. 2020. *Fundamentals of Psychodrama.* New York City: Springer.
Warin, Megan J. 2005. 'Transformation of Intimacy and Sociality in Anorexia: Bedrooms in Public Institutions', *Body & Society* 11(3): 97–113.
Warin, Megan J. 2006. 'Reconfiguring Relatedness in Anorexia', *Anthropology & Medicine* 13(3): 41–54.
Warin, Megan J. 2010. *Abject Relations: Everyday Worlds of Anorexia.* New Brunswick, NJ: Rutgers University Press.
Warren, Cortney S., et al. 2013. 'Demographic and Work-Related Correlates of Job Burnout in Professional Eating Disorder Treatment Providers', *Psychotherapy* 50(4): 553–64.

Watson, Hunna J., Amy O'Brien and Shiri Sadeh-Sharvit. 2018. 'Children of Parents with Eating Disorders', *Current Psychiatry Reports* 20(11): 101.
Watson, Hunna J., et al. 2021. 'Genetics of Eating Disorders in the Genome-wide Era', *Psychological Medicine* 51(13): 2287–97.
Weiss, Gail. 1999. 'The Abject Borders of the Body Image', in Gail Weiss and Honi Fern Haber (eds), *Perspectives on Embodiment: The Intersections of Nature and Culture*. London: Routledge, pp. 41–59.
Welbourn, Richard B. 1992. 'The Emergence of Endocrinology', *Gesnerus* 49(2): 137–50.
Wilson, G. Terence. 1999. 'Cognitive Behavior Therapy for Eating Disorders: Progress and Problems', *Behaviour Research and Therapy* 37: S79.
Wind, Gitte. 2008. 'Negotiated Interactive Observation: Doing Fieldwork in Hospital Settings', *Anthropology & Medicine* 15(2): 79–89.
Winnicott, Donald W. 1957. *The Child and the Family*. London: Tavistock.
Winnicott, Donald W. 1965. *The Family and Individual Development*. London: Tavistock.
Yanagisako, Sylvia J. 2002. *Producing Culture and Capital: Family Firms in Italy*. Princeton, NJ: Princeton University Press.
Yanagisako, Sylvia J. 2018. 'Reconfiguring Labour Value and the Capital/Labour Relation in Italian Global Fashion', *Journal of the Royal Anthropological Institute* 24: 47–60.
Yates, Alayne. 1989. 'Current Perspectives on Eating Disorders: History, Psychological and Biological Aspects', *Journal of the American Academy of Child & Adolescent Psychiatry* 28(6): 813–28.
Zaman, Shahaduz. 2004. 'Poverty and Violence, Frustration and Inventiveness: Hospital Ward Life in Bangladesh', *Social Science & Medicine* 59(10): 2025–36.
Zaman, Shahaduz. 2008. 'Native among the Natives: Physician Anthropologist Doing Hospital Ethnography at Home', *Journal of Contemporary Ethnography* 37(2): 135–54.
Zelizer, Viviana. 1985. *Pricing the Priceless Child: The Changing Social Value of Children*. New York: Basic Books.
Zigon, Jarret. 2007. 'Moral Breakdown and the Ethical Demand: A Theoretical Framework for an Anthropology of Moralities', *Anthropological Theory* 7(2): 131–50.

Index

www.ingramcontent.com/pod-product-compliance
Ingram Content Group UK Ltd.
Pitfield, Milton Keynes, MK11 3LW, UK
UKHW021836150926
8656IPUK00004B/22

9 781836 955245